THE HUNTING OF LEVIATHAN

THE HUNTING OF LEVIATHAN

SEVENTEENTH-CENTURY REACTIONS TO THE
MATERIALISM AND MORAL PHILOSOPHY OF
THOMAS HOBBES

BY

SAMUEL I. MINTZ

CAMBRIDGE
AT THE UNIVERSITY PRESS
1969

PUBLISHED BY
THE SYNDICS OF THE CAMBRIDGE UNIVERSITY PRESS
Bentley House, 200 Euston Road, London, N.W.1
American Branch: 32 East 57th Street, New York, N.Y. 10022

Standard Book Number: 521 05736 1

First published 1962
Reprinted 1969

First printed in Great Britain by The Whitefriars Press Limited
Reprinted in Great Britain by Stephen Austin and Sons, Ltd., Hertford, Herts.

CONTENTS

PREFACE

Hobbes was the *bête noire* of his age. The principal objection to him, the one to which all other criticisms of him can ultimately be reduced, was that he was an atheist. He was the 'Monster of Malmesbury', the arch-atheist, the apostle of infidelity, the 'bug-bear of the nation'. His doctrines were cited by Parliament as a probable cause of the Great Fire of 1666. His books were banned and publicly burnt, and the ideas which Hobbes expressed in them in his lucid and potent style were the object of more or less continuous hostile criticism from 1650 to 1700.

The present study is an examination of this contemporary reaction in England. I have isolated Hobbes's materialism and moral philosophy because these two parts of Hobbes's system provoked the strongest reaction in their own time. Hobbes's critics viewed his denial of spirit and his ethical relativism as defections from the fundamental order of things, as heresies with the most dangerous consequences for religion; moreover a number of Hobbes's critics recognized that his materialism and his assumptions about morality were cardinal principles from which most of his other ideas flowed.

In our own time Hobbes is read chiefly as a political philosopher who developed a severely logical theory of absolutism. Hobbes's contemporaries would have regarded such an approach to his thought as too narrow: they considered his religious and metaphysical opinions and his political doctrines to be inseparable. The theory of commonwealth concerned them most for its Erastian implications, but even that was subordinated by them to the generally irreligious outlook which they detected in Hobbes's work. By studying their reactions we can gain a wider perspective of Hobbes's ideas, besides enriching our knowledge of seventeenth-century intellectual history. Modern scholars have, I believe, neglected the contemporary reaction at their peril. Even so closely-argued and brilliant a book as Howard Warrender's *The Political Philosophy of Hobbes: His Theory of Obligation* (Oxford, 1957) suffers from the absence

vii

of an appropriate historical context against which the analysis of Hobbes's ideas can be measured.[1]

Seeing Hobbes against the background of his age is valuable not only for the light it sheds on Hobbes himself, but also for the revealing glimpses it affords us of seventeenth-century thought. Hobbes's impact was subtle: he provoked intense hostility, but he also obliged his critics to employ his own method of rational argument. Their absorption of his method while they resisted his ideas is an extremely interesting feature of seventeenth-century rationalism.

For the most part the critics were men of high intellectual attainment. It is fascinating to watch them grapple with the perennial problems of philosophy, to recall the strong religious convictions which animated their attacks on Hobbes, to sense the urgency and depth of their feeling, to realize that Hobbes was more than an abstraction; he was a real and vital challenge to their most cherished beliefs. The literature against Hobbes is charged with the drama of different world-views in collision.

The first chapter of this study offers a biographical sketch of Hobbes, with special regard to the controversies in which he was personally engaged. I have also thought it worth while in this chapter to indicate the wide range of Hobbes's interests, and to convey some sense of his personality. The second chapter is a retrospective view of Hobbes's system, and especially of his nominalism, materialism, legal positivism, and

[1] Only three modern scholars have studied the literature against Hobbes as a separate subject. They are John Laird, in his *Hobbes* (London, 1934), pp. 247–317; Sterling Lamprecht, in 'Hobbes and Hobbism', *American Political Science Review*, xxxiv (1940), 31–53; and John Bowle, in *Hobbes and His Critics: A Study in Seventeenth Century Constitutionalism* (London, 1951). Laird has studied Hobbes's influence from the contemporary period to the present day; his treatment of the contemporary reaction is brief, and is largely confined to rapid characterizations (in a few sentences each) of the major critics, with bibliographical notes on the minor writers. Some of Laird's comments are shrewd, but his study, though a readable survey of the whole subject, is cursory. Lamprecht defends Hobbes against misrepresentations, both contemporary and modern, and argues that the contemporary criticism was based very largely on misreadings and biased interpretations of Hobbes's works. Lamprecht's own reading of Hobbes is sympathetic and perceptive, but his treatment of Hobbes's critics is something less than fair. He does not analyse or even cite from the work of a single critic, and is thus able to leave the erroneous impression that all of the critics shared the misconceptions of the very worst among them. Bowle confines his book entirely to the political criticisms of Hobbes, excluding the attacks on Hobbes's metaphysics and religious opinions. It is with the latter two types of criticism that this present study is chiefly concerned.

ethics. The third chapter provides a rapid chronological survey of the criticism, plus a discussion of such questions as Hobbes's 'atheism' and the personal motives, if any, which moved his critics to attack him. In the remaining chapters, I have examined the separate reactions to Hobbes, which I have arranged by topics, following the order in which Hobbes himself presented his ideas in the *Leviathan*. Although I have only occasionally alluded to Hobbes's literary achievements, I have been conscious always of his role as a man of letters, a part which he played with great distinction, not merely because he was an accomplished prose stylist, a minor poet of some merit, and a literary critic of undoubted influence, but because his philosophical system itself attains to the status of art. He regarded his work as part of the long literary tradition of historiography, political theory, metaphysics, and ethics, and I have myself assimilated this broad and venerable conception of literature into my view of Hobbes as a man of letters.

In writing this book I have received sympathetic criticism and advice from many scholars and friends. It is a pleasure to record my debt of gratitude to them. Professor Marjorie H. Nicolson, who has supervised my work through all its stages, has been the best of all mentors—kindly, penetrating, instructive. Professor Rosalie L. Colie, besides encouraging me to write, has read my manuscript and offered the most valuable insights. Professors Sidney Gelber and Sidney Burrell have provided their own philosophical and historical criticism, and have saved me from many errors. I am indebted to Professor Allen T. Hazen for bibliographical advice, given with his usual generosity, and I acknowledge with thanks the help of Mrs Matilda Streichler. My colleagues at the City College of New York, Professor Philip P. Wiener and Professor Albert Friend, have made suggestions from which I have benefited. I am also grateful for a grant from the Research Fund of the City College.

A portion of this book was written at Cambridge University, where I was a Fulbright Fellow in 1955-6, and from which place, I may add, came the greatest number of Hobbes's contemporary critics. I cannot thank enough Professor Basil Willey for his cordiality and kindness, and Dr Dorothea Krook, for her 'chivvying', and for her stimulating advice. Mr Peter Laslett of

Trinity College was an invaluable guide, both to Hobbes and to Cambridge. I must also thank the many librarians who have helped me locate books, and especially Mr A. N. L. Munby, Fellow and Librarian of King's College, who placed at my disposal Lord Keynes's rich collection of Hobbesiana; Mr J. P. T. Bury, Fellow and Librarian of Corpus Christi College, who directed me to manuscript sources for the career of Daniel Scargill; and Mrs Hugh N. Foster, Curator of the McAlpin Collection at the Union Theological Seminary, for her tireless and cheerful service in my behalf. My greatest debt, for sustaining me with patience and tolerance through many years of labour, is to my wife.

S. I. M.

The City College
The City University of New York

CHAPTER I

HOBBES'S LIFE

Thomas Hobbes, 'the infamous author of *Leviathan*', was born on 5 April 1588 in the village of Westport, adjacent to Malmesbury, in Wiltshire. His mother was brought to bed prematurely by the shock of hearing that the Spanish Armada had invaded British waters, so that Hobbes said in his verse autobiography many years later that his mother 'did bring forth Twins at once, both Me, and Fear'.[1] We have his own word for it that fear dogged his steps. He was afraid of 'Nights darkest shade',[2] of thieves, of persecution by his enemies, of death, which he called 'a Leap in the Dark'.[3] His critics liked to say that his fear was a sort of inner confession of sin. It was his conscience plaguing him for his atheism.[4] But Hobbes was a paradox: he was a fearful man with an adventurous and searching mind. His intellect was bold and virile. He never shrank from the violence he did to tradition. He deserved the epithet *temerarius* applied to him by his continental opponent, the German legal historian Conringius.[5] It was indeed 'prodigious', as a contemporary found, that 'the timorousness of his Nature from his Infancy . . . should not have chilled the briske Fervour and Vigour of his mind, which did wonderfully continue to him to his last'.[6] He lived for ninety-one years, *timor mortis* and all, and he was never afraid of new or audacious ideas.

[1] Thomas Hobbes, *The Life of Mr Thomas Hobbes of Malmesbury. Written by himself in a Latine Poem. And now Translated into English* (London, 1680), p. 2. Other contemporary sources for Hobbes's biography are an unfinished prose autobiography in Latin completed by Richard Blackburne and printed as 'Vitae Hobbianae Auctarium' in *Tracts of Thomas Hobb's* (London, 1681), and John Aubrey's biographical sketch in *Brief Lives*, ed. Andrew Clark (Oxford, 1898), I, 321–403.
[2] Hobbes, *The Life*, p. 4.
[3] *The Last Sayings, or Dying Legacy of Mr Thomas Hobbs of Malmesbury* (London, 1680). [Broadside.]
[4] See, e.g., Thomas Tenison, *The Creed of Mr Hobbes Examined* (2nd ed. London, 1671), p. 7; Bishop Francis Atterbury, sermon on 'The Terrors of Conscience', cited by John Hunt, *Religious Thought in England* (London, 1870), I, 397 n.
[5] Hermann Conringius, *Conringiana Epistolica* (2nd ed. Helmstadt, 1719), p. 76.
[6] Cited by John Aubrey, I, 390.

In Malmesbury Hobbes spent a placid boyhood. He fished in the twin rivers that formed a graceful arch around the town; he played among the ruins of a castle, or else he wandered through the neighbouring meadows which Athelstane had 'moistened with the blood of *Danes*'. The five tuneable bells of St Mary's Church gave him pleasure. So did the horse-fair opposite his house.

His father, John Aubrey tell us, was an amiable, semi-literate vicar; 'one of the Clergie of Queen Elizabeth's time, a little Learning went a great way with him and many other ignorant Sir Johns in those days'.[1] He was certainly an indiscreet man. After a night of card-playing he fell asleep in his church and was heard to utter: 'Trafells [clubs] is troumps.'[2] Later he struck a parson at the church door and in consequence was obliged to leave Malmesbury. The care of his family passed to his more affluent brother, Francis, a glover, who maintained the young Thomas both at grammar school and later at Oxford.

When he was seven Thomas Hobbes came under the tutelage of Robert Latimer, 'a good Grecian', who grounded him solidly in Latin and Greek, and when he was fourteen, he matriculated at Magdalen-hall in Oxford. Here he did not flourish. Like so many others of his age he found the scholastic curriculum unpalatable and arid—as Milton called it, 'an asinine feast of sowthistles and brambles'. He appears to have liked the rhetoric well enough, but logic and physics as they were then taught left him wholly unimpressed.

> And sedulously I my Tutor heard,
> Who Gravely Read, althou' he had no Beard.
> *Barbara, Celarent, Darii, Ferio, Baralypton,*
> These Modes hath the first Figure; then goes on
> *Caesare, Camestres, Festino, Baroco, Darapti,*
> This hath of Modes the same variety.[3]

These things, Hobbes told us, he learnt slowly, and then dispensed with. He wanted to 'prove things after my own sense'.[4] To release his imagination from the confinement of a narrow and rigid curriculum he indulged his love of astronomy and geography.

[1] *Ibid.* [2] *Ibid.* p. 387. [3] Hobbes, *Life*, p. 3. [4] *Ibid.*

2

My Phancie and my Mind divert I do,
With Maps Celestial and Terrestrial too.
Rejoyce t'accompany *Sol*, cloath'd with Rays,
Know by what Art he measures out our Days;
How *Drake* and *Cavendish* a Girdle made
Quite round the World, what Climates they survey'd. . . .
Nay there's a Fulness in Geography;
For Nature e'r abhor'd Vacuity.[1]

We have no exact information about Hobbes's reading at this time. Years later his critics were to charge him with not having read enough,[2] an opinion which Hobbes encouraged by boasting that if he had read as much as other men, he would have known no more than other men.[3] But Hobbes *was* widely read. He deliberately suppressed evidence of his reading as a pose, partly from vanity, so as to give weight to his conception of himself as innovator, and partly from an honest impatience with the habit of venerating the past uncritically. In the Battle of the Books Hobbes classed himself as a 'modern'. 'Though I reverence those men of ancient time, that either have written truth perspicuously, or set us in a better way to find it out ourselves; yet to the antiquity itself I think nothing due. For if we will reverence the age, the present is the oldest.'[4] Hobbes was willing to give the past its due, but not, as was 'the custom of late time', to grovel before it. Let no man, he says, argue from authority, unless (and in this Hobbes is human enough) the authority is Hobbes himself.

At Oxford Hobbes must have read sufficiently to satisfy his tutors, for in due course he took his bachelor's degree, and in 1608 was recommended by the Principal of his college to be tutor to the son of William Cavendish, Baron Hardwick, soon to become the first Earl of Devonshire. This appointment was

---

[1] *Ibid.* pp. 3–4.

[2] 'Mr *Hobbes* consulted too few Authors, and made use of too few Books'. Clarendon, *Brief View and Survey of The Dangerous and Pernicious Errors to Church and State, In Mr Hobbes's Book . . . Leviathan* (2nd ed. Oxford, 1676), 'Epistle Dedicatory', sig. *3 v.

[3] Aubrey, p. 349.

[4] *Leviathan*, ed. Michael Oakeshott (Oxford, 1946), p. 467. Hobbes is echoing Bacon. Cf. Francis Bacon, *Works*, ed. Spedding, Ellis, Heath (London, 1879–90), III, 291; IV, 82. (All page references to *Leviathan* will be to Oakeshott's edition.)

of the utmost significance for Hobbes's later development. A new world was opened to him, offering him travel, leisure, the company of famous and sophisticated men. The tall, grave, black-haired boy with 'hazel-quick' eyes, who had suffered from 'contemplative melancholinesse' at Oxford, was introduced to the splendours of Chatsworth and Welbeck Abbey. In the Cavendish household he was spared the grinding, humiliating poverty which was the usual lot of the tutor in the seventeenth century.[1] His masters were generous, and their kindness soon ripened into friendship. Hobbes mingled with their guests: discoursed on philosophy with Lord Herbert of Cherbury, on Arminianism with Lucius Cary, Lord Falkland, on poetry with Ben Jonson. His connection with the 'Noble and Conspicuous' Cavendish family lasted, with minor interruptions, for the rest of his long life.

Most particularly he welcomed the salubrious intellectual climate of Welbeck Abbey, where William, Earl of Newcastle, and his brother Charles Cavendish, a gifted mathematician, had established an outpost of the new science.[2] The Earl of Newcastle was a brilliant administrator of his estates, and later a very able commander in the royalist army. He was less proficient at science, but he showed a perennial curiosity in it, and maintained a private laboratory where, according to a biased source (his famous wife Margaret), he discovered that the sun is 'nothing else but a very solid body of salt and sulphur, inflamed by its own motion upon its own axis'.[3] He had, too, a special interest in optics and geometry and combined these with his passion for horses by persuading Hobbes to write a curious treatise called 'Considerations Touching the Facility or Difficulty of the Motions of a Horse on Straight Lines, or Circular'.[4] It was on his behalf that Hobbes spent many hours

---

[1] John Eachard, *Grounds and Occasions of the Contempt of the Clergy* (London, 1670), *passim;* Macaulay, *The History of England from the Accession of James II* (London, 1877), I, 160.

[2] Cavendish's scientific achievements are studied in Jean Jacquot, 'Sir Charles Cavendish and his Learned Friends,' *Annals of Science*, VIII (1952), 13–27, 175–95.

[3] See Margaret Cavendish, Duchess of Newcastle, *Philosophical and Physical Opinions* (London, 1663), p. 463.

[4] A. S. Turberville, *A History of Welbeck Abbey and its Owners* (London, 1938), p. 54. The manuscript is printed in *A Catalogue of Letters and Other Historical Documents Exhibited in the Library at Welbeck*, compiled by S. Arthur Strong (London,

searching the London bookshops in vain for a copy of Galileo's *Dialogues*.[1]

In these early years with the Cavendish family Hobbes had leisure to think and access to good libraries. Chatsworth was to him what Horton was to Milton. Here he read hundreds of romances and plays, which Aubrey points to as the source of his 'copie of words'.[2] Here he also deepened his knowledge of the classical poets and historians, as well as of their best commentators. At Chatsworth he found the university he had missed at Oxford.[3]

These benefits did not accrue to Hobbes all at once. At first he was rather a companion than a tutor to his pupil, who was only three years Hobbes's junior, seventeen when they met in 1608, though already a married man. The young Earl's bride was a twelve-year-old Scottish heiress who was allowed to mature some years more before assuming her wifely duties,[4] so that her husband was, for all practical purposes, a bachelor. He and his tutor rode hunting and hawking together, and Hobbes was set such unpleasant tasks as raising money for his pupil's creditors. He did not strenuously object to this mode of life, though he caught cold frequently on his borrowing missions, and he worried about forgetting his Latin. In 1610 he and his charge embarked on the grand tour. They visited France and Italy where they applied themselves to the study of foreign tongues. On their return Hobbes continued his reading of the classical historians, and in 1629 produced his first published work, a translation of Thucydides's *Peloponnesian War*. There are anticipations of the *Leviathan* in this book, both in the political overtones of Hobbes's preface and in the pithy phrases of the translation. 'There's none', said Hobbes, 'that pleased me like Thucydides.'

1903). The editor refers to this treatise as 'an irrelevant superfluity of reasoning' such as was produced by 'the tailor in *Gulliver's Travels* who measures his men with the help of a sextant and other mathematical instruments' (p. vii).

[1] Portland MSS., *Historical Manuscripts Commission*, II, 124.
[2] Aubrey, p. 361.
[3] Cf. Hobbes's statement: '... there was not any ... in whose house a man should less need a university'. Thomas Hobbes, *English Works*, ed. Molesworth (11 vols., London, 1839–45), VIII, iv. (This collected edition will henceforth be referred to as *Works*.)
[4] Francis Bickley, *The Cavendish Family* (Boston, 1914), p. 41.

He says Democracy's a Foolish Thing,
Than a Republick Wiser is one King.
This Author I taught *English*, that even he
A Guide to Rhetoricians might be.[1]

Some time before the Thucydides appeared, Hobbes served a brief period as secretary to Francis Bacon.[2] He accompanied the deposed Lord Chancellor in his 'delicious walkes' at Gorhambury; on these occasions Hobbes kept pen and paper in readiness against any sudden philosophic thought from his master. Bacon considered Hobbes the best of his amanuenses because the most understanding, and allowed him to help with the translation into Latin of several of the English essays.[3] It was from Hobbes that Aubrey derived his anecdote about the death of Bacon: the philosopher impulsively alighted from a coach in mid-winter to buy a chicken, which he eviscerated and stuffed with snow in order to test a theory about food-freezing, and as a consequence he contracted pneumonia and died.

In 1628 Hobbes lost another friend, his pupil-companion, Cavendish, who succumbed to 'excessive indulgence in good living'.[4] Hobbes was forced to seek employment elsewhere, and was engaged as cicerone to the son of Sir Gervase Clinton, with whom he immediately embarked on a tour of France and Switzerland. Hobbes was now forty years old and had not yet begun his career as philosopher. It was during this second tour, however, that he discovered Euclid and first turned his thoughts to the possibilities of mathematical philosophy. He had come upon a copy of Euclid in a private library in Geneva.[5]

'By G—,' sayd he, 'this is impossible!' So he reads the demonstration of it which referred him back to such a proposition; which proposition he read. That referred him back to another, which he

---

[1] Hobbes, *Life*, pp. 4–5. Hobbes consulted Ben Jonson and the Scottish poet Sir Robert Ayton about the prose style of his translation. Little is known about the relations between Hobbes and Ben Jonson. It is possible that Jonson's tribute to Bacon in the *Discoveries* is borrowed from Hobbes. See Arthur T. Shillinglaw, 'Hobbes and Ben Jonson', *T.L.S.* 18 April 1936, p. 336.

[2] Aubrey's chronology is vague. Bacon died in 1626. Precisely when Hobbes's connection with Bacon began and ended is not known.

[3] Aubrey, p. 331, remembers only one: Essay XXIX: 'Of the True Greatness of Kingdoms and Estates'.

[4] Bickley, *The Cavendish Family*, p. 43.

[5] The place is fixed in a recently discovered letter. See G. R. De Beer, 'Some Letters of Hobbes', *Notes and Records of the Royal Society*, VII (April 1950), 205.

also read. Et sic deinceps, that at last he was demonstratively convinced of that trueth. This made him in love with geometry:[1]

So began Hobbes's lifelong infatuation with 'the only science that it hath pleased God hitherto to bestow on mankind'.[2] In the company of many other thinkers of his age, Hobbes thought he perceived in mathematics a certitude which the flux of human opinion could not alter. He considered 'Truth' to be a function of reasoning, its discovery an analytical process in which definitions are placed in their proper order. This type of truth is best arrived at by geometry, which is propositional in character, and which, when practised correctly, is immune to contradiction. The unity and logical structure of geometry produced in Hobbes an almost aesthetic emotion, comparable to that 'sense for beauty' which Matthew Arnold says the born scientist can apply even to the most unpromising subject matter.[3] The language of geometry, moreover, is lucid, free of verbal confusions, a perfect analogue of the kind of style which Hobbes hoped to achieve in his non-mathematical writings. And finally, geometry harmonized most easily with the cosmology that Hobbes was soon to develop: a universe that consists only of extended body is best described in geometrical terms.

Algebra, on the other hand, held no such attractions for Hobbes. It could not properly be applied to figures in space, since these are ultimately described only in qualitative terms. Hobbes was suspicious of all attempts, whether by Archimedes or John Wallis, to 'arithmetize' geometry;[4] the truth is that Hobbes grossly underestimated the scope of algebra. For him it was a minor branch of arithmetic, 'to the theory whereof two or three Days at most are required, though to the Promptitude of Working, perhaps the Practice of three Months is necessary'.[5] Even the use of symbols offended him, possibly because he

[1] Aubrey, p. 332.
[2] Leviathan, p. 21.
[3] Matthew Arnold, 'Literature and Science', Discourses in America (London, 1885), p. 113.
[4] Thomas Hobbes, Seven Philosophical Problems (1662), in Works, VII, 67–8.
[5] Thomas Hobbes, Rosetum Geometrum (1671), translated by Venterus Mandey as Book II of Mellificium Mensionis (4th ed. London, 1727), p. 125. Hobbes later 'lamented [to Sir William Petty] that he had not taken the art of algebra more into his studies'. The Petty-Southwell Correspondence, ed. Marquis of Lansdowne (London, 1928), p. 322.

contrasted them with the pleasing abstract forms of geometrical drawings. Wallis's 'scab of symbols'[1] simply disfigured the page, 'as if a hen had been scraping there'.[2]

By thus holding himself aloof from algebra—as well as from calculus—Hobbes remained outside the mainstream of mathematical thought in his century. Nor did he make any significant contributions to geometry. Much of his energy was spent in pursuit of such *ignes fatui* as the quadrature of the circle and the duplicate of the cube. His dogmatic assertions, which he later modified, of success in these attempts amused his critics, and led him into long and futile controversy with the acrimonious but vastly superior mathematician, John Wallis.[3] Of this dispute it may be said that Wallis was right, but Hobbes was more of a gentleman, though neither conducted himself precisely according to the rules of fair play. At least we ought to remember that Hobbes was not unique in his preoccupation with circle-squaring; the same problem engaged the minds of other and better mathematicians in the century, such as John Pell; and it was not until the nineteenth century that the solution of this problem was finally shown to be impossible.[4]

Hobbes was soon to assimilate his interest in geometry to the new physics. In 1630 he returned to the Cavendish household, this time as tutor to the Earl of Devonshire's young son, and with his pupil again made the inevitable continental tour. On this third and longest journey, 'whether on Horse, in Coach, or Ship', Hobbes meditated on the problems of motion; at Pisa he sought out Galileo, whom he ever afterward held in veneration. 'Galileus . . . was the first that opened to us the gate of natural philosophy universal, which is the knowledge of *motion*. So that

[1] Thomas Hobbes, *Six Lessons to the Professors of the Mathematics* (1656) in *Works*, VII, 316.
[2] *Ibid.* p. 330.
[3] The controversy (which lies outside the scope of the present study) is treated fully in J. F. Scott, *The Mathematical Work of John Wallis* (London, 1938), and may be supplemented in G. Udney Yule, 'John Wallis, D.D., F.R.S.: 1616–1703', *Notes and Records of the Royal Society* (April 1939), pp. 74–82. The bibliography of the dispute is recorded in Hugh Macdonald and Mary Hargreaves, *Thomas Hobbes: A Bibliography* (London, 1952).
[4] Florian Cajori, *A History of Mathematics* (New York, 1894), p. 2. A. De Morgan, *A Budget of Paradoxes* (London, 1915), p. 110, says that Hobbes was 'very wrong in his quadrature, but . . . he was not the ignoramus in geometry that he is sometimes supposed. His writings, erroneous as they are in many things, contain acute remarks on points of principle.'

neither can the age of natural philosophy be reckoned higher than to him.'[1] In Paris, possibly through the offices of Sir Kenelm Digby,[2] he met Marin Mersenne, the Franciscan monk who conducted in his cell an informal scientific academy where some of the best scientists of the age gathered and exchanged views. To Mersenne Hobbes communicated the results of his early speculations in optics and sensation.[3]

When he returned to England he continued to correspond with Mersenne about physics. He had by then already formulated the outlines of his philosophical system. It was to have three parts—of Body, of Man, of Citizenship—to be developed in that order. As Hobbes was provided with leisure and books at Welbeck Abbey, and was stimulated by his recent contacts with Mersenne and Galileo, he set about formulating the first section of his system, that concerning Body. The fruits of these early labours are three manuscripts,[4] none published in Hobbes's lifetime, and all apparently drafts of *De Corpore*, Hobbes's finished statement on this subject, which he published in 1655.

But Hobbes's political interests, which all his life were to compete with his metaphysical speculations, soon asserted themselves. In 1640 he produced two treatises, *Humane Nature; or the Fundamental Elements of Policie*, and *De Corpore Politico, or the Elements of Law*, both of which circulated widely in manuscript until they were combined and published in 1650. Hobbes hoped

[1] Hobbes, *Elements of Philosophy*, 'De Corpore', *Works*, I, viii. Tönnies believes, on very slight evidence, that at their interview Galileo first suggested to Hobbes the notion of treating ethics in a geometrical manner. See Ferdinand Tönnies, 'Hobbes-Analekten', *Archiv für Geschichte der Philosophie*, III, 232.

[2] John Stoye, *English Travellers Abroad*, 1604–67 (London, 1952), p. 438.

[3] These were summarized by Mersenne in his *Cogitata Physico-Mathematica* (Paris, 1644), preface to 'Ballistica'.

[4] The first, in English, was entitled 'A Short Tract on First Principles', edited by Tönnies, who printed it in his edition of Hobbes's *Elements of Law* (2nd ed. Cambridge, 1928), pp. 152–67. It is dated 1630 by Frithiof Brandt, *Thomas Hobbes's Mechanical Conception of Nature* (Copenhagen, 1928). The second, in Latin, was discovered in 1945 in the National Library of Wales by Mario M. Rossi, who believes that it is a copy made by Lord Herbert of Cherbury for his own use. From this premise Rossi dates the manuscript 1637. R. I. Aaron ('A Possible Early Draft of *De Corpore*', *Mind*, LIV (1945), 342–56) does not believe the handwriting is Herbert's, but is willing to accept the date on other grounds. The third, also in Latin, was discovered at the Bibliothèque Nationale in 1952 and is quite obviously a chapter-by-chapter refutation of Thomas White's *De mundo dialogi tres quibus materia* (1648), which is itself an attack on Galileo's *Dialogue upon the two systems of the world*. This third manuscript is described by Jean Jacquot in *Notes and Records of the Royal Society*, IX (1952), 188–95.

9

that these philosophical and relatively abstract treatises might help cool the political and religious passions which were then boiling over in England; but his monarchical bias could not, in 1640, placate a Parliament soon to assume power. Hobbes feared for his safety; though the Parliament at that time made no move against him, nevertheless Hobbes thought it prudent to remove himself to France, where he remained, mostly in Paris, for eleven years.

In Paris Hobbes set himself at once to perfect his philosophy. In 1642 he published *De Cive;* then, abetted by Mersenne, he returned to his physical speculations, and was almost immediately engaged in controversy with Descartes. Hobbes was already acquainted with Descartes's work, having received a copy of the *Discourse on Method* from Sir Kenelm Digby in 1637, only a few months after the book was published.[1] The controversy with Descartes turned on a question which brought credit to neither man: which of the two had first announced that colours do not inhere in objects, but are rather functions of the mind? Descartes claimed priority and called Hobbes a plagiarist. Hobbes said he had expressed the doctrine verbally to Newcastle and Charles Cavendish as early as 1630.[2] Neither was actually first; the principle that secondary qualities are subjective was enunciated clearly and at great length by Galileo in *Il Saggiatore* (1623). But Hobbes and Descartes were both too proud to acknowledge this debt; and for the rest of their lives they alluded to each other's works with the utmost reserve and coolness. Of course their differences are more fundamental: Hobbes banished spirit from the universe; Descartes separated it from matter, but never denied that spirit was real. It is true that Descartes's critics thought this segregation of matter and spirit had the same effect as banishing spirit altogether, but in fact, Cartesian dualism remains a view of the world essentially different from the Hobbesian view. It is a difference which

---

[1] Digby's letter accompanying the book is printed from manuscript by Marjorie Nicolson, 'The Early Stage of Cartesianism in England', *Studies in Philology*, XXVI (1929), 358. The letter is sometimes referred to as containing the first English allusion to Descartes, but it is actually preceded in this respect by a passage in Samuel Hartlib's *Ephemerides* of 1635, describing a meeting between Descartes and John Dury which took place some time earlier. See C. De Waard, 'Un entretien avec Descartes en 1634 ou 1635', *Archives Internationales d'Histoire des Sciences*, XXII (Janv.–Mars 1953), 14–16.

[2] René Descartes, *Oeuvres*, ed. C. Adam and P. Tannery (Paris, 1899), III, 342.

helps also to define the Cartesian and Hobbist spheres of influence. The great philosophic problem of seventeenth-century science was to find a way of working out its mechanical principles without abandoning spirit and God. Cartesianism offered just the kind of support the burgeoning scientific movement needed, namely, a rigorously mechanical view of the material world, accompanied always by the certainty that the spirit-world also exists. Scientists and theologians alike—indeed they were often the same persons—could derive no comfort from contemplating a Hobbist universe, however mechanical, when that universe was devoid of spirit and only distantly related to a material God. These larger issues were touched upon in the debate between Hobbes and Descartes which Mersenne published as a portion of the *Objectiones* to Descartes's *Meditations*.

Hobbes was soon embarked on a second controversy, with John Bramhall, Bishop of Derry, in which questions of real substance were tried with much heat, as was customary, but also with considerable light and perspicuity. In 1645 Bramhall was, like Newcastle, one of a growing number of English refugees in Paris. In Newcastle's house, Bramhall, an ardent Arminian and the very type of Laudian bishop, sounded Hobbes out on the question of free will and found in him a ready but amiable opponent. Bramhall committed his side of the debate to paper; Hobbes wrote a rejoinder.

> The Question at that Time was, and is still,
> Whether at God's, or our own Choice We Will.
> And this was the Result proceeding thence,
> He the Schools follow'd, I made use of Sense.[1]

Both men agreed not to publish what they had written, but Hobbes allowed his manuscript to be translated into French for the use of a friend. The translator, one John Davys of Kidwelly, appropriated a copy of the English text for himself, and published it without Hobbes's knowledge in 1654. Bramhall, thus publicly attacked in print, and with his own side of the matter ignored, considered Hobbes entirely responsible, and was moreover outraged by a preface written by Davys containing a scurrilous attack on priests.

He consequently published a reply in which he printed not only what he had originally written in defence of free-will, but

[1] Hobbes, *Life*, p. 14.

also an appendix attacking Hobbes for the impiety and free-thought of *Leviathan*, then already in print. Thus was launched a controversy which continued intermittently until Hobbes had the last (posthumous) word with the publication of *An Answer to a Book Published by Dr Bramhall . . . Called The Catching of the Leviathan* (1682).[1] The details of the controversy will be considered in a later chapter. Here it may suffice to note that Bramhall was learned, witty and more than usually skilled in scholastic disputation. His magniloquent periods are in sharp contrast to Hobbes's blunt and pithy phrases. The two styles are good illustrations of the changes then taking place in English prose: Bramhall's tropes and cadences were yielding in popular favour to the 'plain' style so admirably exemplified in Hobbes.

Bishop Bramhall was not the first cleric to attack Hobbes for his irreligion. In 1645, probably through the influence of New-castle, Hobbes was appointed tutor in mathematics to the Prince of Wales, who was then in exile at St Germain. The appointment aroused widespread fears that Hobbes might contaminate the Prince with atheistical principles. From Scotland Robert Baillie reported that 'the placeing of Hopes [Hobbes] (a professed Atheist, as they speak) about the Prince as his teacher, is ill taken. . . . Let such wicked men be put from about him'.[2] Moreover the anti-papal sentiments which Hobbes had already expressed in *De Cive* irritated Queen Henrietta Maria. Hobbes was therefore obliged to promise that he would teach mathematics only, and not politics.[3] How far he succeeded in keeping this promise is not shown in the record; Charles II at any rate embodied no Hobbist principles in his statecraft in so far as he practised statecraft at all; his libertinism must also surely be charged to other causes than tutorial sessions with a bookish philosopher. What Charles may have received

[1] For a full discussion of the origin of the Hobbes–Bramhall controversy see G. Groom Robertson, *Hobbes* (Edinburgh, 1886), pp. 163–7. The bibliography of the controversy is recorded in Hugh Macdonald, *Hobbes: A Bibliography, passim*. Davys's unauthorized printing of Hobbes's manuscript was entitled *Of Libertie and Necessity* (London, 1654). Pepys read it in bed on 20 November 1661, thought it 'a little but very shrewd piece'.

[2] Robert Baillie, *The Letters and Journals of Robert Baillie*, ed. David Laing (Edinburgh, 1841–42), II, 388, 395.

[3] Ferdinand Tönnies, 'Hobbes-Analekten' in *Archiv für Geschichte der Philosophie*, III, 194.

from Hobbes was an interest in science strong enough for him to bestow his royal favour on the Royal Society when that body was chartered in 1662.

Notwithstanding the criticisms directed against him Hobbes persevered in his studies and gave his metaphysical and political beliefs their most finished statement in his masterpiece, *Leviathan*, which he published in 1651. Hardly anyone at the English court in France liked it; it was absolutist enough, but it expressed no particular bias in favour of monarchy. By insisting that a subject submit to any government which has *de facto* control so long as that control is firm enough to secure internal peace, Hobbes appeared to give more comfort to the Puritans than to the Royalists. Besides, its materialism and peculiar religious doctrines offended the Anglicans, while its anti-clericalism and barbed attacks on Rome were anathema to the French Jesuits and to English Catholics like Wat Montagu.[1] For these reasons Charles banished Hobbes from the Court in 1652 and the philosopher, now sixty-four years old, returned to England.

After the Restoration Hobbes's critics liked to say that the *Leviathan* was written in order to curry favour with Cromwell. Clarendon alluded to the book's Review and Conclusion as 'a sly address to Cromwell'.[2] Wallis, who conveniently forgot that he had himself performed valuable services for Cromwell as a cryptographer, said the book 'was written in defence of Oliver's title, or whoever, by whatsoever means, can get to be upmost'.[3] Still later a groundless rumour was circulated that Cromwell had offered Hobbes a secretaryship.[4] The truth is, as Hobbes himself said,[5] Cromwell was not yet Lord Protector in 1651, and Hobbes had no way of knowing that Cromwell would assume that office. Hobbes was obliged to return to England when he did because his position in France was precarious, but it does not seem likely that he wrote the *Leviathan* to ensure his safety at home. Its basic principles, at any rate, had been germinating

[1] According to the *Nicholas Papers* (Camden Society, 1886), p. 285, 'Wat Montague and other Papists' were responsible for the expulsion of Hobbes from the English court in France.
[2] Clarendon, *Brief View and Survey*, p. 317.
[3] John Wallis, *Hobbius Heauton-timorumenos* (Oxford, 1662), p. 5.
[4] John Dowel, *The Leviathan Heretical* (London, 1683), p. 137.
[5] Hobbes, *Works*, IV, 415.

in his mind for a considerable period, extending back at least as far as 1640, when he gave them an attenuated but not essentially different expression in *The Elements of Law*.

In London, Hobbes worked at his geometry, and for greater leisure retired in 1653 to the Cavendish estate at Derbyshire. After the Restoration, when he was anxious to regain the good opinion of the Court, Aubrey arranged an appointment for him at a limner's at a time when the King would be there.[1] Hobbes was well received; the King admired his wit and agreeable conversation, and was not in the slightest degree disturbed by the charges, now more frequently heard, that Hobbes was an atheist. The clergy, said Charles, tormented Hobbes as dogs bait a bear, for exercise.[2] For his part the King would have none of this; and he must have irritated hundreds of (silent) clergymen when he awarded Hobbes a pension of one hundred pounds a year, which, however, the Crown did not always remember to pay.

In his later years Hobbes devoted such time as he could spare from the paper war with Wallis to the continued refinement of his philosophical system. He produced a Latin translation of the *Leviathan*, published in Amsterdam in 1670, which differed from the original English text in a lesser emphasis on personalities and a greater preference for monarchy.[3] 'Of late', wrote Archbishop Tenison, '[Hobbes] hath set forth his *Leviathan* in the Latine Tongue; declaring his desire (as is the manner of infected persons) of spreading his Malady throughout the World.'[4] The book did not however lash such a storm as the English *Leviathan* did.

As a man of letters Hobbes's total output was small, but it was by no means without merit. We have already mentioned the translation of Thucydides, which proved to be enduringly

---

[1] Anthony Powell, *John Aubrey and His Friends* (London, 1948), p. 99.
[2] Samuel Sorbière, *Voyage to England* (London, 1709), p. 40.
[3] The Latin and English texts are compared in Julius Lips, *Die Stellung des Thomas Hobbes zu den Politischen Parteien der grossen Englischen Revolution* (Leipzig, 1927), ch. VII, and in Zbigniew Lubienski, *Die Grundlagen des ethisch-politischen Systems von Hobbes* (Munich, 1932), pp. 260 ff.
[4] Thomas Tenison, *The Creed of Mr Hobbes Examin'd* (London, 1671), sig. A 4. Cf. Tillotson's remark in a letter to Worthington, April 1669: 'Some things in it seem to be knavishly intended, but the greatest part is very foolish.' John Worthington's *Diary*, ed. J. Crossley and R. C. Christie in the *Publications of th~ Chetham Society*, CXIV (1886), 316.

popular in the seventeenth and early eighteenth centuries. It went through five editions, the last in 1723, and a portion of it —'Lib. 2. As it is excellently translated by Mr Hobbs'—was six times reprinted as an addendum to Thomas Sprat's *The Plague of Athens*. Hobbes's second published work was an original composition, the long descriptive Latin poem *De Mirabilibus Pecci* (1636), which gave an account of a tour Hobbes made in the Peak country near Chatsworth. In its English version, produced in 1678 by 'a Person of Quality',[1] the poem enjoyed a considerable vogue. The verses themselves are, for the most part, pedestrian, but occasionally they achieve a stately rhythm:

> On th' English *Alps*, where *Darbies* Peak doth rise,
> High up in Hills, that Emulate the Skies,
> And largely Waters all the Vales below,
> With Rivers that still plentifully Flow,
> Doth *Chatsworth* by swift *Derwins* Channel stand . . .[2]

Apart from its abundant topographical and meteorological lore, *De Mirabilibus Pecci* is interesting for two very extravagant 'metaphysical' conceits, and for the glimpses it affords us of Hobbes's personality in the 1620's. Hobbes shared in the widespread, though not universal, detestation of mountains. He called them obscene excrescences. The two humps of the Peak were the 'Devil's Arse', and the mouth of a huge pit below resembled the privities of a woman. Hobbes thought these were 'apt' similes, since 'To small things . . . thou may'st compare what's great'. But the obvious pleasure he took in delivering these conceits in no way dimmed his feeling that the mountain is an ugly deformation. Such a feeling may seem odd in a man who, as a traveller, had already had wide experience of mountains on the continent; Hobbes was, however, merely following a classical tradition. Even so, he endowed the convention with vivid touches furnished from the recesses of his own personality. He had a genuine phobia of heights and of darkness; as he scales the Peak, or as he enters a cave, he communicates to us his very real sense of fear. Fear of the Peak and a sense of

---

[1] *De Mirabilibus Pecci: Being the Wonders of the Peak in Darby-shire. . . . The Latine Written by Thomas Hobbes of Malmesbury. The English by a Person of Quality* (London, 1678).
[2] *Ibid.* p. 2.

15

wonder are compounded in equal measures in *De Mirabilibus Pecci.*

Of greater significance than either his translations or Latin poem are Hobbes's critical doctrines, expressed mainly in his prefaces to Davenant's *Gondibert* (1650, 1651), although some additional views can be found in Hobbes's redactions of Aristotelian rhetoric (1637, 1651), and in the prefaces to his *Homer* (1673). The Davenant papers are written so concisely as to be not entirely free of obscurity. They do not, as is commonly supposed, mark a clean break with orthodox criticism. Both Hobbes and Davenant (though Davenant to a greater degree) believed in the didactic purpose of the heroic poem: it must teach Christian virtue. For Hobbes the poet's judgment, by which he means his apprehension of the truth, is united with his imagination to produce a work that pleases while it instructs. 'All that is beautiful or defensible in building; or marvellous in engines or instruments of motion; whatsoever commodity men receive from the observations of the heavens, from the description of the earth, from the account of time, from walking on the seas; and whatsoever distinguisheth the civility of Europe from the barbarity of the American savages; is the workmanship of fancy, but guided by the precepts of true philosophy.'[1]

It can be seen from this passage that Hobbes does not explicitly argue a separation of thought and feeling, or what is referred to so often in T. S. Eliot's phrase as a 'dissociation of sensibility'. Fancy and judgment are not precisely one, but both together and in harmony produce a good poem. On the other hand it is clear that in Hobbes's scheme the imagination plays a distinctly subordinate role. 'Judgment begets the strength and structure, and fancy begets the ornaments of a poem.'[2] This is consistent with Hobbesian psychology, which Hobbes assimilated into his literary criticism. Imagination is rooted in sensation, but it is 'decaying sense', and because decaying gives rise to apparitions, phantasmogoria, a belief in witchcraft, and other similar errors and credulities. The poet who uses imagination alone does so at his own peril; he may attribute to those long-received and now decaying half-remembered sense-impressions a truth-value which they do not possess. Even so the imagina-

---

[1] Hobbes, 'The Answer to the Preface to Gondibert', *Works*, IV, 440–1.
[2] *Ibid.* p. 449.

tion can still delight; but it cannot teach, because it enables the poet to know only what is in his own mind, and not what lies about him. The good poet allows his imagination to be ruled by his judgment, 'the severer sister', that which is confirmed by experience and right reasoning. Hence Hobbes believed that the poet draws his best themes from his observations of men in society and achieves his best effects by a perspicuity of style which holds a tight rein on his straining imagination.

In his tone, in his insistence on the pre-eminence of judgment, in his feeling, obviously derived from his materialist and sceptical outlook, that the supernatural apparatus of epic is purely ornamental—the mere outward trappings of poetry— in his emphasis on the manners of men and on perspicuity, Hobbes looked forward to Augustan critical theory. I cannot therefore agree with Professor Thorpe that Hobbes was the founder of a school of psychological literary criticism favouring freedom of the imagination,[1] but I think that Professor Thorpe was certainly right in calling attention to the element of realism in Hobbes's aesthetics. In so far as Hobbes insisted that the heroic poem *must* teach virtue, his theory was didactic and in this respect it owed much to earlier Renaissance criticism. But Hobbes's critical statements were more descriptive than they were legislative. He wanted to say what a poem was before he would say what it ought to be. Moreover he would not allow his didactic purpose to influence his account of the creative process and of the nature of poetry. He approached the subject of poetry in the same realistic spirit that marked his treatment of physics, psychology, and politics. 'To Hobbes', observed Professor Thorpe, 'more than to any other single Englishman, later criticism may be said to have owed its distrust for trad- ition and dogma and its gradual return to the spirit of Aristotle in basing its judgments on a close study of works of literature and on an anaylsis of facts in relation to literature.'[2]

Hobbes was a literary figure in a sense which the term 'man of letters' does not properly convey. His whole body of work attains to the status of art. This is so not merely because he possessed a powerful and subtle prose style which was by turns

---

[1] See Clarence De Witt Thorpe, *Aesthetic Theory of Thomas Hobbes* (Ann Arbor, 1940).
[2] *Ibid.* p. 8.

17

witty, ironical, didactic, and sententious. He was an artist because his philosophical system was a grand imaginative conception—a complex structure of ideas having unity, order, coherence. Professors Wellek and Warren, the very brilliant theoreticians of literature, would probably exclude Hobbes's work from the category of 'pure' literature, but even they insist that 'every work of art imposes an order, an organization, a unity on its material'.[1] Hobbes's system is nothing if it is not ordered.

No doubt there are flaws in his organization and strains on his unity which his more perceptive critics have not failed to point out. '... [To] fasten *de Homine* and *de Cive* cleverly together', John Eachard told Hobbes, 'requires a little more knocking and hammering.'[2] So indeed it does, but it is the knocking and hammering of the artist's chisel, perfecting what he has already created as a work of art. Hobbes himself said that philosophy is a creative activity.

If you will be a philosopher in good earnest, let your reason move upon the deep of your own cogitations and experience; those things that lie in confusion must be set asunder, distinguished and every one stamped with its own name set in order; that is to say, your method must resemble that of the creation.[3]

Hobbes followed this method with the most striking results. 'The *Leviathan*', Michael Oakeshott avers,

is a myth, the transposition of an abstract argument into the world of the imagination. In it we are made aware at a glance of the fixed and simple centre of a universe of complex and changing relationships. The argument may not be the better for this transposition, and what it gains in vividness it may pay for in illusion. But it is an accomplishment of art that Hobbes, in the history of political philosophy, shares only with Plato.[4]

In his old age Hobbes returned to the classics, ending his career as he began it, with translations. At the age of eighty he produced complete versions of the *Iliad* and the *Odyssey* in English verse. 'Why, then, did I write it?' he asks in his preface.

---

[1] René Wellek and Austin Warren, *Theory of Literature* (London, 1949), p. 14.
[2] John Eachard, *Mr Hobbs's State of Nature Considered* (London, 1672), p. 39.
[3] Hobbes, *Works*, I, xiii.
[4] Michael Oakeshott, Introduction, *Leviathan* (Oxford, 1946), p. xviii.

Because I had nothing else to do. Why publish it? Because I thought it might take off my adversaries from showing their folly upon my more serious writings, and set them upon my verses to show their wisdom. But why without annotations? Because I had no hope to do it better than it had already been done by Mr Ogilby.[1]

Dryden's wry comment on the translations is that Hobbes studied poetry 'as he did mathematics, when it was too late'.[2] The best that his critics would say about his interest in Homer is that it kept him out of mischief:

> O that he had spent all the time
> In hard translations and in rhyme
> Which he spent in opposing truths by
> which to Heaven we climb.[3]

Hobbes's old age was not unpleasant. He spent most of his time at Chatsworth or Hardwick, in the company of his beloved Cavendishes. He read, dictated to his amanuenses—from his sixtieth year onward Hobbes was afflicted with palsy—and meditated. He smoked and drank moderately; Aubrey estimates that he was drunk no more than one hundred times, or an average of slightly more than once for every year of his life, which in the seventeenth century amounted to almost total abstinence. He was a bachelor, but, as Aubrey tells us with splendid ambiguity, 'he was not a woman-hater'. He indulged his great passion for music by playing frequently on the bass viol and singing aloud from a book of prick-songs, although he showed a nice regard for the feelings of his neighbours by doing these things only when his doors and windows were shut. Except for the palsy and a serious case of typhus in 1647, his health was good. Hobbes was a valetudinarian; he believed that profuse sweating was the best protection against disease. Consequently he submitted to vigorous massages, took long walks, dressed warmly, even in mild weather, and played tennis up to his seventy-fifth year.

He died at Hardwick at age ninety-one, in 1679. According to Southwell[4] he died in all the forms of a good Christian,

---

[1] Hobbes, *Works*, x, x.
[2] John Dryden, *Fables Ancient and Modern* (2nd ed. London, 1713), 'Preface', sig. a3v.
[3] [Anon.], *The True Effigies of the Monster of Malmesbury* (London, 1680), p. 8.
[4] Ormonde Papers, *Historical Manuscripts Commission*, n.s. IV, 13 December 1679.

though when death had stared him in the face in France during his siege of typhus, he rejected the offices of English and French divines by saying: 'Let me alone, or else I will detect all your cheates from Aaron to yourselves.'[1] According to rumour, Hobbes wished that his tomb would bear the following inscription: 'Here is the true philosopher's stone.'[2] But it bears instead an epitaph which Hobbes wrote and which reads in part: 'Vir probus, et fama eruditionis Domi forisque bene cognitus.'[3] This estimate of himself is not wholly unjust. Even some of his severest critics, like Ross and Clarendon, acknowledged the depth of his learning and the probity of his character. And although the curve of his reputation was at its lowest point in his own lifetime, he had still his friends and admirers, as well as sympathetic critics both at home and abroad. He was intimate with Harvey, Pell, Petty, Cowley, Selden, Waller, Gassendi, Mersenne. Harrington, who could find nothing to admire in Hobbes's politics, was nevertheless moved to compliment him extravagantly as one who 'is and will in all future ages be accounted the best writer at this day in the world'.[4] One of Cowley's finest odes is a touching tribute 'To Mr Hobbes', that great 'Columbus of the golden land of new philosophies'.[5] On the continent Puffendorf disputed with him about natural law, but praised him for the acuity of his thought, while Velthuysen[6] greeted *De Cive* with warm enthusiasm.

To these men Hobbes was a philosopher of the first order. But to the greater majority of his contemporaries he was the *pontifex maximus* of infidelity. His epitaph would have been more representative of contemporary opinion if it had contained the lines which appeared in an anonymous broadside published after his death:

---

[1] Aubrey, I, 368. (Hobbes saw a divine coming to administer the last rites to the dying Selden. 'Sayd Hobbes: "What, will you that have wrote like a man, now dye like a woman?" So the minister was not let in.' Aubrey, II, 221.)

[2] *The Last Sayings or Dying Legacy of Mr Thomas Hobbes of Malmesbury* (London, 1679). [Broadside.]

[3] Aubrey, I, 386.

[4] James Harrington, *Oceana* (London, 1656), p. 259.

[5] Abraham Cowley, 'To Mr Hobs', *Works* (London, 1668), sig. z.

[6] Lambertino Velthuysen, *Epistolica Dissertatio de Principiis Justi et Decori* (Amsterdam, 1651).

Here lies *Tom Hobbes*, the Bug-bear of the Nation,
Whose *Death* hath frighted *Atheism* out of *Fashion*.[1]

In the popular mind Hobbes's biography did not end with his death. He continued to have an existence *sub terris*, and details of his after-life were reported in parody news-sheets, popular dialogues, and other ephemera. Dialogues set in hell belonged to a distinct genre of English literature in an unbroken tradition from the sixteenth to the eighteenth centuries;[2] pictures of Hobbes in hell were soon added to the canon, and naturally enough, since who was a better candidate for hell than the Arch-Atheist and Monster of Malmesbury? We hear in 1680 that the *Leviathan* had recently been printed in 'Gemorrah the Lower'. A special place was reserved for its author:

> *Old Tom*, with a Recanting Verse,
> Must his *odde Notions* dolefully rehearse
> To *new Disciples* in the *Devils-Ar*——.[3]

Hobbes himself was seen either as more monstrously atheistic, or else as repentant and in torment. In the role of the proud sinner he proclaimed his contempt for the clergy who 'repined at *Leviathan*':

I was never dismay'd at their Fulminations or afraid of being toss'd upon the Horns of their Altars; their Ecclesiastical Nets were too weak to resist the power of my *Leviathan*; and *Bramhall* and *Clarendon* were sufficiently assured at the long run, they cou'd not make a *Hook* strong enough to fasten him. . . .

The Clergy of our own Nation took me in the right Sense . . . for whilst I spoke against the Power of the Pope and the Roman-Church, I was shoving at theirs, and striving to overturn both. When I blamed the *Aristotelian* Philosophy and the Doctrines and Managements of the University beyond Sea, you may easily suppose what my Sentiments were of *Oxford* and *Cambridge*. In fine, my aim was to overturn all Models of Religion, and Constitutions of all Churches whatsoever. . . .

---

[1] *An Elegie upon Mr Thomas Hobbes of Malmesbury, Lately Deceased* ([London], 1679). [Broadside.] This elegy is discussed briefly by Betty T. Stocks, 'Two Broadsides on Hobbes', *Elizabethan Studies and other Essays in Honor of George F. Reynolds* (University of Colorado Press, 1945), pp. 211–14. The 'Epitaph' of the elegy is reprinted by S. I. Mintz, 'A Broadside Attack on Hobbes', *History of Ideas News Letter*, I, 3 (1955), 19–20.

[2] See Benjamin Boyce, 'News from Hell', *P.M.L.A.*, LVIII (1943), 402–37.

[3] *An Elegie Upon Mr Thomas Hobbes of Malmesbury*. [Broadside.]

I invalidated the Miracles of *Moses*, and all the *Major* and *Minor* Prophets of the Old Testament: I made their Inspiration no more than common Dreams, and ordinary Visions: I lessened the stupendous Actions of our blessed Saviour; I levelled the cures of the Dumb, the Leperous and the Blind, as things incident to an ordinary Physician; nor stopp'd I at any thing, but perverted one Text by another, till I shook the Belief of them all. . . .[1]

In a later dialogue popularly but wrongly ascribed to John Bunyan, Hobbes modulated his voice and appeared as a contrite sinner:

I am one of the most wretched persons in all these sooty territories. Nor is it any wonder that my voice is changed, for I am now changed in principles, though changed too late to do me any good. For now I know there is a God; but oh! I wish there were not! for I am sure he will have no mercy on me, nor is there any reason that he should. I do confess that I was his foe on earth, and he is mine in hell. . . . Oh, that I could but say, I feel no fire! How easy would my torments be to that which I now find them. But oh, alas! the fire that we endure ten times exceeds all culinary fire in fierceness.[2]

And so the philosopher's soul continued to burn, 'the smoke of his Torment ascending for ever and ever'.

---

[1] [Anon.], *Visits from the Shades* (London, 1704), pp. 32–4.
[2] [Anon.], *The Visions of John Bunyan* (London, 1725), p. 7. [The author of this dialogue may have been George Larkin. See Frank Mott Harrison, *Bibliography of the Works of John Bunyan* (Oxford, 1932), p. 77.]

CHAPTER II

HOBBES'S SYSTEM IN RETROSPECT

Hobbes was a nominalist and materialist; he elaborated his system on the basis of a fundamentally nominalistic account of knowledge and a fundamentally materialistic account of the universe. It was the consequences he deduced from these philosophical foundations which did so much violence to contemporary opinion. For these consequences were plainly irreligious; in Hobbes's hands nominalism and materialism became the instruments of a powerful scepticism about the real or objective existence of absolutes, and in particular about such absolutes as divine providence, good and evil, and an immortal soul.

As a materialist, Hobbes believed that the universe is a great continuum of matter, devoid of spirit, created and set in motion by a material God. Our knowledge of the universe is derived, either directly or ultimately, from our sense impressions. That is to say, by the impact of external objects on our organs of sense, 'seemings' or 'phantasms' are produced in the brain and these constitute the ultimate data of our knowledge. But—Hobbes continued, arguing now as a nominalist—the knowledge which we derive from our senses is a knowledge of singulars only, of particular things. Such knowledge—which is the only knowledge we can have—gives us no authority for believing in the independent existence of universals or absolute ideas, or in classes of things as separate entities; on the contrary, universals are functions of the human mind—they are the products of thought operating through the medium of language. When we speak of them we speak only of names, no doubt useful devices for communicating our thoughts to others, but corresponding only to our thoughts, and not to external reality. Those who

do seriously contend, that besides Peter and John, and all the rest of the men that are, have been, or shall be in the world, there is yet somewhat else that we call man, (viz.) man in general, [are] deceiving themselves by taking the universal, or general appellation, for the thing it signifieth. For if one should desire the painter to make him the picture of a man, which is as much as to say, of a man in general; he meaneth no more, but that the painter shall choose what man he pleaseth to draw, which must needs be some of them that are, have been, or may be, none of which are universal.[1]

Thus is it plain for Hobbes (as it was for his great predecessor Ockham) that 'there is nothing universal but names'. Names however are not mere objects of contempt. They are a sort of Ariadne's thread to guide us through the labyrinth of sense-impressions; they are the artifacts of reasoning, and by their proper ordering and manipulation in the form of definitions and propositions they yield a type of analytic knowledge which is rooted in sense-experience, but which the senses alone cannot provide.

All knowledge, Hobbes tells us, is bound up with names; we give names to objects in nature (such as *a stone* or *a tree*), or to other names (such as *universal* or *predicate*), or even (in Hobbes's view) to meaningless combinations (such as *incorporeal substance* or *round quadrangle*). True knowledge consists in reasoning correctly about names; that is to say, it is possible by a method of syllogistic reasoning closely analogous to computation in arithmetic to deduce correct conclusions from postulates and definitions, which are themselves names joined together by predicates. And so for Hobbes truth is arrived at by a purely logical procedure. '*True*, truth, and true proposition are equivalent to one another.'[2] And this entails the view that truth is a function of language. To say that the proposition *a man is a living creature* is true, is to affirm only that the name 'a man' contains within its definition the name 'a living creature', the link between both names having been established by arbitrary linguistic convention. The truth of the proposition is thus only logical and 'analytical', not ontological. 'For *true* and *false* are attributes of speech, not of things. And where speech is not there is neither *truth* nor *falsehood*.'[3]

We may now begin to perceive the radical element in Hobbes's nominalism; there are no universals but names; nor is there

[1] Thomas Hobbes, *The Elements of Law*, ed. F. Tönnies (Cambridge University Press, 1928), p. 15.
[2] Thomas Hobbes, 'Of Logic or Computation' in *Works*, ed. W. Molesworth (London, 1839), I, 35.
[3] Hobbes, *Leviathan*, ed. M. Oakeshott (Oxford, 1946), p. 21.

a scale or order of values except such as is created by the mind of man. To discover order in the universe one must look into one's own mind; to create order one must reason correctly about the constructions of the mind, and about the sense-experiences which gave rise to them. 'If you will be a philosopher in good earnest, let your reason move upon the deep of your own cogitations and experience; those things that lie in confusion must be set asunder, distinguished, and every one stamped with its own name set in order; that is to say, your method must resemble that of the creation.'[1] Order and meaning are conceptual, and are brought into being by reason. Nor is reason the 'Right Reason' of the Cambridge Platonists, or of Puritan thinkers such as Milton and John Owen. It is not an inward illumination, 'the candle of the Lord', an intuitive apprehension of external reality. 'Reason' for Hobbes means 'reasoning'; it means the processes of logical thinking, and right reasoning the processes of logical thinking correctly applied to propositions about names. The truth which reason yields for Hobbes is the truth about words, not things; it is a hard truth to find because words are such notorious snares; their meanings shift according to the 'nature, disposition, and interest of the speaker', or else they are used metaphorically 'in other sense than that they are ordained for', or they are wholly devoid of meaning, like 'the canting of the schoolmen', or like the insignificant speech which (Hobbes says) is heard so frequently in the universities. That is why it is so essential to fix definitions and use them consistently, else the speaker 'will find himself entangled in words, as a bird in lime twigs, the more he struggles, the more belimed'.[2]

Now as language is by 'arbitrary institution', and the meanings of words conventional and fixed by agreement, it follows that the names given to ethical judgments, such as 'good', 'evil', 'just', 'wicked', are also conventional, their meaning fixed by arbitrary institution.

For these words of good, evil, and contemptible, are ever used with relation to the person that useth them: there being nothing simply and absolutely so; nor any common rule of good and evil, to be taken from the nature of the objects themselves; but from the person of the man, where there is no commonwealth; or in a common-

1 *Works*, I, xiii. 2 *Leviathan*, pp. 19, 21.

25

wealth, from the person that representeth it; or from an arbitrator or judge, whom men disagreeing shall by consent set up, and make his sentence the rule thereof.[1]

So a primary consequence of Hobbes's nominalism is this doctrine of ethical relativism.

As a corollary to this doctrine Hobbes developed his concept of positive law. Law, says Hobbes, represents a positive injunction, prohibition, or command; it is the sense of the magistrate or sovereign; in its absence there is no justice or injustice, no right or wrong, and no sin. Law is artificial, and like truth, established by arbitrary institution. 'Where there is no common power, there is no law; where no law, no injustice.' Justice and injustice 'are qualities that relate to men in society, not solitude',[2] and they derive their meaning from the pronouncements and enforcements of the civil magistrate.

What then becomes of the doctrine of natural law, of an eternal and immutable morality antecedent to political institutions and implanted by God in the hearts of men? Hobbes retained the name of this doctrine, but little else; whereas for Hooker, whose views carried immense authority in the seventeenth century, the laws of nature are the laws eternal originating 'in the bosom of God',[3] self-evident and hence known to all reasonable men, and providing the foundation upon which positive civil law rests, for Hobbes the laws of nature are not really laws at all; rather they are theorems of conduct for the ordering of men's lives in a commonwealth so as to ensure civil peace. They are a *method*, suggested to men by reason, and deduced from human, not divine, nature. It is true that Hobbes called them 'eternal' but we may presume that he meant by this what John Laird has called 'the timelessness of logical implications'.[4] They are secular and utilitarian articles of peace which reason suggests and reasonable men will follow; but they do not coerce except as they are assimilated into positive law. The only sense therefore in which they may be said to be antecedent to positive law is the sense in which any principle of logic is antecedent to a law based upon it. The sovereign is not

[1] *Ibid.* p. 32. [2] *Ibid.* p. 83.
[3] Richard Hooker, *Ecclesiastical Polity*, Book I, xvi, in *Works* (London, 1825), I, 226.
[4] John Laird, *Hobbes* (London, 1934), p. 62.

obliged to lay down civil law on the basis of these 'natural laws'. No doubt if he is a reasonable man he will do so; and then these 'articles of peace' will become laws and not mere precepts. But if he does not do so they remain reasonable suggestions. And so they are not really the traditional 'laws of nature', not really, that is to say, moral laws which exist prior to positive law and oblige even in the absence of positive law, and which draw their authority from the will of God. What Hobbes has done is to secularize the traditional concept of natural law; he has removed it from the sphere of absolute morality; he has deduced it, not from the idea of man's perfection, not from what man ought to be, but from what man is, or at any rate from what Hobbes thought man is.[1]

To his contemporaries the doctrine of ethics grounded in positive law conveyed irresistibly the notion of atheism. Hobbes, it was felt, had cut the laws of nature off from their divine source, and had cast them into a secular and utilitarian mould

[1] It must be said that to describe Hobbes's doctrine of natural law in this way is to shear away a great many of the subtleties and refinements, as well as a number of equivocations and inconsistencies, with which he has surrounded it. But I think it is a fair description, and I cannot find with Professor Leo Strauss that 'Hobbes distinguishes no less precisely than any other moralist between legality and morality', or with Professor Sterling Lamprecht that Hobbes deliberately over-stated his case in order to bring home the important concept that morality can never profitably be separated from its social context. Both these interpretations of Hobbes's doctrine seem to me to be mistaken, as do the views recently expressed by Howard Warrender in *The Political Philosophy of Hobbes: His Theory of Obligation* (Oxford, 1957). Of the several eminent commentators who have argued that Hobbes's natural law theory depends upon a doctrine of absolute morality, Mr Warrender is perhaps the most persuasive. His position is that certain obligations of the citizen and all the obligations of the sovereign to his subjects are, according to Hobbes, grounded in a natural law antecedent to civil law. Against this view Professor Oakeshott has argued (Introduction to Hobbes's *Leviathan*, Blackwell's Political Texts, 1946) that the citizen's right of self-preservation, which is immune to sovereign authority, as well as all the obligations of the sovereign himself, are *rational*, not *moral*, obligations. They arise when a man is 'prevented from willing a certain action because he perceives that its probable consequences are damaging to himself.' (p. lix). They are 'natural' laws only because they follow naturally from a man's rational consideration of his own self-interests; and they are 'laws' only in the sense that they are precepts or principles of conduct. Dr Dorothea Krook has argued similarly ('Mr Brown's Note Annotated', *Political Studies*, 1, [1953], pp. 216–27; 'Thomas Hobbes's Doctrine of Meaning and Truth', *Philosophy*, XXXI [1956], 3–22), and, in a general way, the same position had been taken by the nineteenth-century commentators Croom Robertson and Leslie Stephen. My own view of this matter follows Professor Oakeshott's closely. I am, however, in the chapters that follow, primarily concerned to show what Hobbes's critics thought about this question.

27

entirely alien to the Christian tradition. His rejection of absolute values was read as an attack on specifically Christian values. The point is made succinctly by a recanting 'Hobbist' who declared publicly at Cambridge that in the propagating of atheism a leading role is played by those who adopt such 'execrable Positions' as 'that all moral Righteousness is founded only in the Law of the Civil Magistrate'.[1]

The same theme was sounded repeatedly in the literature against Hobbes. There could be no compromise with Hobbes on this point. Natural law, the critics declared, is absolute and immutable; its final arbiter is God, not man; it is not the creation of the civil magistrate: it precedes positive civil law, and positive law presupposes it. It is morally as well as logically binding; it is eternal, laid up in the bosom of God. To think otherwise is, as Bishop Cumberland observed, 'to come to a pitch of madness'.[2]

But Hobbes thought otherwise, and he argued further that just as civil law originates in the first instance in the dictates of the sovereign, so Scriptural law derives its authority from the interpretations of the sovereign. For the Bible is peculiarly subject to private constructions, and these can be seditious if they are not strictly subordinated to the interpretation of the sovereign. Indeed, Hobbes developed this point with extraordinary logical rigour, and was led to adopt the thoroughgoing Erastian[3] principle that the state must be supreme in all matters affecting religion, else the power of the sovereign to protect the security of his subjects would be eroded by religious factionalism. Hobbes found no difficulty in deducing his Erastianism from his relativist assumptions. Consider, for instance, how he concluded that it is only the civil authority which may dictate the forms of public worship:

Because words, and consequently the attributes of God, have their signification by agreement and constitution of men, those attributes are to be held signi-

[1] Daniel Scargill, *The Recantation of Daniel Scargill* (Cambridge, 1669), p. 1.
[2] Richard Cumberland, *A Treatise of the Laws of Nature*, trans. John Maxwell (London, 1727), p. 199.
[3] I use this term as it was commonly applied to Hobbes in the seventeenth century, and not as it was originally intended by Erastus. 'The main object of Erastus,' wrote Figgis, 'was not to magnify the State, nor to enslave the Church, but to secure the liberty of the subject.' Erastus was, therefore, 'Less Erastian than Whitgift, perhaps less so than Cranmer, far less so than Selden or Hobbes.' John Neville Figgis, *The Divine Right of Kings* (2nd ed. Cambridge, 1934), pp. 335, 337.

ficative of honour, that men intend shall be so; and whatsoever may be done by the wills of particular men, where there is no law but reason, may be done by the will of the commonwealth, by laws civil. And because a commonwealth hath no will, nor makes no laws, but those that are made by the will of him, or them that have the sovereign power; it followeth that those attributes which the sovereign ordaineth, in the worship of God, for signs of honour, ought to be taken and used for such, by private men in their public worship.[1]

The same applies to any other religious practice: it is to be per-mitted only at the sovereign's discretion—for only then does it have the force of law, since law, for Hobbes, is exclusively positive law, and positive law represents the will of the sovereign.

Hobbes's critics were alive to all the implications of this ultra-Erastian position. They recognized that it swept away ecclesiastical power and privilege at the same time that it curbed sectarianism and religious dissension. They saw also a larger danger; it was a threat to Christianity itself. For Hobbes's view that the sovereign must impose a uniform religion does not include the guaranty that the religion so imposed will be Christianity. On the contrary, Hobbes implied that the citizen of a commonwealth must accept the religion imposed by the sovereign and enforced by the laws of the commonwealth whether that religion is Christianity or not and regardless of the private beliefs of the citizen. The citizen (argues Hobbes) will do so—as Naaman the Syrian did and as any reasonable man will do—because he knows that his security depends upon the absolute and effective power of the civil authority.

As if [one of the critics wrote scornfully], as if the favour of our Lord, the Prince of Glory, towards his sincere, and faithful, patient, and undaunted subjects . . . were not of more value than the thin shelter of worldly power; which, if it could hide us under Rocks and Mountains, could not secure us from the stroke of him, who is, in the first place, to be feared.[2]

For the critics wordly power is a 'thin shelter'. It cannot deliver a sinful man from the retribution of a just God. The

---

[1] *Leviathan*, p. 240. (Italics mine).
[2] Thomas Tenison, *The Creed of Mr Hobbes Examined* (2nd ed. London, 1672) p. 208.

apostate Christian who submits to a false religion is purchasing a short-lived security; it cannot protect him in the eternal life hereafter from 'the stroke of him who is in the first place to be feared'. Hobbes, of course, was impervious to such argument. For him what is to be feared in the first place is not a life of torment after death, but rather the evils which men inflict upon each other in the present life. Even when he enlarges the subject of his discourse to include eschatological questions he does so only because he is persuaded that such discussion will throw further light on the purely temporal problems of men. The *summum malum*, 'the chiefest of all natural evils', is death, and especially violent death, because that puts a premature and painful period to life, and hence cuts off the possibility of achieving the only kind of 'felicity' that the Hobbesian scheme of salvation permits of, namely, the power of men to satisfy their shifting and continually renewing human desires. Hobbes, the complete materialist, never invoked the tradition of *memento mori*, never, that is to say, dwelt on the mortality of bodily life as a prelude to the immortality of spiritual life. If he bids us remember death it is because death represents the practical limit of his interest in human personality. His attention is on that most 'general inclination of all mankind, a perpetual and restless desire of power after power, that ceaseth only in death'.[1]

Within the framework of materialism Hobbes developed his views on human nature. Man, for Hobbes, is in the first place a mechanism of matter in motion. His sense impressions are defined as movements in the organs of sense caused by the pressure of external things, and leading in turn to movements in the brain, called ideas. Imagination is the consciousness of ideas still present in the mind after the original movements in the organs of sense have died away. Memory is the recollection of these ideas. All these activities can be carried out without the use of speech, and hence they are, in Hobbes's view, the properties of animals as well as of men. Also, men and animals are alike in having emotions or 'passions', a set of voluntary movements in the internal organs, responding this time to ideas or images in the brain and not to movements in the organs of sense. Human desires or appetites are constantly being renewed, and felicity consists not merely in the satisfying of single

[1] *Leviathan*, p. 64.

desires, but in the assurance that future desires will also be satisfied; so that felicity can have no *finis ultimus*—it is 'a continual progress of the desire, from one object to another'.[1] It does, however, have an absolute ending, and this is death. Fear of death is thus a positive cause of infelicity, and security from violent death a necessary condition of felicity.

In short, man is a complicated structure of matter in motion; and a part of that structure is the internal motions which are called the passions, of which the most fundamental are man's 'appetites' and 'aversions'. He is happiest when his capacity to satisfy his successive desires is most nearly unimpaired. What are the conditions of life in which this sort of happiness is most likely to be attained? Hobbes did not answer this question immediately, but put the question first in a negative form. What, he asked, are the conditions of human life *least* likely to induce felicity?

For the answer Hobbes asked us to consider what men would be like in the total absence of civil restraint. They would be in what he called the 'state of nature'. Where there is no civil law every man is 'free' to satisfy his desires as best he can. He will try to do so by all possible means because of the pressure and intensity of his appetites. But he is faced with a dilemma. His individual nature is a tissue of desires and varying capacities to satisfy them; but in this he is no different from other men. All men are equal—equal, that is, in having desires, in desiring roughly the same things, and in having roughly the same capacity to obtain them. The solitary part of man's nature, that which isolates him from other men, compels him to seek the fulfilment of his desires at the expense of every other man's 'felicity', and the presence of other men with similar desires frustrates the individual will. As Professor Oakeshott has put it: 'Man is solitary; would that he were alone'.[2] He is not alone; and so there results a competition of human desires, a 'perpetual contention for honour, riches, and authority',[3] a struggle between every man against every other man, in which, because law is absent, force and fraud become the cardinal virtues. In such a condition, says Hobbes, in one of his most frequently-quoted phrases, the life of man is 'solitary, poor, nasty, brutish,

---

[1] *Ibid.* p. 63. [2] Michael Oakeshott, Introduction, *Leviathan*, p. xxxv.
[3] *Leviathan*, p. 460.

and short'.[1] Man's need to secure himself from violent death (the right to preserve his life is his fundamental and inalienable 'right of nature') combines with his (equally natural) rapacity and greed to create that condition of maximum insecurity which Hobbes calls the 'state of nature'. And men are powerless to escape from this predicament so long as they live without law and according to the dictates of their own passions.

Such is Hobbes's view of the 'state of nature'. One observation about its impact on contemporary thought may be made here. It was believed by a number of critics that the 'state of nature' represented Hobbes's view of what human conduct *ought* to be. It announced a programme for libertinism. It told men that unbridled lust, greed, stealth, and force were their right 'by nature', and hence that such conduct was entirely 'justifiable', and was limited only by the need for self-preservation. Now I believe it is clear that this represents a misreading of Hobbes's doctrine, similar to seventeenth-century misconceptions about Epicurus. (Hobbes was himself called 'epicurean' on a number of occasions.) There is nothing in Hobbes's doctrine to suggest that he ever sanctioned 'licence'. On the contrary, the whole force of his philosophy is directed towards the suppression of 'licence'. The 'state of nature' is a state of chaos in which all human conduct is dominated by self-interest. But it is an unenlightened self-interest, because it is essentially self-defeating: the uninhibited pursuit of power in a society where all men seek power brings with it a train of miseries—pain, or death, or at the very least, fear of death. When Hobbes says that it is the 'natural right' of every man in the 'state of nature' to prey upon his neighbour,[2] the term 'right' is used in a strictly descriptive sense. It is simply a datum of human nature: it means that man *will* behave in this way because he is compelled to do so by his own nature—so long as he is free of external legal restraint. It does not mean that he is 'morally justified' in behaving this way: for, as we have seen, Hobbes allowed no meaning at all to 'justice' in a society where positive civil law was absent. 'Natural right' is, then, no invitation to 'licentiousness', but a horrible example of what could happen to men in the total absence of effective civil government. And so Hobbes's account of the 'state of nature' is not to be taken as

[1] *Ibid.* p. 82. [2] *Ibid.* p. 85.

historical: it is a generalization from his theory of the passions. Hobbes thought that he could detect some near approaches to the 'state of nature' in history—for instance, in the social disorder attending civil war, or in the predatory habits of one nation against another, or in the deplorable conditions of life in America. But these serve only to confirm, not to establish, the theory, which depends in the first place upon correct reasoning from the definitions of the passions. The 'state of nature' is the logical extreme of human society without law. It is neither a historical picture nor a practical guide to conduct.

How can man avoid the extreme of the 'state of nature'? How can he escape from a predicament to which he is driven by his own human nature? The answer, says Hobbes, can be discovered by the proper exercise of reason. So that while it is one side of human nature—the passions—that brings him to this predicament, it is another side of human nature reason— which can deliver him from it. Indeed the passions do play a role in man's deliverance; for it is the fear of death, which increases as man's insecurity increases, and which in the state of nature is thus a total and consuming fear—it is the fear of death which inspires man's search for a way out of the dilemma. And it is reason which provides the way.

Instructed by his reason man can discover those 'natural laws' or general theorems of behaviour conducing to peace. All these theorems can be summed up in an adaptation of the Golden Rule: 'Do not that to another, which thou wouldest not have done to thyself.'[1] Do not, that is to say, unless you are truly alone, pursue your felicity without let or hindrance, for your own self-interest is bound to collide with the self-interest of others. It is reason, says Hobbes, which brings men to an understanding of this fundamental principle, and it is reason which announces the method by which this principle may be translated into the closest approach to human felicity that the shifting desires of men will allow.

The method consists in the generation of a commonwealth. According to Hobbes, the relationship between men which appears in 'agreement' or 'covenant' is a foretaste of the condition of peace which he supposes all men to seek. But in the state of nature

[1] *Ibid.* p. 103.

there is no reasonable security for any of them that so covenant. . . . For seeing the wills of most men are governed only by fear, and where there is no power of coercion, there is no fear, the wills of most men will follow their passions of covetousness, lust, anger, and the like, to the breaking of those covenants, whereby the rest also, who otherwise would keep them, are set at liberty, and have no law, but from themselves.[1]

Therefore, what is required in order to escape from this condition is an authority capable of compelling all men to keep the covenants they enter into. And, as Hobbes understands it, an authority of this sort can spring only from a special kind of covenant, namely, one in which each man agrees with every other man to transfer his natural *right* to govern himself to a sovereign authority (a single person or a group of persons) and in which each man in common with every other man confers upon this sovereign authority his *power* to govern himself. 'This is the generation of that great LEVIATHAN . . . to which we owe our peace and defence'; and thus only may a multitude of men come to compose a commonwealth.[2]

The sovereign, in whose person the multitude is united, 'may use the strength and means of them all, as he shall think expedient, for their peace and common defence'.[3] The power of the sovereign is supreme, although his subjects may resist him if they find that he fails to act in such a way as to guarantee civil peace, since the reason the subjects created their sovereign in the first place was to provide security against the hazards and miseries of life engendered by their own natural passions. Hobbes laid down as a general rule that the danger of tyranny resulting from the concentration of power in the hands of the sovereign was a necessary risk for men to take, because the greatest danger of all is civil disorder and social chaos, from which men can be delivered only by the rule of indivisible and absolute power wielded in a commonwealth which Hobbes called 'that great Leviathan' and 'mortal god'.

If in the opinion of his critics Hobbes had espoused and promoted the cause of irreligion, he also offended his contemporaries in another way. His system was not merely irreligious— it was barbed with irony. It delivered outrageously heterodox

---

[1] *Works*, IV, 129. [2] *Leviathan*, p. 112. [3] *Ibid.*

opinions at the same time that it professed to be orthodox. And it used the language of orthodoxy as a means of exploding orthodox beliefs. Consider for example Hobbes's conception of natural law. When he says that the laws of nature are eternal and immutable and that they can be apprehended through the exercise of right reason, he is investing the concept 'natural law' with an appearance of orthodoxy which his meaning belies. The 'laws of nature' are for Hobbes eternal and immutable only as logical deductions, not as moral precepts. They have no legal character—they are not binding, except, again, as logical implications are binding—so that they hardly deserve the name of law. They are in fact no more (or no less) than theorems of conduct, 'convenient articles of peace' suggested by right reason for the melioration of man's hard condition. Hobbes has thus stripped them of their absolute moral character; but he chose nevertheless, out of a fine sense of irony, to retain their traditional name, and to describe them in traditional language. Similarly, as he uses the term 'right reason', it is shorn of its divine afflatus; it is no more than correct reasoning applied to the theory of the passions, and as it yields knowledge which is rooted in sense-experience and in language, it can never attain to a knowledge of God.

In his theology Hobbes reveals the same mixture of heterodox opinions couched in the language of orthodoxy. He does not deny the existence of God and angels, but declares them to be corporeal. He does not reject the term Trinity, but asserts that it consists of Moses, Jesus, and the Apostles. Heaven and hell certainly exist, but they are terrestrial abodes. The damned are surely tormented, but only for a limited time, after which they are annihilated altogether. Witches ought to be punished, not because they are witches—for witchcraft is an imposture—but for thinking they are witches, because their delusion is apt to cause social mischief. Miracles can be performed, but most of them can be explained away as superstition, vain beliefs, or events which have as yet imperfectly understood natural causes. Martyrs there certainly were, but none after the time of Christ's death and ascension.

Hobbes's irony is nowhere blunter than in the peroration to *Leviathan* called 'Of the Kingdom of Darkness', where he gives the freest expression to his anti-clerical feelings.

The heathens had also their *aqua lustralis*, that is to say, *holy water*. The Church of Rome imitates them also in their *holy days*. They had their *bacchanalia;* and we have our *wakes*, answering to them: they had their *saturnalia*, and we our *carnivals*, and Shrove-Tuesday's liberty of servants: they their procession of *Priapus*; we our fetching in, erection, and dancing about *May-poles*; and dancing is one kind of worship; they had their procession called *Ambarvalia*; and we our procession about the fields in the *Rogation-week*. Nor do I think that these are all the ceremonies that have been left in the Church, from the first conversion of the Gentiles; but they are all that I can for the present call to mind; and if a man would well observe that which is delivered in the histories, concerning the religious rites of the Greeks and Romans, I doubt not but he might find many more of these old empty bottles of Gentilism, which the doctors of the Roman Church, either by negligence or ambition, have filled up again with the new wine of Christianity, that will not fail in time to break them....

The *ecclesiastics* are *spiritual* men, and *ghostly* fathers. The fairies are *spirits*, and *ghosts*. Fairies and *ghosts* inhabit darkness, solitudes and graves. The *ecclesiastics* walk in obscurity of doctrine, in monasteries, churches, and churchyards.

The *ecclesiastics* have their cathedral churches, which, in what town soever they be erected, by virtue of holy water, and certain charms called exorcisms, have the power to make those towns, cities, that is to say, seats of empire. The *fairies* also have their enchanted castles, and certain gigantic ghosts, that domineer over the regions round about them.

The *fairies* are not to be seized on; and brought to answer for the hurt they do. So also the *ecclesiastics* vanish away from the tribunals of civil justice.

The *ecclesiastics* take from young men the use of reason, by certain charms compounded of metaphysics, and miracles, and traditions, and abused Scripture, whereby they are good for nothing else, but what they command them. The *fairies* likewise are said to take young children out of their cradles, and to change them into natural fools, which common people do therefore call *elves*, and are apt to mischief.

In what shop, or operatory the *fairies* make their enchantment, the old wives have not determined. But the operatories of the *clergy* are well enough known to be the universities, that received their discipline from authority pontifical. ....

The *fairies* marry not; but there be amongst them incubi, that have copulation with flesh and blood. The *priests* also marry not.[1]

[1] *Ibid.* pp. 435, 457–8.

Hobbes delivered these sentiments under the guise of an attack on the Church of Rome, but he left no doubt that he had in mind the Protestant clergy as well. 'For it is not the Roman clergy only, that pretends the kingdom of God to be of this world, and thereby to have a power therein distinct from that of the civil state.'[1]

In almost all the attacks on Hobbes there is an undercurrent of resentment against the general excellence of his style. It was almost as if the critics were saying that it was unfair of Hobbes to be so wrong and yet to write so well—unfair, and moreover, dangerous, because a wicked man in possession of a good prose style was like the Devil quoting Scripture: he was perverting a good thing to his own evil purposes. Hobbes 'had so fine a Pen', wrote John Dowel in 1683, 'that by the clearness of his Style, and exactness of his method, he gain'd more Proselytes than by his Principles'.[2] 'He hath, long ago', said Archbishop Tenison

publish'd his Errours in Theologie, in the English Tongue, insinuating himself, by the handsomeness of his style, into the mindes of such whose Fancie leadeth their Judgements: and to say truth of an Enemy, he may, with some Reason, pretend to *Mastery*, in that Language. Yet for this very handsomeness in dressing his Opinions, as the matter stands, he is to be reproved; because by that means, the poyson which he hath intermixed with them is, with more readiness and danger swallowed.[3]

To Lord Clarendon also Hobbes's style was a subtle and powerful instrument for the perpetrating of subversive opinions. Clarendon had a just appreciation of Hobbes's style. 'Mr *Hobbes* is plentifully endowed' with

order and method in Writing, and his clear expressing his conceptions in weighty, proper, and significant words, are very remarkable and commendable; and it is some part of his art to introduce, upon the suddain, instances and remarques, which are the more grateful, and make the more impression upon his Reader,

---

[1] *Ibid.* p. 459.
[2] John Dowel, *The Leviathan Heretical* (Oxford, 1683), sig. A3.
[3] Thomas Tenison, *The Creed of Mr Hobbes Examined* (London, 1670), sig. A4. Hobbes's style was praised unreservedly by Thomas Sprat, *Observations on Mons. de Sorbiere's Voyage into England* (London, 1708), p. 163, and Henry More paid tribute to 'the excellency of [Hobbes's] natural wit'. *The Immortality of the Soul* in *A Collection of Several Philosophical Writings* (4th ed. London, 1712), p. 33.

by the unexpectedness of meeting them where somewhat else is talk'd of.[1]

It is a good style, but it is for this reason all the more dangerous. It disarms the reader. In an age inclining to 'all kind of Paradox', said Clarendon, the unwary reader may come to believe Hobbes's 'Propositions to be more innocent, or less mischievous, then upon a more deliberal perusal [he] will find them to be'.[2] As an example of this Clarendon cites a discussion in the *Leviathan* of 'Dreams, and Fayries, and ghosts, and goblins, Exorcisms, Crosses, and Holy-water', into which 'Philosophical Discourse' Hobbes gratuitously introduced a 'Comical mention of the power and goodness of God, and of the Devil's activity and malignity'. The effect of this intrusion,

in a place so improper and unnatural for those reflexions, will the more incline his Disciples to undervalue those common notions of the goodness and assistance of God, and of the malice and vigilance of the Devil . . . and prepare them to believe, that all the Discourses of Sanctity, and the obligations of Christianity, and the essentials of a Church, Faith, and Obedience to the dictates of God's spirit, are but the artifice and invention of Churchmen, to advance their own pomp and worldly interest, and that Heaven and Hell are but words to flatter or terrifie men.[3]

Hobbes's opponents set out to penetrate the ironical façade of Hobbes's system, so as to expose in all its nakedness the irreligious temper which lies beneath it and to refute those 'loose and licentious reflections' which, said Clarendon, Hobbes 'collected . . . into such a Mass of impiety, that the very repeating all the particulars, without which they cannot be replied to, must be more grievous and offensive to most devout Persons, than the most unclean discourse can appear to the chastest eares'.[4]

---

[1] Edward Hyde, Earl of Clarendon, *A Brief View and Survey of the Dangerous and Pernicious Errors to Church and State in Mr Hobbes's Book, Entitled Leviathan* (Oxford, 1676), pp. 16–17.
[2] *Ibid.* sig. *3.
[3] *Ibid.* pp. 17–18.
[4] *Ibid.* pp. 274–5 (mispaged 264–5).

CHAPTER III

THE CONTEMPORARY SETTING

'Atheism' in the seventeenth century was a hydra-headed term. When it was not being used as an epithet of abuse having only emotional content, it referred in general to the denial of God's existence; but it also meant any arguments which tended in that direction, even if only by implication. Hence it was flexible enough to include a variety of doctrines, many of them dissimilar in their premises, but all of them conceived of as leading to the same conclusions and as having the same consequences— the disavowel of the deity and the undermining of Christian faith.

Many of the intellectual positions associated with atheism are embodied in the following 'Atheists' Catechism' which Sir Charles Wolseley appended to an anti-Hobbist diatribe he wrote in 1666. It is interesting enough to quote *in extenso*:

Q. Do you believe there is a God?
A. No: I believe there is none.
Q. What is the true ground of your belief?
A. Because I have no mind there should be one.
Q. What other reason do you give for it?
A. Because I never saw him.
Q. If there be no God, how came this world to be?
A. It made itself by meer chance.
Q. After what manner was it first pieced together?
A. By a casual hit of Atoms one against another.
Q. How came those Atoms so to hit one against another?
A. As they were eternally dancing about, in an infinite space.
Q. Whence came the reason of mankind; and all that order and regularity we find in the world?
A. From the meer accidental conjunction of those Atoms.
Q. What is it that men call Religion?
A. A politick cheat put upon the world.
Q. Who were the first contrivers of this cheat?
A. Some cunning men that designed to keep the world in subjection and awe.

Q. What was the first ground of it?
A. Men were frighted with Tales, that were told them, about invisible nothings.
Q. When did this fright first seize men?
A. 'Tis very long ago: and (for ought we can find) 'tis as old as the world itself.
Q. Has this fright upon men been general?
A. Yes: The whole world, in all ages of it, have been possessed with a fear of nothing.
Q. What is the great end that every man is to live to?
A. To please himself.
Q. How prove you that?
A. Because there is nothing above him: and so he is his own Law.
Q. Are men to make any distinction in their actions?
A. No further, nor upon no other account, but as they please or displease themselves.
Q. Is there any such thing as good or evil?
A. No: 'tis a distinction the world hath been couzened with.
Q. When was that distinction first brought into the world?
A. 'Tis of the same date with those fables about a Deity; and related wholly to them.
Q. Is there anything for a man to hope for or stand in fear of, beyond this world?
A. No, nothing at all.
Q. What becomes of a man when he dyes?
A. He returns into his first Atoms.
Q. What becomes of those Atoms?
A. They still help to carry on the great round of the world.[1]

From this passage it is possible to distinguish a number of traditional strands of thought which the seventeenth-century controversialist would have catalogued as scepticism, naturalism, atomism (otherwise called 'Epicureanism' or 'Lucretianism'), blasphemy, and heresy, besides certain loosely-defined attitudes of mind such as cynicism and general irreverence. All of these were atheism under its various heads, and all of these were attributed by various critics to Hobbes. It is clear that Wolseley's 'Catechism' is supposed to represent the beliefs of a 'Hobbist'. The Atheist's characterization of religion as 'Tales ... about invisible nothings' with which 'men were frighted' is

[1] Sir Charles Wolseley, *The Unreasonablenesse of Atheism made manifest* (2nd ed. London, 1669), pp. 197–9.

a free and unscrupulous adaptation of Hobbes's definition: *'Fear* of power invisible, feigned by the mind, or imagined from tales publicly allowed, RELIGION; not allowed, SUPER-STITION.'[1] I call Wolseley's adaptation unscrupulous because it omits entirely Hobbes's corollary: 'And when the power imagined, is truly such as we imagine, TRUE RELIGION.'[2] Even so, Hobbes's corollary does not succeed completely in taking the edge off his preliminary definition, and as in the seventeenth century atheism was attributed as much to a writer's tone or habit of mind as it was to his overt statements, Wolseley's omission of the corollary has its own rough justification.

One aspect of atheism which Wolseley's catechist did not stress but which was widely discussed in contemporary polemics on the subject is the denial of spirit, or else the rejection of its primacy in the scale of being. Glanvill called this doctrine 'Sadducism', and saw it as the inevitable prerequisite to the denial of theism. Henry More, too, read it as 'a dangerous Prelude to Atheism itself, or else a more close and crafty Profession and insinuation of it. For assuredly that Saying is not more true in Politick, *No Bishop, no King*; than this is in Metaphysick, *No Spirit, No God*'.[3] This was a hit at Hobbes, and it went home far more directly than Wolseley's crude implications that Hobbes was an atomist (he was actually a plenist) or that Hobbes rejected the notion of personal immortality (he believed in a type of resurrection after the Last Judgment). What was perfectly clear and straightforward in Hobbes was his thoroughgoing materialism, which to all the critics meant either a 'crafty Profession' of atheism or else 'a dangerous Prelude' to it.

Was Hobbes an atheist? He professed not to be one; he resented the charge that he was one. But the question is difficult. If it is taken to mean, did Hobbes renounce theism, the answer must be 'no'. God, Hobbes said, exists; he is material; he is the First Cause; he is omnipotent; whatever other attributes he may possess are ineffable, though we describe him in various ways by way of honouring him. Hobbes

---

[1] *Leviathan*, p. 35. [2] *Ibid.*
[3] Henry More, *An Antidote Against Atheism* (1653) in More's *A Collection of Several Philosophical Writings* (4th ed. London, 1712), p. 142.

collected these opinions into a pamphlet apologia which he published in 1662, in reply to an attack by Wallis.

There has hitherto appeared in Mr *Hobbes* his Doctrine no sign of Atheism; and whatsoever can be inferr'd from the denying of *Incorporeal Substances*, makes Tertullian, one of the ancientiest of the Fathers, and most of the Doctors of the Greek Church, as much Atheists as he; for Tertullian in his Treatise *De Carne Christi*, says plainly, *Omne quod est, corpus est sui generis, nihil est incorporale, nisi quod non est.* . . .

. . . What kind of attribute I pray you is *immaterial*, or *incorporeal substance*? Where do you find it in the Scripture? Whence came it hither, but from *Plato and Aristotle*, Heathens, who mistook those thin Inhabitants of the Brain they see in sleep, for so many *incorporeal* men; and yet they allow them motion, which is proper only to things *corporeal*. Do you think it an honour to God to be one of these? And would you learn Christianity from *Plato* and *Aristotle*? But seeing there is no such word in Scripture, how will you warrent [*sic*] it from natural reason? Neither *Plato* nor *Aristotle* did ever write of, or mention an *incorporeal Spirit*; for they could not conceive how a Spirit, which in their language was πνεῦμα (in ours *a Wind*) could be *incorporeal*. Do you understand the connection of *substance* and *incorporeal*? If you do, explain it in English; for the words are Latine. It is something, you'l say, that being *without Body, stands under*——! Stands under what? Will you say, *under Accidents*? Almost all the Fathers of the Church will be against you; and then you are an Atheist. Is not Mr *Hobbes* his way of attributing to God, that only which the Scripture Attribute to him, or what is never anywhere taken but for honour, much better than this bold Undertaking of yours, to *consider* and decypher Gods *nature* to us?[1]

In Hobbes's view the material nature of God is a deduction from natural reason. Whatever is, is material; ergo, God is material. But we must notice the implication that God exists, a point which in fact Hobbes never explicitly denied. Nor did he reject the notion of God as First Cause and of God's omnipotence, both attributes being in his opinion a matter of Scriptural knowledge. What he was sceptical of were all the other traditional attributes of God—God's goodness, holiness, blessedness, justice, wisdom, mercy, infinity, eternity—attributes which he

[1] Hobbes, *Considerations Upon the Reputation, Loyalty, Manners & Religion of Thomas Hobbes of Malmesbury* (London, 1680) pp. 32–7. This work is a posthumous second edition of Hobbes's *Mr Hobbes Considered*. . . (London, 1662). Wallis's attack was *Hobbius Heauton-timorumenos* (London, 1662).

construed as mere 'Expressions of Reverence, such as are in use amongst men for signs of Honour'.[1] We delude ourselves if we believe that such terms of honour refer to the facts about God, because the facts are unknowable. Neither a careful reading of Scripture nor the exercise of natural reason will yield this kind of knowledge to us. Scripture is of no avail because it is inexplicit on these points; the argument from authority and the argument *ad consensum gentium* are equally unavailing; while the arguments from natural reason, such as the ontological argument and the argument from design, have not only failed to shed any light on the question, but might very possibly 'have made it more doubtful to many men than it was before'.[2]

So far we have no grounds for doubting Hobbes's theism. It is no doubt unorthodox theism, but not atheism in its strictest sense. The difficulty arises when we try to gauge the sincerity of Hobbes's belief. And here we meet a curious fact. Hobbes maintained that Scripture, and not reason, is our only warrant for believing in God's existence. But in the *Leviathan* he subjected the scope, authorship, and general authenticity of the Bible to a corrosive and searching criticism, in fact to a type of the 'higher criticism' in which he anticipated Père Simon and Spinoza. He insisted that the Pentateuch, except for the Mosaic laws in Deuteronomy, could not have been written by Moses, but must have been composed afterwards, and that the Books of Samuel, Joshua, Kings, Judges, Esther, Ruth, Job, the Psalms, the Proverbs, the Prophets, etc., are similarly riddled with anachronisms and interpolations which call their avowed authorship, and in some places their very authority, in doubt.[3] Hence he concluded that the truth of revelation cannot be known with certainty but must, for the sake of civil peace, be left to the interpretation of the civil magistrate.

What then are we to make of Hobbes's theism? Did he

[1] Hobbes, *Considerations*, p. 20.

[2] *Ibid.* p. 35. Cf. *Leviathan*, p. 239: 'When men, out of the principles of natural reason, dispute of the attributes of God, they but dishonour him: for in the attributes which we give to God, we are not to consider the signification of philosophical truth, but the signification of pious intention, to do him the greatest honour we are able. From the want of which consideration, have proceeded the volumes of disputation about the nature of God, that tend not to his honour, but to the honour of our own wits and learning.'

[3] *Leviathan*, Ch. xxxiii, 'Of the Number, Antiquity, Scope, Authority, and Interpreters of the Books of Holy Scripture', pp. 246–55.

sincerely believe in it, or was he merely following his own precepts in obeying the dictates of the civil authority? Or was he, perhaps, to ensure his own personal safety, disguising his true atheism and 'accommodating' his views to the general view? Of the latter theory Professor Leo Strauss made the following interesting comment:

Many present-day scholars . . . do not seem to have a sufficient notion of the degree of circumspection or of accommodation to the accepted views that was required, in former ages, of 'deviationists' who desired to survive or to die in peace. Those scholars tacitly assume that the pages in Hobbes's writings devoted to religious subjects can be understood if they are read in the way in which one ought to read the corresponding utterances, say, of Lord Bertrand Russell. In other words, I am familiar with the fact that there are innumerable passages in Hobbes's writings which were used by Hobbes and which can be used by everyone else for proving that Hobbes was a theist and even a good Anglican. The prevalent procedure would merely lead to historical errors, but for the fact that its results are employed for buttressing the dogma that the mind of the individual is incapable of liberating itself from the opinions which rule his society. . . .[1]

I doubt that Hobbes's 'theism' was a screen thrown up for his own safety. It is hard to credit such a theory when we remember that Hobbes's *openly-avowed* opinions on the nature of God were profoundly unorthodox and aroused the most intense opposition in their own time. Hobbes must have known that the line between his brand of theism and seventeenth-century atheism was a thin one and that for many of his contemporaries this line did not exist at all. If safety and a peaceful life were his object he would have had to express his opinions far more circumspectly than Professor Strauss would have us believe.

In fact there is no evidence in our present knowledge of Hobbes's life and thought which can lead us to any certain conclusions about the depth and sincerity of Hobbes's theism. All that we can say is that Hobbes never displayed what we might call a true religious sensibility, that if he did believe in God, it was in a remote, abstract, intellectualized deity who could give little comfort to Hobbes's contemporaries. And we certainly know that his critics thought he was an atheist. They

[1] Leo Strauss, *Natural Right and History* (Chicago, 1953), p. 199.

arraigned him as arch-atheist for the whole bent of his thought, which was secular and naturalistic, but they also believed that his religious opinions in particular successfully met every test for atheism which his age could devise. Hobbes said plainly enough that the universe is body, that God is part of the world and therefore body, that the Pentateuch and many other books of Scripture are redactions or compilations from earlier sources, that the members of the Trinity are Moses, Jesus and the Apostles, that few if any miracles can be credited after the Testamental period, that no persons deserve the name of 'martyr' except those who *witnessed* the ascension of Christ, that witchcraft is a myth and heaven a delusion, that religion is in fact so muddled with superstition as to be in many vital places indistinguishable from it, that the Church, both in its government and its doctrine, must submit to the dictates of Leviathan, the supreme civil authority which alone can curb religious dissension and the civil disorder which it breeds.

These views may be read both as logical deductions from Hobbes's central thesis about government and as necessary supports for it. But their sweeping unorthodoxy is self-evident, and it is therefore not surprising that few of the critics were able to get beyond them to the fundamental principle which they asserted. Alexander Ross, for instance, one of the first of the critics, treats the *Leviathan* as a tissue of heterodox opinions, never noticing its logical structure. If he had been able to perceive it as the expression of a coherent and closely-knit philosophical system, he might have pitched his criticism on a loftier plane; but he did not, and it would be unhistorical to expect that he should have done so. *Leviathan* was first of all irreligious, and more than that, corrupting and toxic, 'swallowed down by some young Scoliasts without nauseating'.[1] The first task of a seventeenth-century divine would be to destroy *Leviathan*; the second might be to understand it.

It was atheism then which was at the heart of the controversy about Hobbes, the source of all the fears and seething indignation which Hobbes's thought inspired, the single charge which is most persistently made, and to which all other differences between Hobbes and his contemporaries can be reduced. Fearing the spread of atheism, and seeing it writ large in the works of

[1] Alexander Ross, *Leviathan drawn out with a Hook* (London, 1653), sig. A3.

45

a very acute thinker, Hobbes's enemies were able to sink their political and sectarian differences, and unite in what they conceived to be the common defence of the Christian faith.[1]

Three classes of critics may be discriminated here: the clergy and sectaries of all persuasions, the university teachers, and the lawyers. It is convenient to single these out for two reasons: first, because Hobbes did so himself, having reserved for them some of his most special scorn, and second, because the individual turns which they gave to their replies reflect their special background and, in a sense which I hope to make clear, their vested interests.

Hobbes's indictment of the first two of these classes is best seen in his history of the Long Parliament, *Behemoth* (first authorized edition 1682), which was intended to show that a society not ordered according to the correct (i.e. Hobbist) precepts of government is doomed to suffer rebellion and civil disorder. According to Hobbes the Civil War was fomented by the seditious opinions in divinity and politics of the Presbyterians, the Papists, and the Independents. Of these the Presbyterians were the worst offenders. They maintained the dominion of the spiritual arm over the secular (a doctrine which is ultimately derived from Rome), and they further allowed every man, 'nay every boy and wench that could read English',[2] to judge the Scriptures according to the dictates of their own consciences, which is a certain prelude to religious dissension and civil disturbance. Some of their strength they drew also from ambitious and 'democraticall' gentry.

As for the Independents, Hobbes affirmed that they were 'a brood of Presbyterian hatching'[3] and so deserved no separate discussion. The same was true of the minor sects, whether Anabaptist, Brownist, Fifth-monarchy men, or Quakers;[4] they all resisted lawful authority and plunged the nation into chaos. Hobbes was far more circumspect when he came to discuss the Church of England, but even here he was able to get off a sally about Archbishop Laud's imprudent and un-statesmanlike

---

[1] Future scholars will undoubtedly develop other interpretations of what is coming to be called the 'psychology of controversy'. I am deliberately limiting myself to the issues as they emerge in the pages of Hobbes and his opposition.

[2] Hobbes, *Behemoth*, ed. Ferdinand Tönnies (London, 1889), p. 21.

[3] *Ibid.* p. 136.   [4] *Ibid.*

'punctilios' concerning 'the service book and its rubrics'.[1] It was in fact the *whole* English clergy which ignored Hobbes's ultra-Erastian dictum about the need for a single church establishment dominated by secular authority. In Hobbes's view the doctrines and practices of the Church are a matter of civil law, which when once enacted must never be contravened.

But the clergy opposed this, and Hobbes traces its opposition to the Universities which had always been 'an excellent servant to the clergy' as the clergy had always been 'an excellent means to divide a kingdom into factions'.[2] Hobbes's quarrel with the Universities was two-fold: they had first of all instilled 'democratical principles'[3] into their pupils—the future clergy of the nation—by training them on the worst classical authors, such as Plato, Aristotle, Cato, Cicero, and Seneca (but not Thucydides). Thus they planted the seeds of rebellion and sedition. And second, they adopted and perpetuated the worst features of scholastic thought—the interminable refinements of quiddities, separated essences, immaterial substances, and other such arrant nonsense. Logic-chopping may seem innocuous enough, but it is actually dangerous, for it has the effect of making the clergy read into their divinity more subtleties than are necessary or indeed prudent for a nation to absorb.[4] And of course as a means of arriving at the truth of any doctrine scholastic philosophy is hopelessly ineffectual.[5]

In the same way, said Hobbes, the education of lawyers was also defective. They were trained in the arid subtleties of legal disputation, and from this they drew the unwarranted inference that the law was an absolute entity independent of the sovereign's control, or else (as in the Civil War) opposed to it. For Hobbes the law was simply what was legislated in the name of the sovereign, and if such legislation ran counter to customary usages then those usages were no longer to be construed as law.[6] To argue as the common lawyers did that custom is an indepen-

[1] *Ibid.* p. 73. [2] *Ibid.* p. 148. [3] *Ibid.* p. 158. [4] *Ibid.* p. 90.

[5] *Ibid.* p. 42–3. Laird, *Hobbes*, p. 55 n. cites two contemporary opinions which seem unintentionally to justify Hobbes's views of the university. Bramhall in *Serpent Salve* (1643) described the attack on the universities—'the two eyes of the kingdom'—as part of an attack on the clergy (*Works*, III, 478). And John Edwards in *A Brief Vindication* (1679) wrote: 'See how naturally a man passes from arraigning and vilifying the Universities to affront and abuse religion.' (Ep. Ded.)

[6] *Leviathan*, pp. 174, 176.

dent source of law is, again, to weaken the authority of the sovereign and to invite civil war.

It will thus be seen that Hobbes's attacks on the clergy, the universities, and the lawyers have a common basis. All three classes contributed to the decline of sovereign power so essential to the stability of the commonwealth: the clergy by asserting that the Church is either independent of the state or superior to it; the lawyers by upholding the view that the common law is an independent entity exempt from the royal prerogative; and the universities by fostering the opinions of the other two classes. If a commonwealth is to avoid civil strife it must curb the power of these three groups.

To this argument the critics replied in two ways: first, as members of their own party defending the interests of their party, and second, and more important, as Christians who shared a common faith in the validity of religious belief however they may have disagreed about its details. When they wrote as party-men they naturally associated themselves with the programme of their party, or else they reflected the special position which they had adopted within the party. When they wrote as fellow Christians they laid aside (perhaps ignored is the better word) their sectarian and political differences and attacked a common enemy. Thus Richard Baxter, writing from the vantage-point of an unorthodox brand of Presbyterianism, was obliged to distinguish between his own theocratic solution to the problems of church and state and Hobbes's Erastian method. This he did by affirming that theocratic government preserves and promotes Christianity by making the state itself an arm of the Church, while Hobbes's 'way of absolute Impious monarchy . . . pretendeth not to any such thing as the securing a succession of the Christian Religion, without which a Righteous government is not to be expected'.[1] At the same time Baxter praised the 'learned Dr Ward (now Bishop of Exeter), and that clear-headed primate of Ireland, Dr Bramhal' for their castigations of Hobbist metaphysics. Similarly, Samuel Parker, Bishop of Oxford, while admitting that when his work is misquoted it 'savours not a little of the Leviathan',[2] was still

[1] Richard Baxter, *A Holy Commonwealth* (London, 1659), p. 225.
[2] Samuel Parker, *A Defence and Continuation of the Ecclesiastical Politie* (London, 1671), p. 279.

48

able to show that the type of absolute sovereignty which he advocated upheld the Christian character of government by enjoining the sovereign from actions contrary to the principles of Christian morality,[1] while a Hobbist prince could violate God's law with impunity. For Parker the rights and obligations of ruler and subject were circumscribed by absolute standards of morality; for Hobbes such standards simply did not exist, they belonged to that which is *quid nominis*, and in their place stood the positive law of the civil magistrate, from whom standards of right and wrong were derived. Against Hobbes, therefore, Baxter the sectary and Parker the bishop were united by a common Christian outlook, while between them and Hobbes stood the impassable gulf of opposing world-views.

What was true of the clergy who opposed Hobbes was true also of the lawyers and dons. Roger Coke, Clarendon and Sir Matthew Hale wrote as Christians first and lawyers second.[2] Each devoted as much space to an attack on Hobbes's theology as they did to a refutation of his theory of law. Seth Ward, writing as a young professor of mathematics at Oxford, vindicated the universities from the 'calumniations' of Hobbes by saying, first, that the universities were by 1654 no longer the citadels of scholastic thought which Hobbes in the *Leviathan* had supposed them to be,[3] and second, that what Hobbes really was objecting to was the universities' 'crime' of asserting 'the Attributes of God and the Naturall Immortality of the Soules of Men'.[4] On one point the universities and Hobbes were agreed. Both seemed to be saying that if you want to influence the nation, let the winds of your doctrine blow over the quadrangles and courts of Oxford and Cambridge. The question, of

---

[1] [Samuel Parker], *A Discourse of Ecclesiastical Politie* (London, 1670), pp. 137–38.
[2] For Coke and Matthew Hale, see: Roger Coke, *A Survey of the Politicks of Mr Thomas White, Mr Thomas Hobbs, and Mr Hugo Grotius* (London, 1662): and Sir Matthew Hale, 'Reflections by the Lrd. Cheife [*sic*] Justice Hale on Mr Hobbes His Dialogue of the Laws', British Museum, *Harleian MS* 711, fols. 418–39. Hale's short treatise is the most brilliant contemporary reply to Hobbes's theory of positive law. Hale argued, as did the elder and younger Coke, that the law is 'an artificial perfection of reason'. Its decisions rest upon a conception of absolute right and wrong. 'The obligation of Naturall Justice bindes Princes and governors as well as others to stand to their Pacts and agreemts.' (Fol. 437) Hale's treatise is greatly esteemed by Sir Frederick Pollock and W. S. Holdsworth, who have printed it, together with brief apparatus, in *The Law Quarterly Review*, CXLVII (1921), 274–303.
[3] Seth Ward, *Vindiciae Academiarum* (Oxford, 1654), p. 58.
[4] *Ibid.* p. 60.

course, was which doctrine. The universities were determined that it should not be Hobbism, and to this end they instituted a number of repressive measures designed to protect the young and impressionable 'sophister' from Hobbist influence. John Fell, the Dean of Christ Church College and later Bishop of Oxford, besides pronouncing the *Leviathan* 'monstrosissimum' and compelling Anthony Wood to revise the life of Hobbes in the *Historia Universitatis Oxoniensis* so as to put Hobbes in the worst possible light, was also instrumental in having the *Leviathan* and *De Cive* formally banned by university decree in 1683 and publicly burnt. In Cambridge an incident occurred, which, because it illustrates perfectly the intensity of feeling against Hobbes in the universities as well as the manner in which the university critics sought to link Hobbes with infidelity, deserves to be set out in some detail.

In March, 1668 one Daniel Scargill, Fellow of Corpus Christi College, Cambridge, was expelled from the University for having 'asserted several Impious and Atheistical Tenets to the great dishonour of God, the scandal of the Christian Religion and of the University'.[1] Ralph Cudworth, the Master of Christ's and Cambridge Platonist, who was Hobbes's most intellectually formidable opponent, was one of those who signed the expulsion order.[2] At the same time Scargill was deprived of his fellowship at Corpus. Some months later he was informed that he could be restored to the University provided that he make a public recantation. This he agreed to do, and in 1669, after the University had first rejected two drafts of his recantation,[3] he was allowed to deliver the following remarks in the University Church of St. Mary the Great:

Whereas I Daniel Scargill, late Batchelour of Arts, and Fellow of Corpus Christi Colledge; in the University of Cambridge, being through the instigation of the Devil possessed with a foolish proud conceit of my own wit and not having the fear of God before my eyes: Have lately vented and publickly asserted in the said University divers wicked, Blasphemous, and Atheistical positions (particularly, That all right of Dominion is founded only in Power: That all moral Righteousness is founded only in the positive Law of the Civil Magistrate . . .), professing that I gloried to be an *Hobbist*

[1] Cambridge University Library, *Baker MSS.*, Mn. 1. 38, fol. 143.
[2] *Ibid.*   [3] *Ibid.* fols. 143, 144.

and an Atheist; and vaunting, that Hobbs should be maintained by *Daniel*, that is, by me. Agreeably unto which principles and positions, I have lived in great licentiousness; swearing rashly; drinking intemperately; boasting myself insolently; corrupting others by my pernicious principles and examples: to the Dishonour of God; the Reproach of the University; the Scandal of Christianity; and the just offence of mankinde. . . .

Wherefore, I do here in the presence of God, Angels, and men, cast my self down in a deep dread of the just judgements and vengeance of God upon the accursed Atheism of this age, acknowledging my self to be highly guilty of the growth and spreading thereof, having contributed what my profane wit could devise, or my foul mouth express, to instill it into others or confirm them therein. . . . In a deep sense of that wretched part I have acted in the propagating thereof, I do now abhor my self in dust and ashes, and from the bottom of my heart, I do disclaim, renounce, detest, and abhor those execrable Positions asserted by me or any other: particularly. . . that there is a desirable glory in being and being reputed an Atheist: which I implied when I expressly affirmed that I gloried to be an *Hobbist* and an Atheist.[1]

Scargill's recantation is remarkable for the light it sheds on the mental atmosphere of the times. Here we see a university scholar submitting (with what disingenuousness we cannot at this distance tell) to the overwhelming pressures of university and Church opinion, united in their detestation of Hobbes. It is true that Scargill was obliged only to give up his fellowship and make a public recantation; in an earlier age he might have been burnt. But his words have the traditional recantatory ring, and behind them we can sense the revulsion amounting almost to horror which Hobbes produced in his time. Also, we find Scargill condemning libertinism, or what was conceived of in his time as practical rather than doctrinal atheism. Here Scargill interprets his own libertinism as the inevitable practical consequence of his having adopted two typical Hobbist positions—ethical relativism and Erastianism. In thus associating

---

[1] Daniel Scargill, *The Recantation of Daniel Scargill publickly made before the University of Cambridge in Great St Maries*, 25 *July* 1669 ([Cambridge], 1669), pp. 1–4. There is a reprint in Somers' *Tracts*, VII (London, 1812), a brief but perceptive notice by Dorothea Krook in 'The Recantation of Daniel Scargill', *Notes and Queries*, 198 (1953), 159–60, and a short memoir plus a reprint by C. L. S. Linnell, 'Daniel Scargill', *Church Quarterly Review*, CLVI (July–Sept. 1955), 256–65.

Hobbes's thought with the debasement of public morality, Scargill was repeating a commonplace of anti-Hobbes criticism after the Restoration.

Hobbes himself may have seen in the Scargill incident a crystallization of opinion against him; at any rate, he was moved to write an apologia in reply. Unfortunately, this document was never printed and has not survived. Hobbes asked Sir John Birkenhead to see it through the press, but Birkenhead, for reasons known only to himself, suppressed it.[1] The incident, however, had another sequel of great interest. After Scargill's expulsion a friend of his, not now known to us but presumably a man of influence, interceded on his behalf with the Archbishop of Canterbury, hoping to have Scargill restored to his fellowship. Two letters from Archbishop Sheldon to Dr Spencer, the Master of Corpus Christi College, are preserved among the Harleian manuscripts in the British Museum. The first asks Spencer to reinstate Scargill. This must have met with a firm refusal, for in the next letter we find the Archbishop acknowledging that it is better for one foolish fellow to perish rather than endanger a whole society—and he promises no longer to press for Scargill's readmittance.[2] Thus is recorded one of Archbishop Sheldon's rare defeats. As his letter-book covering the period 1669 to 1681 shows him to have been a resolute and forceful administrator, seldom crossed, almost never frustrated,[3] his defeat in the present instance and at the hands of a Doctor of Divinity in the Church of which he was Primate is all the more significant. Perhaps it should be added that Scargill was never restored to his fellowship and that he afterwards held various livings in Norfolk, where he appears to have suffered extreme poverty.

While we do not have Hobbes's comments on this affair, we have an earlier statement of his concerning the motivation of the criticism against him. He argued that the critics who attacked him in the guise of defenders of the faith were in fact inspired by a wholly different motive: they feared the loss of their power. The view that 'I had made the civil powers too

[1] Wood, *Athenae Oxonienses*, III, 1215; Aubrey, I, 362.
[2] British Museum, *Harleian MSS*, 7377, fol. I and IV.
[3] See E. A. O. Whiteman, 'Two Letter Books of Archbishops Sheldon and Sancroft', *Bodleian Library Record*, IV (April, 1953), 215.

large' was, he said, 'most bitterly excepted against . . . but this by ecclesiastical persons. That I had utterly taken away liberty of conscience; but this by sectaries. That I had set princes above civil laws; but this by lawyers'.[1] How blunt and scornful these phrases are, but also how self-assured, as if there can be no doubt whatever that the attacks reflected the vested interests of these various groups.

In a certain sense Hobbes's view of his critics' motives is correct. It is clear that he touched his opponents in the sensitive area of power and privilege; and I think it will also be granted that the thirst for power and privilege is a compelling if not a fundamental human motive, and that in the present controversy the powerful interests of clergy, university and common law were heavily engaged and just as vigorously defended. This I say is true; but it is not the whole truth. The clergy who attacked Hobbes had a vested interest; so had the universities; so had the lawyers. But any explanation of their motives is incomplete which attempts to rationalize away the intensity and depth of their religious belief, the suasive power of religion itself to move them to its defence against what they considered to be the dangerous strictures of an atheist. Again and again the critics return to this point: that if the creeds and practices of the Church are made to subserve the interests of the state, then not only the Church but Christian faith itself will wither away. Here, for instance, is Sir Charles Wolseley, who if not the most edifying is at least one of the most representative of Hobbes's critics:

To bottom all Religion upon humane authority, and derive it from the power and pleasure of men, tends . . . to destroy all Religion, and at last to bring men to no Religion. If we once take away divine Authority from Religion we have made an inrode upon its best defence . . . If once it be taken for granted that the Scriptures have no Authority but what the Civil Power give them [cf. *Leviathan*, ch. 24], they will soon come, upon a divine account, to have none at all.

[1] Thomas Hobbes, *Philosophical Rudiments Concerning Government and Society* in *Works*, II, xxiii. Hobbes wrote to the same effect in 1662: 'There is nothing in [the *Leviathan*] against episcopacy. I cannot therefore imagine what reason any episcopal man can have to speak of me, as I hear some of them do, as of an atheist or man of no religion, unless it be for making the authority of the church depend wholly upon the regal power'. *Seven Philosophical Problems* (1662) in *Works*, VII, 5.

Nothing gratifies the Atheist more, when he is pulling down the pillars of Religion, than positions of this nature.[1]

Thus the critics were agreed that Hobbes did not merely threaten their own power; he was assaulting the validity and truth of religion itself; and the critics maintained this argument not merely as bishops, vicars, sectaries, dons, lawyers, but as devout men whose total view of the world was coloured by religious feeling. Though the tone of the criticism varied considerably from one writer to the next, it betrayed always the emotions of a religious man. Baxter, for example, paused in the midst of an attack on Hobbes's materialist doctrine of the soul to insert a prayer which is as revealing of the differences between him and Hobbes as any of the conventional arguments which preceded it:

Even in the panting, languishing desires and motions of my soul, I find that thou [my God], and only thou, are its resting place . . . The creature were dead if thou wert not its life; and ugly, if thou wert not its beauty; and insignificant, if thou wert not its sense. The soul is deformed which is without thine image; and lifeless, which liveth not in love to thee, if love be not its pulse, and prayer, and praise, its constant breath. The mind is unlearned which readeth not thy name on all the world, and seeth not 'Holiness to the Lord' engraven upon the face of every creature. He doteth that doubteth of thy being or perfections; and he dreameth who doth not live to thee. O let me have no other portion, no reason, no love, no life but what is devoted to thee, employed on thee, and for thee here, and be perfected in thee, the only perfect, final Object for evermore.[2]

If we set this passage against any in Hobbes we find in it an intense religious feeling conveyed in a lyrical, incandescent prose, while Hobbes's will show a utilitarian and secular outlook expressed in hard, direct, hammer-like clauses. The difference is the profound difference between opposing sensibilities, between a religious temper and a sceptical one. Baxter's prose style is remote from the banter of John Eachard, another of Hobbes's critics, or even from the solemn, measured periods of Clarendon, but all three critics, and all the others as well, shared the same assumptions about Christianity, and it was

[1] Wolseley, *Unreasonablenesse of Atheism*, pp. 15–16.
[2] Richard Baxter, *The Reasons of the Christian Religion* in *The Practical Works*, XXI (London, 1830), 391.

these assumptions which moved them as much as anything else to repudiate Hobbes.[1] The first full-scale polemic against Hobbes as atheist was Alexander Ross's *Leviathan drawn out with a Hook* (1653). The Leviathan Ross hooked was a queer heretical fish, and Hobbes the very type of heresiarch; Ross called him an Anthropomorphist, Sabellian, Nestorian, Sadducean, Arabian, Tacian, Manichee, Mohammedan, Cerinthian, Tertullianist, Audean, Montanist, Aetian, Priscillianist, Luciferian, Originist, Socinian, and Jew.[2] Ross was learned, an Aristotelian, and a gifted and prolific controversialist with a pungent style. None of the critics was able to ferret out as many heresies in Hobbes as he was able to do; still, he announced the theme and set the direction for all the critics who followed. *Leviathan*, he wrote, is 'a piece dangerous both to Government and Religion'.[3]

These sentiments were quickly echoed by Seth Ward, who between 1653 and 1656 produced a volume attacking Hobbes's materialism, the tract in defence of the universities, and an elaborate refutation in Latin of Hobbes's most typical ideas.[4] Ward was determined not to rail; his only weapon would be the power of Reason itself. But the effort proved too much for him, and we soon find him lapsing into abuse, his limbs 'numb with horror and indignation'[5] when he contemplates the impiety of his opponent.

Hobbes's name was now a by-word for infidelity. In 1657 it was classed by Lord Saye and Sele with pirates, thieves, and atheists.[6] In 1658 Bishop Bramhall published his *The Catching of the Leviathan, or the Great Whale*, in order to demonstrate, *inter alia*, 'out of Mr Hobbs his own Works, That no man who is thoroughly an Hobbist can be a good Christian'.[7] 'The wild

---

[1] Eachard's criticisms of Hobbes are *Mr Hobbs's State of Nature Considered* (London, 1672), and *Some Opinions of Mr Hobbs Considered* (London, 1673).
[2] Ross, sigs. A 14–16.
[3] *Ibid.* sig. A 16.
[4] Seth Ward, *A Philosophical Essay Towards an Eviction of the Being and Attributes of God* (Oxford, 1655); *Vindiciae Academiarum, op. cit.; In Thomae Hobbii Philosophiam* (Oxford, 1656).
[5] Ward, *In Thomae Hobbii Philosophiam*, p. 199.
[6] See 'A Letter from Lord Saye and Sele to Lord Wharton, 29 December 1657', printed by C. H. Firth in *English Historical Review*, x (1895), 107.
[7] Quoted from the collected edition of Bramhall's *Works* (Dublin, 1677), Tome III, 3rd Discourse, t.p.

Bore hath been in the Vineyard', wrote Bishop Lucy in 1663, 'and hath . . . digged at the roots of Religion . . . and surely if any one man for some hundreds of years might be called that Bore, it is Mr Hobbes, no man ever writing so destructively to the principles of Christianity as he hath done.'[1]

And so the criticism, with the theme of atheism running constantly through it, proliferated. In 1673 Robert Sharrock thundered from the pulpit against Hobbist infidelity, and entertained his parishioners with a vivid picture of Hobbes in hell, 'the smoke of his Torment ascending for ever and ever'.[2] In the same year a Norfolk divine named Robotham contributed a remarkable Latin ode to a feeble criticism of Hobbes by Dr John Templer.[3] 'Who', asked Robotham, 'is this Colossus lying stretched out in the sea in all his enormity, his dreadful jaws gaping fiercely, and with obscene regurgitations belching forth abominable dogma which befouls the British coastlines?' It is the

Malmesburian Hydra, the enormous Leviathan, the gigantic dragon, the hideous monstrosity and British beast, the Propagator of execrable doctrines, the Promulgator of mad wisdom, the Herald and Pugilist of impious death, the Insipid Venerator of a Material God, the Renowned Fabricator of a monocondyte Symbol, the Depraved Renewer of old heresies to the faith, the Nonsensical roguish vendor of falsifications, a strenuous hoer of weeds and producer of deceits——

and so on for some twenty lines more, the imagery becoming more febrile, classical, and confused (the great sea-monster wielding a hoe), until the beast is slain by John Templer in the person of Theseus.

Some of the quality of Robotham's rhetoric is preserved in Bishop Vesey's remarks on Hobbes which he inserted in his *Life of Bramhall* (1677). 'Tho this great *Leviathan* takes pleasure in that deluge of *Atheism* he has spued out of his mouth, and roules with great wantoness in the deep, attended with a numerous shoal of his own spawning, yet the *hook is still in his*

[1] William Lucy, *Observations, Censures and Confutations of Notorious Errors in Mr Hobbes His Leviathan* (London, 1663), 'To the Christian Reader', sig. b2.
[2] R[obert] S[harrock], *De Finibus Virtutis Christianae* (Oxford, 1673), p. 198.
[3] Charles Robotham, Ode prefaced to John Templer's *Idea Theologiae Leviathanis* (London, 1673), sig. A7 (Templer is chiefly remembered as Dryden's tutor in Trinity College, Cambridge.)

nose.' Hobbes is 'a pandor to bestiality' and his 'doctrines have had so great a share in the debauchery of his Generation, that a good Christian can hardly hear his name without saying of his prayers'.[1] William Howell in 1679 expressed 'a just resentment of the Affronts Mr Hobbs hath cast, and Injuries he hath done to our Religion';[2] in 1680 appeared the anonymous *True Effigies of the Monster of Malmesbury: or, Thomas Hobbes in His Proper Colours*, showing the Leviathan sailing 'i' th *Ocean* of the most *Profound Impiety*';[3] in 1686 Bishop South preached at Westminster Abbey against 'the lewd, scandalous and immoral doctrine' put forward 'by the infamous author of *Leviathan*';[4] in 1694 James Lowde heard the tenets of Hobbism buzzing in his ear 'like the troublesome Fly, [which] is always busie about the sores of Human Nature; not with an intent to cure 'em but to make 'em worse'.[5]

On the continent Hobbes received the same hard usage. His English critics were quoted with approval, and in some instances translated. In Germany, for example, a translation of John Eachard's *Mr Hobbs's State of Nature Considered* (1672) appeared in 1680 and went through two editions,[6] while the *Leviathan* itself had to wait until 1794 for a German translation. The background of the continental reaction to Hobbes is complicated by historical and intellectual developments which lie outside the scope of the present discussion. One aspect of this criticism, however, is worth noting as having its parallel in England. Spinoza published his *Tractatus Theologico-Politicus* in 1670 and the *Tractatus Politicus* was published posthumously in 1677. Both works gained wide publicity on the continent and were quickly linked (though quite uncritically) with Hobbes as

[1] J. Vesey, 'The Life of primate Bramhall', in Bramhall, *Works, op. cit.*, sig. nv.
[2] W[illiam] H[owell], *The Spirit of Prophecie* (London, 1679), 'To the Reader', sig. A3 (This work is wrongly ascribed to William Hughes by Wing, *STC*, following a false attribution by Halkett and Laing, v, 345. It is attributed to Howell by his contemporary, Richard Blackburne, in his *Tractatuum contra Hobbium editorum Syllabus* (London, 1681), p. 196. Hughes was a writer on horticulture, Howell the vicar of Fittleworth in Sussex).
[3] [Anon.], *The True Effigies of the Monster of Malmesbury; or, Thomas Hobbes in his Proper Colours* (London, 1680), p. 8.
[4] Robert South, *Sermons Preached Upon Several Occasions* (London, 1730), ii, 322.
[5] James Lowde, *A Discourse Concerning the Nature of Man* (London, 1694), sig. A8 v.
[6] See Baron Cay von Brockdorff, 'Friedrich Maximilian Klinger und Hobbes', *Veröffentlichungen der Hobbes-Gesellschaft* (Kiel, 1935), p. 3.

tending toward the same irreligious conclusions. Thus a score of theologians and scholars (many of high reputation) laboured to establish the origins of Spinoza's religious thought in Hobbist philosophy.[1] Their task was made easier by a number of striking similarities between the two thinkers: both (though in different ways) preached a doctrine of determinism; both were violently anti-clerical; both were sceptical of witchcraft, or of miracles, or of the Divine authorship of the Bible. Their critics found it convenient to ignore their differences, however large these may be, as these were not felt to diminish the strength of their threat to Christian religion. Spinoza was read as an apostle of atheism who took his cue from Hobbes. 'Sonderlich Spinoza,' observed an anonymous critic in 1702, 'scheinet vol recht vom Satan dazu gedinget zuseyn die Atheisteren auf guten Fuss zu setzen. Was Hobbes nur halbicht angefangen das hat er mit grosser Werwegenheit zu Ende gebracht. GOTT behüte uns für solcher unweisen Philosophie!'[2]

In England Spinoza was read from the first by informed thinkers like Richard Baxter and the Cambridge Platonists Cudworth and More, as well as by More's intellectually-alert friend Lady Conway. To their number may be added the name of Thomas Browne, an obscure parson who in 1683 published an intelligent criticism of Hobbes and Spinoza on miracles.[3] All these writers attacked Hobbes and Spinoza together as fellow conspirators in the cause of atheism.[4] The burden of their attacks is that Hobbes and Spinoza were both concerned to

[1] See, e.g. Franciscum Cuperum, *Arcana Atheisme Revelata* (Rotterdam, 1676), p. 121, where both Spinoza and Hobbes are said to deny the absolute certainty of knowing about the existence of the external world; Christian Kortholt, *De tribus Impostoribus Magnis—Herbert, Hobbes, Spinoza* (Kiel, 1680); Michael Berns, *Altar der Atheisten, der Heyden und der Christen* (Hamburg, 1692), cited in C. Güttler, *Eduard Lord Herbert* (Munich, 1897), p. 142; Jacobus Staalkopf, *Ab Impiis Detorsionibus Thomae Hobbesii & Benedicti de Spinoza* (Gryphiswald, [1707]); etc.

[2] [Anon.], *Fürstellung vier neuer Welt-Weisen, nahmentlich, I. Renati Des Cartes, II. Thomae Hobbes, III. Benedicti Spinosa, IV. Balthasar Beckers* ([Frankfurt a. M.?], 1702), 'Beneigter Leser', Sig. Alr.

[3] [Thomas Browne], *Miracles Work's Above and Contrary to Nature* (London, 1683).

[4] Richard Baxter, *The Defence of the Nonconformist's Plea for Peace* (London, 1680), p. 12; Ralph Cudworth, *True Intellectual System of the Universe*, ed. Mosheim, II, 564; Henry More, *Demonstrationes Duarum Propositium* in *Opera Omnia* (London, 1678), p. 615, quoted by Mackinnon, ed. More's *Enchiridion Metaphysicum*, p. 295; also More's letter to Joseph Glanvill, 25 May 1678, in Glanvill, *Sadducismus Triumphatus* (London, 4th ed.; London, 1726), pp. 9–10; Lady Anne Conway, *The Principles of the Most Ancient and Modern Philosophy* (London, 1692), *passim*.

deny the existence and power of spirit, and consequently of God. Even the once-venerated and now-despised Descartes was to Lady Conway free at least of the materialist taint which she found in the work of Hobbes and Spinoza.

For *Cartes* acknowledges God to be plainly Immaterial, and an Incorporeal Spirit. *Hobbs* affirms God himself to be Material and Corporeal; yea, nothing else but Matter and Body, and so confounds God and the Creatures in their Essences, and denies that there is any essential difference between them. These and many more the worst of Consequences are the Dictates of *Hobbs's* Philosophy; to which may be added that of *Spinosa*; for this Spinosa also confounds God and the Creatures together, and makes but one Being of both. . . .[1]

Baxter, it is true, addressed himself to the central thesis of Spinoza's *Tractatus Theologico-Politicus*, which is that the right to free thought and discussion is consistent with true piety and good government, a position which Baxter repudiated but which he could not conceivably attribute to Hobbes. So he redirected his argument to include Hobbes and Spinoza's unorthodox treatment of Scripture. 'This apostate Jew' has written a 'pernicious book' which most 'subtily assaulted the text of the Old Testament [and] is greedily sought and cried up (with Hobbes his equal) in this unhappy time . . .'[2]

Hobbes did not share Spinoza's view that the right to free discussion was an essential ingredient of good government. For Hobbes, thought and opinion are free when they are unexpressed, since there is then no conceivable way in which the civil authority can interfere with them. But once thought and opinion are communicated to others and are freed from civil restraint, they have the power to weaken the authority of the magistrate, who must rule absolutely if he is to rule at all. Hence, a stable commonwealth will stamp out dissent or risk the consequences that may follow.

This is harsh and uncompromising enough, but it had no effect whatever on those of Hobbes's critics who wished to see *his* works suppressed. They pursued their aim without regard to Hobbes's views on toleration, or even in spite of them, because they were agreed that every definition of freedom,

[1] Lady Conway, *op. cit.*, pp. 148–9.
[2] Baxter, *op. cit.*, p. 14.

whether of the Presbyterian type offered by Baxter or of the more liberal Independent sort put forward by Milton, must exclude utterances against religion such as are to be found in Hobbes. In *Areopagitica* Milton argued that although the right of one Protestant Christian to attack the views of another is inviolable, no similar right exists for papists, infidels, and blasphemers. These are beyond the pale and must be suppressed. Milton wrote too early (1644) to be thinking of *Leviathan*, but he may have had Hobbes's *De Cive* (1642) in mind. Indeed it has been pursuasively argued by one modern scholar that Milton's vision of the good man who rejects evil by the exercise of free choice and right reasoning is a conscious refutation of Hobbes's contrary views in *De Cive*.[1] In any case, though Milton was not explicit about which books he would exempt from his passionate plea for freedom of the press, it is entirely plausible to assume that Hobbes's works were among them.

Two later appeals addressed to Parliament on the same subject as *Areopagitica* were explicit in naming Hobbes as a writer dangerous to the idea of religion itself and therefore deserving of censorship. The first of these was made in 1652 (the year after *Leviathan*) by a London bookseller named Luke Fawn and endorsed by a number of his colleagues. The second was Baxter's 'Humble Advice' to the Parliament in 1655. Fawn called upon the Parliament to amend the language of the licensing act then pending so as to list specifically certain 'Popish, blasphemous and apostate' works, most particularly *Leviathan*.[2] Futher, the act ought to set out in detail what is most offensive in *Leviathan*, namely Hobbes's Erastianism, and several of his heterodox theological views, such as that the soul is mortal, that damnation is not eternal, and that tormentors in hell are not individual devils but mere metaphors for qualities of pain endured by the damned.[3] Two years later Fawn issued a new petition in which he widened the scope of his bigotry to include Quaker literature as well as *A Treatise of Schism* by Philip Scot

---

[1] Marjorie Nicolson, 'Milton and Hobbes,' *Studies in Philology*, XXIII (1926), 405–33. Cf. also Don M. Wolfe, 'Milton and Hobbes', *Studies in Philology*, XLI (1944), 410–26.
[2] [Luke Fawn], *A Beacon Set on Fire* (London, 1652), p. 7.
[3] *Ibid.* pp. 14–15.

(1650), a work written against Hobbes but censorable because by a Jesuit.[1]

Baxter echoed Milton's view that the hard core of religious belief ought never to be challenged. Let the Parliament, Baxter wrote, 'Lay a penalty on him that Prints or sels any Books against the Fundamentals or Essentials of Christianity; and that slander or reproach Magistracy, Ministry or Ordinances of Christ. And burn more of this nature, that you may manifest a disowning of them. Specially *Hobbs* his *Leviathan*.'[2]

It is difficult to say what precise effect this agitation had on the Parliament. I find no record of a Parliamentary ban imposed on Hobbes in the 1650's, but it is clear from the printing history of *Leviathan* that the Stationers' Company tried to suppress the book after its initial appearance. The first English edition bore the imprint 'London, Printed for Andrew Crooke, etc. . . . 1651'. Two subsequent 'editions' appeared, but these contained the identical imprint of the first edition and the same date, 1651. That they were separate and later editions is proved by the presence on their title pages of different printer's ornaments, and by corrections which were merely listed as *errata* in the first edition. All the evidence points to their having been printed in Holland, and probably in Amsterdam,[3] where a Dutch translation of *Leviathan* appeared in 1667. What is the explanation for their false imprints? It must surely be that the *Leviathan* was twice reissued surreptitiously in order to evade a ban and at the same time to satisfy a growing public demand.[4] One consequence of the ban is that the price of *Leviathan* rose from 8s. to 30s.; Pepys considered himself fortunate on 3 September 1668 to find a second-hand copy at 24s.

In 1683 *Leviathan* was again proscribed, this time in the decree already mentioned of the University of Oxford which condemned it to the flames, together with *De Cive* and other 'Pernicious Books and Damnable Doctrines', because they are

---

[1] [Luke Fawn], *A Second Beacon Fired* (London, 1654).

[2] Richard Baxter, *Humble Advice, or the Heads of Those Things which were offered to many Honourable Members of Parliament* (London, 1655), p. 9.

[3] See Macdonald, *Bibliography of Hobbes*, pp. 27–30, where the printing history of *Leviathan* is set out in lucid detail.

[4] This is at least partly confirmed by an entry in the *Calendar of State Papers* for 12 October 1670 which describes the seizure by the Stationers Company of a press as well as sheets from *Leviathan* then being printed in London.

THE HUNTING OF LEVIATHAN

'false, seditious, and impious; and most of them . . . also Heretical and Blasphemous, infamous to Christian Religion, and destructive of all Government in Church and State'.[1] On the continent Hobbes's works proved equally noxious and combustible. *De Cive* was placed on the Index at Rome in 1654, among other books which 'damnati, prohibiti, ac respective suspensi fuerunt.'[2] In 1674 the States General in Holland prohibited *Leviathan* and Spinoza's *Tractatus Theologico-Politicus*.

Hobbes himself was never personally molested, although Aubrey reports that a number of bishops talked of having him burnt. This alarmed Hobbes sufficiently to cause him to destroy some of his papers, and he was given further anxiety in 1666 when the House of Commons cited the atheism of Hobbes and of his friend the Roman Catholic priest Thomas White as a probable 'cause' of the Great Fire and Plague of London, and ordered an investigation of their works.[3] Hobbes's influential friends at Court, however, especially Arlington, the Secretary of State, prevented him from coming to harm.[4]

But his friends could not stem the flood of abuse which continued to pour from the presses throughout the last quarter of the seventeenth century and the early decades of the eighteenth.

From a Bishop down to a Country Curate, [Hobbes] was esteem'd for a dangerous and Sceptical Author; and a Parson wou'd as soon visit a House where there's the Plague, or give away the Tithes of his Parish, than let a Parishioner have the Perusal of [his] Book; they have made it a sort of Damnation to speak in his Defence; and who espouses him with the Pen, is liable to the Inquisition of Doctors Commons, and is sure of being trounced for a Heretick. . . .[5]

---

[1] *The Judgment and Decree of the University of Oxford Past in their Convocation* (Oxford, 1683). Propositions 7 and 10–14 are charged to Hobbes.
[2] Cited by Macdonald, p. 16 from a *Decretum* published at Rome, 16 June 1654.
[3] *Calendar of State Papers*, 20 October 1666.
[4] *Ibid.*, 9 June 1667.
[5] [Anon.] *Visits from the Shades* (London, 1704), p. 33.

CHAPTER IV

MATERIALISM: GENERAL REACTIONS

All that *really* exists, said Hobbes, is body. Those things which are usually considered to be immaterial, such as space and time, or thought, or logical relations, are attributes of mind; they are 'phantasms' of the mind, and mind, in Hobbes's view, is a material phenomenon, a complicated series of physical motions. Whatever is in the universe is material, and as all things are in the universe, all things are material, or else they are nowhere and nothing.[1]

Hobbes tried to make this doctrine clearer by the use of the following hypothetical illustration. Suppose, he said, the whole world were annihilated except for one man in it. What would that man know of the world? He would know what he remembers of the past—that is to say, his mind would be furnished with 'the memory and imagination of magnitudes, motions, sounds, colours, &c. as also of their order and parts'.[2] When the world is restored from its supposed annihilation, only magnitude and motion are actually restored, because these are attributes of body, and body comprises the whole of external reality. Sounds, colours and the like are secondary qualities—not inhering in objects, while space and time are 'accidents of the mind', space being the 'Phantasm' or 'imagination' of a thing which exists outside the mind but which has no other attribute except that it appears outside the mind, and time being 'the phantasm of before or after in motion'.[3] All that *really* exists is body, which is defined as 'that, which having no dependance [*sic*] upon our thought, is coincident or coextended with some part of [imaginary] space'.[4] The two defining properties of body are extension, understood mentally as space, and motion, understood mentally as time.

Motion is defined as 'a continual relinquishing of one place, and acquiring of another'.[5] Its importance in Hobbes's scheme cannot be overestimated. Hobbes, who was enormously ex-

---

[1] *Leviathan*, p. 440.   [2] *De Corpore* in *Works*, I, 92.
[3] *Ibid.* p. 95.   [4] *Ibid.* p. 102.   [5] *Ibid.* p. 109.

cited by the discoveries of Galileo in the field of mechanics, set for himself the task of assimilating motion as the grand unifying principle of his philosophical system. Motion underlies all change; motion *is* in fact change. This follows clearly enough from Hobbes's materialism. For if all reality is body, and body is extended or spatial in character, the only change possible is change of place, that is, motion. Motion also lies at the root of all causes and effects in nature, for effects are produced upon 'bodies contiguous' brought into contact by motion; and these effects in turn become causes affecting other bodies, so that causation is a continuous physical process. Hobbes consistently denied that action at a distance is possible. 'There can be no cause of motion, except in a body contiguous and moved.'[1] This proposition Hobbes treated as largely self-evident, though he attempted a proof based upon the principle which he adapted from Galileo's law of inertia, namely, that 'whatsoever is at rest, will always be at rest, unless there be some other body besides it, which, by endeavouring to get into its place by motion, suffers it no longer to remain at rest.'[2] But this simply assumes that a body cannot move of its own accord, and hence presupposes what was in the first place to be proved. The only kind of motion possible in Hobbes's view is motion externally caused, with the exception of the First Cause itself, which Hobbes thought of in the Aristotelian fashion as both unmoved and uncaused. And causation represents the action of one moving body upon another contiguous body in a continuous chain of motions.

Hobbes responded to the idea of motion with so much intellectual excitement that he tended at times to treat the concept as though it were an ultimate reality. Thus for example he wrote that 'the things that really *are* in the world without us,

---

[1] *Ibid.* p. 124. Hobbes evolved two separate theories to explain how contiguous bodies are moved. In the *Little Treatise* (so named by Brandt and first printed by Tönnies as Appendix I to the *Elements of Law* (Cambridge, 1928), Hobbes argued that all bodies emit particles (or species) which move across space to affect other bodies. By the time he came to write *De Corpore* Hobbes had changed his mind on this point and offered instead a mediumistic theory according to which the motion of one body is imparted to another body at a distance by an intervening medium or rarified ether. An admirable study of both theories is to be found in Frithiof Brandt, *Thomas Hobbes's Mechanical Conception of Nature* (Copenhagen, 1928), pp. 17–32, 103–9, 365–7.
[2] *De Corpore*, p. 15.

are those motions by which these seemings are caused.'[1] This statement in particular provoked the scornful comment of one of Hobbes's minor critics, Bishop Lucy, who ridiculed the 'universe of motion madly fancied by Mr Hobbes'. 'Is all *without us* nothing but *motion?*' Lucy asked. 'Is the standing still of the earth nothing but *motion?* Is the thing that *Moves* nothing but motion?'[2] But motion for Hobbes meant the motion of bodies. The reason he considered motion to be so vitally important was his feeling that motion holds the key to all knowledge. Change in nature—that is to say, the generation, mutation and corruption or decay of bodies—is represented by the motions of bodies. Similarly, cause and effect in nature can be understood only as a sequence of events in which one moving body collides with another. This is as true of the causes of sense-experience, in which human knowledge is rooted, as it is for any other natural phenomenon. So that while body remains the ultimate reality, a proper understanding of the motion of body provides the clue to all change and to all causation and hence to all the knowledge which is possible in a material but not a static universe.

Let us examine more closely Hobbes's view that the laws of cause and effect are applicable as much to human as to non-human experience. We remember Hobbes's definition of body as 'that which having no dependance upon our thought, is coincident or coextended with some part of space'. It might have appeared from this definition that Hobbes had established thought as a separate category of existence independent of body. This however he did not do. All that exists is body. Thought, or as Hobbes put it, 'conceptions . . . are nothing *really*, but motion in some internal substance of the *head*'.[3] Mental activity is therefore material, and as such is subject to the same laws of cause and effect as is all matter. Hobbes never considered the possibility that the product of mental activity—thought—is different in kind from the physical processes which give rise to it. The motions 'in some internal substance of the

---

[1] *Human Nature* in *Works*, iv, 8.
[2] William Lucy, *Observations, Censures and Confutations of . . . Mr Hobbes* (London, 1663), p. 49. (It is worth observing that the Copernican hypothesis was still being rejected in 1663.)
[3] *Human Nature* in *Works*, iv, 31.

head' are a reaction to other motions communicated to the head by means of the sense-organs and nerves. The whole process is mechanical and material.

Such a view of man as a mechanico-material being has large and disturbing implications for religion. For if all reality is material, and if 'cogitation is really the same thing with Corporeal Motion', and if there 'can be no cause of motion, except in a body contiguous and moved', then free will is impossible and final causes are utterly rejected. Bacon thought the traditional Aristotelian concept of final cause had no place in an accurate account of macrocosmic nature, but he retained it as a means of explaining human purposive behaviour. Similarly, Descartes rejected final causes in involuntary actions, but retained them for voluntary human behaviour. It remained for Hobbes to banish final causes altogether. 'A *final cause*', he wrote, 'has no place but in such things as have sense and will; and this also I shall prove hereafter to be an efficient cause.'[1] Thus has Hobbes invaded the last natural preserve of final cause—man himself—whose behaviour, both involuntary and purposive, is now reduced to the ineluctable and 'necessitous' movement of bodies. Man's capacity to choose freely and hence to choose between good and evil, that capacity which Milton saw as the most treasured of all human possessions, is in this view rendered meaningless.

In his earliest philosophical treatise Hobbes showed himself to have been a materialist, and to this doctrine he adhered all his life. Why was he a materialist: Why, that is to say, did he reject spirit and adopt a theory of matter as ultimate reality at a time when the notion of spirit as real held a firm grip on the minds of men? To this question research into Hobbes's life and the sources of his thought has not yet produced a satisfactory answer. For our purposes there is a more interesting question: Did Hobbes prove, or even attempt to prove, that matter alone is real? The answer is that he did neither of these things. His

---

[1] *De Corpore*, p. 132. It should be noted that although he did not realize this, Hobbes was not completely liberated from the concept of final cause. He depended upon Aristotle (through Galileo) for his physical hypothesis of simple circular motion, according to which all bodies move in a revolving motion because this type of motion was most natural to fulfil the orderly ends of creation. For Hobbes's debt to Aristotle on this point see Samuel I. Mintz, 'Hobbes, Galileo and the Circle of Perfection', *Isis*, 43 (1952), 98–100, and Brandt, pp. 324–33.

materialist assumptions rested on no surer foundation than his sincere belief that they were true. He identified matter with substance, and on the basis of this was able to show that 'immaterial substance' is a contradiction in terms. But his assumption that there can be no other substance but matter is gratuitous and unproved. Hobbes was most impressive when he worked out the logical consequences of his assumptions; he showed no inclination for proving those assumptions to be true beyond a firm belief that they were self-evident and attainable by all reasonable men who exercise their minds with due and proper care.

All the critics of Hobbes's materialism agreed with Bishop Bramhall that

by taking away all incorporeal substance, [Hobbes] taketh away God himself . . . And *to say that an Angel or Spirit is an incorporeal substance, is to say in effect, that there is no Angel or Spirit at all.* By the same reason, to say That God is an incorporeal substance, is to say that there is no God at all. Either God is incorporeal, or he is finite, and consists of parts, and consequently is no God.[1]

Materialism then was 'that main root of Atheisme, from which so many lesser branches are daily sprouting up'.[2] It had to be extirpated.

The problem of the critics was therefore to establish the absolute, independent existence of spirit. To do this they drew upon the whole armoury of traditional arguments—the argument from design, the ontological argument, the argument from revelation, the argument from the common consent of mankind, the argument from the evidence of witchcraft, demonology, and occult experience. They were particularly anxious to demonstrate that consciousness, reasoning, memory and moral judgments are essentially non-material phenomena, belonging to the activity of the soul, even if these phenomena are accompanied by bodily movements.

Two of the earliest writers against Hobbes's materialism— Alexander Ross in 1653 and Robert Vilvain in 1654—showed no disposition to *argue* the question at all. They considered the matter as settled; spirit is immaterial substance and spirit exists. Ross was a prolific controversialist who consistently

[1] John Bramhall, *The Catching of Leviathan* in *Works* (Dublin, 1676), Tome III, 873.
[2] *Ibid.*

THE HUNTING OF LEVIATHAN

defended conservative positions. All his life he waged war against new ideas, and with so much vehemence that most of his contemporaries, even those who agreed with him, regarded him as an eccentric. Writing from the Aristotelian point of view, he attacked Thomas Browne's 'atomism' and the advanced astronomy of John Wilkins, which Ross described as the 'whimzicall opinion of the earths motion'.[1] Against Hobbes Ross asserted the superiority of Aristotelian philosophy. Everyone who has not taken leave of his senses, he said, knows that there is such a thing as final causes, that inanimate objects have appetites and inclinations. This

is so far from being absurd, that to affirm the contrary were most absurd; for from whence is it that heavy bodies move downward, light bodies upward, but from this natural appetite or inclination? There would be no generation if there were not in the matter an appetite to the form; neither could there be motion or action, if there were not an appetite of entities in possibility, to become entities in act.[2]

This same bias for traditional opinion, which Ross delighted in upholding against the advocates of the new science, appears in his attack on Hobbes's materialism:

If there were no real parts of the universe but bodies, then the universe were not universe, but an imperfect system, as deficient in the most noble of all created entities, to wit, incorporeal substances; but God made the world perfect, consisting both of material and immaterial substances; such are Angels and mens souls, which are neither corporeal in their being, nor operation; for if they were corporeal, they must be mortal and corruptible, and compounded at least of matter and form, they must be also quantitative, local by circumscription, and movable by physical motion; all which are absurd: and if a substance be the same that a body is, then he must make God corporeal, for he is a substance. . . .[3]

Not Aristotle but Revelation is the final authority on which Robert Vilvain rested his case against Hobbes. Vilvain was a Salisbury physician, an amateur theologian, and a collector of rarities who 'enjoyed a certain notoriety . . . from being the

---

[1] Alexander Ross, *Leviathan drawn out with a Hook*, p. 93. Ross's attack on Wilkins is to be found in *The New Planet no Planet* (London, 1646), and against Browne in *Arcana Microcosmi . . . With a Refutation of Doctor Brown's Vulgar Errors* (London, 1658).
[2] *Leviathan drawn out with a Hook*, p. 4. [3] *Ibid.* pp. 35–6.

possessor of a skull "no bigger than a bean" which was alleged to be that of one of three hundred and sixty-five children brought forth at a birth by Margaret, Countess of Henneberg'.[1] Vilvain wrote his book against Hobbes[2] in his old age (which he called, not untruthfully, his dotage); it is a curious, rambling book, full of 'Supplements subjoined', 'Postscripts subnected' and interpolations of Latin and English doggerel verses. Vilvain's purpose was to refute Hobbes's theology and political theory, and his method may be illustrated by the following: '. . . the Souls Verity, Unity and Immortality shall be farther proved by a few select places of Sacred Scripture, promiscuously collected and congested together for the present occasion'.[3] And where Scripture was silent, or, what is worse, where Scripture puzzled the understanding by saying too much too variously, Vilvain was content to accept received opinions on faith alone. This was his solution to the problem of spirit.

Wher none can answer or satisfy that words Sense in Scripture, it falls not under Human understanding, and Faith consists not in our Opinion, but submission: specialy wher God is said to be a Spirit, or wher by Spirit is meant God. For his nature is incomprehensible; and we know not what he is, but that he is.[4]

Ross and Vilvain represented an older generation to which a belief in the primacy of immaterial spirit was an ingrained habit of mind; so secure were they in this belief that its contrary seemed to them wholly inconceivable. The best way therefore for meeting the challenge of Hobbist philosophy was to call it absurd, as Ross did, or to set against it the authority of Scripture and the conviction of faith. To the critics who came after Ross and Vilvain this method seemed inadequate; it needed the support of rational argument which was a more persuasive means of weaning away Hobbes's disciples than the bare appeals to the authority of Scripture or of scholastic thought. And the argument against Hobbes's materialism which they thought was the strongest was the one which asserted that matter in motion cannot by itself account for thought.

This argument—that matter is incapable of perception—

---

[1] William Addison, *Worthy Dr Fuller* (New York, 1951), p. 136. Pepys has a reference to this skull in the *Diary*, 19 May 1660.
[2] Robert Vilvain, *Theoremata Theologica* (London, 1654).
[3] *Ibid.* p. 226. [4] *Ibid.* p. 230.

was the most persistent theme in the attacks on Hobbes's materialism. Mental activity, Seth Ward asserted in his *In Thomae Hobii Philosophiam* (1656), lies outside the sphere of corporeal motions: '. . . adduci quod excedat operatione sua mens humana, Sphaeram omnem corporeae actionis, eaque perficiat quae *neq motus Corporei neq. phantasiae* (quae hominibus cum brutis communis creditur) actiones assequuntur'.[1] Similarly Henry More wrote in 1659 that 'Spirits do act really upon the Senses, by acting upon Matter that affects the Senses, and some of these Operations being such that they cannot be rationally attributed to the Matter alone, Reason, by the information of the Senses, concludes that there is some other more noble Principle distinct from the Matter'.[2] 'You are not wont to be so great a friend to Mr *Hobbes*', said George Rust, 'as to think that *matter* by what name soever it be called, dead or living, hath any sense or perception at all, much less can it be vertuous or vicious . . . which being grossly false, and the widest inlet that is unto *Atheisme* . . .'[3]

The same general point was made by Stillingfleet in 1662, by Tenison in 1670, by Cudworth in 1678, and by Glanvill in 1682. To Cudworth the opinion of 'a modern atheistic pretender to wit' that 'mind is nothing else but local motion in the organic parts of man's body' is a paradox such as 'none but either a stupid and besotted, or else an enthusiastic, bigotal, or fanatic Atheist could possibly give entertainment to';[4] while Glanvill declared that 'if the *soul* be *matter*, then whatever *perceptions* or *apprehensions* it hath, or is capable of, they were let in at the *senses*. And thus the great Patron of the *Hypothesis* states it, in his *Leviathan*, and other writings. But how clear it is that our souls have some *conceptions*, which they never received from eternal sense. . . .'[5]

Let us see in detail how this argument was conducted by two of the critics—Edward Stillingfleet and Thomas Tenison.

[1] Seth Ward, *In Thomae Hobii Philosophiam* (Oxford, 1656), p. 29.
[2] Henry More, *The Immortality of the Soul* (1st ed. 1659) in *A Collection of Several Philosophical Writings of Dr Henry More* (4th ed. London, 1712), p. 37.
[3] George Rust, *A Letter of Resolution Concerning Origen and the Chief of His Opinions.* Reproduced from the edition of 1661 (New York: Facsimile Text Society, 1933), p. 129.
[4] Ralph Cudworth, *The True Intellectual System of the Universe*, ed. J. L. Mosheim (London, 1845), III, 418–19.
[5] Joseph Glanvill, *Lux Orientalis* (London, 1682), p. 17.

Stillingfleet, the Bishop of Worcester, was an immensely popular preacher, theologian, and antiquary-historian, who is best remembered today for his vigorous prose style and for his controversy with Locke on the doctrine of the Trinity, which he believed Locke had rejected in the *Essay on the Human Understanding*. Stillingfleet's first book, *The Irenicum* (1659), called for peace among all contending religious factions, arguing that the precise form of church government had never been settled by the Apostles, and was immaterial. But it also argued (in a very Hobbist way) that non-conformism is destructive of civil peace. Stillingfleet may therefore have been influenced by Hobbes on this point, but he could never accept Hobbes's larger materialist assumptions, which he examined and rejected in his second book, *Origines Sacrae* (1662).

The purpose of *Origines Sacrae* was to find a rational and historical basis for revealed religion—that is to say, to bring Scripture into harmony with reason and with pagan accounts of history. I do not propose to say whether Stillingfleet accomplished this ambitious aim. He at any rate believed that his book was a valuable antidote to the 'large spread of Atheism among us', particularly to the sort of 'Philosophical Atheism' exemplified by Hobbes. The arguments against Hobbes, which are scattered throughout the book, are reducible to the single argument that '*there are some beings in the world which cannot depend on matter or motion, i.e. that there are some spiritual and immaterial substances or Beings*'.[1]

In order to prove this assertion Stillingfleet was willing to accept, for argument's sake, the doctrine that 'all sensation in man doth arise from corporeal motions'. If then

it can be proved that there is a *principle* of *action* in *man* which proceeds in a different *way* of *operation* than *sensation* does . . . it will be clear that there is a principle in man higher than *matter* and *motion*. . . . If our *minds can* and *do* form apprehensions of *things* quite *different* from those which are conveyed by *sense*, there must be a *higher principle* of *knowledge* in man than *imagination* is.[2]

Such apprehensions of things not conveyed by sense are illustrated, according to Stillingfleet, by man's perception of the sun. No telescope can convey to the brain an image of the sun

---

[1] Edward Stillingfleet, *Origines Sacrae* (London, 1662), p. 411. [2] *Ibid.* p. 412.

which 'answers to its just *magnitude, viz* that it is 160 times *bigger* than the earth'.[1] How then can the apprehension of the *bigness* of the sun possibly come in at our senses? If it is argued, as Stillingfleet grants, that the mind has learnt from experience that the magnitude of objects diminishes as their distances increase, then it is already granted that the mind is capable of apprehending '*proportions* and *distances* which are mere *respects*, and can have no *corporeal phantasms* whereby to be represented to it; so that by this very way of *ratiocination* it is *evident*, that there is some *principle* in *man* beyond imagination'.[2]

Again, how can we explain cogitation—'the reflex acts of the mind upon itself'—how account for the mind's awareness of itself, except by recourse to some higher principle of supersensory activity? Surely, Stillingfleet insisted, the materialists will not argue that imagination is the seat of reflection, for by Hobbes's own definition in *Humane Nature* [Ch. III, Sect. 1] imagination is decaying sense, and thus is still dependent for its force on some prior sensation. So it is inconceivable that decaying sense, which is nothing more than the slowing-down of a mechanical process, can *imagine* that it *imagines*. The latter phenomenon can be understood only as the operation of the spirit upon senseless matter. In fact Hobbes's whole theory of mind may be dismissed with the simple observation that no material objects in motion can attain velocities which equal the celerity of thought.[3]

Thomas Tenison amplified these arguments and added a number of others in an eminently readable book, *The Creed of Mr Hobbes Examined* (1670). This was Tenison's first book, written while he was a parish priest in Huntingdonshire, and before he rose to eminence as Archbishop of Canterbury. Throughout his long career as ecclesiastic and publicist Tenison showed the same irenical tendencies which characterized the work of Stillingfleet, and he is associated with the group of Latitudinarian churchmen which included also Tillotson and Bishop Burnet.[4] *The Creed of Mr Hobbes Examined* is a dialogue, and was written (as Tenison tells us in his preface), partly to vindicate religion from the errors of Hobbes and partly to show

[1] *Ibid.* p. 413. [2] *Ibid.* [3] *Ibid.* p. 415.
[4] For a full-scale biography of Tenison, see Edward Carpenter, *Thomas Tenison* (London, 1948).

that Tenison himself was not a Hobbist, although he had been compassionate toward the recanting Hobbist Scargill who was first his pupil and later a fellow don at Corpus Christi College, Cambridge.

The tone of Tenison's criticism is relaxed, and remarkably (if not perfectly) free of the rancour which marks so much seventeenth-century controversy. We are told, for instance, that Tenison will 'keep distance enough from the crime of *Albutius* the Rhetorician, who desired to speak, in every Cause, not all that was fitting, but all that he could say'.[1] So Tenison presented a fictional debate between Hobbes and a student of divinity, and put into Hobbes's mouth accurate quotations or else faithful adaptations of Hobbes's printed utterances. Tenison read Hobbes carefully and was willing to meet him on his own grounds. Only when he felt that Hobbes had been overwhelmed by the superior force of the student's arguments did he allow the philosopher to lapse into abuse, and for this purpose he inserted, quite unscrupulously, a number of pungent epithets which Hobbes had hurled at Wallis in a wholly different context.

After a few preliminary remarks about Hobbes's moroseness and ill-temper, supported by 'evidence' from the printed comments of Descartes, Henry More and others, the debate proceeded to the subject of materialism. Hobbes first affirmed that there is a God, for he cannot conceive of matter as eternal, and must therefore return to some eternal principle of creation. This principle is God. But God is also material; neither Scripture nor common sense warrants any other opinion of his nature. To this the student replied that in this view God must be everywhere, since Hobbes had elsewhere maintained that all that is, is body. How then is God to be distinguished from mundane matter? 'If the Universe be God, then *Cain*, and *Cham*, and *Pharoah*, and *Herod*, and *Pilate* and *Judas*, and (that I may say it with sufficient emphasis) the Teacher also of this doctrine is part of the Deity'.[2] But Hobbes refused to accept pantheism. God, he said, is not the same as nature, for a cause cannot be the same as its effect. God's material nature is a deduction from natural reason, and is not contradicted by Scripture or by the best pagan and patristic authorities. It was after all Tertullian

[1] Thomas Tenison, *The Creed of Mr Hobbes Examined*, sig. A5.
[2] *Ibid.* p. 13.

who said: 'In quantum omne corporale possible est, in tantum quod possible est, corporale est'.[1]

Tenison's scholarly instincts were aroused by this allusion to Tertullian, and he attempted to overwhelm Hobbes with a flood of quotations from pre-Christian and early Christian sources, all arguing for the reality of spirit. The Scripture, he said, clearly implies, if it does not state, a belief in incorporeal substance. 'Lay hold of me', Christ said in Luke 24:39, 'handle me, and see that I am not an incorporeal Daemon'.[2] As for Plato, he had Socrates praise Hospes, in the *Politicus*, for his belief in incorporeal beings. Similarly Aristotle, in his doctrine of separate intelligences meant, according to Maimonides in his *More Nevuchim*, part II, Chapter 6 (a work known also to More and Cudworth) 'the same with those who maintain the existence of incorporeal Angels'.[3] And Aristotle taught in his *Analytics* (l.l.c.l.) that the rational soul is separable from the body because it is not the 'entelech' of any body. And if this were not convincing enough, Tenison asked us to consider the testimony from a cloud of patristic witnesses, from Ignatius, Justin Martyr, Athenagoras, Theophilus, Tatianus, Eusebius, Athanasius, St Ireneus, St Basil, St Gregory Nazienzen, St Gregory Nyssen, St Epiphanius, 'and a long order of others', who were all utterly persuaded of the reality of spirit. But what are we to make of Tertullian? We might say that he was merely a single witness, or that his testimony was invalid because it was heretical, or that 'he was better skilled in the laws of the Roman Empire, than in those of nature', etc.; but we will do him more justice if we explain one place in him by another, and when we follow this method we are able to show that he used the term *corpus* to mean 'essence' and not 'impenetrable matter'.[4]

Tenison, however, realized that Hobbes would not be convinced by an array of impressive authorities. Indeed, Hobbes, when pressed, was perfectly willing to give up Tertullian, for the

---

[1] Tertullian, *De Anima*, cap. vii.

[2] Tenison (pp. 17–18) adds the following gloss to this quotation: 'You will now tell me, that I follow not the true Copy of the New Testament, in the translation of this produced Text. I defend myself, by answering, that I follow holy *Ignatius* . . . in his undoubted Epistle to those of Smyrna cited both by *Eusebius* and *St Hierome* . . .' The text in the King James version reads: 'Behold my hands and feet, that it is I myself: handle me, and see; for a spirit hath not flesh and bones, as ye see me have'.

[3] Tenison, p. 19.   [4] *Ibid.* pp. 17–23.

argument in Hobbes's view rested not on an appeal to authority, but to reason. 'Of Authority enough; let us consult natural Reason, by attending to which I maintain, that Incorporeal Body is not a name, but an absurdity of speech.'[1] Tenison therefore turned his attention to the weightiest part of his undertaking—the defence of spirit on rational grounds. He first affirmed that Hobbes's definition of substance (in the *Objectiones* to Descartes) as *materia subjecta accidentibus et mutationibus* was a piece of colossal dogmatism. 'I deny it, once and again, that the speech Incorporeal Substance, either is, or implies a contradiction: there's a bare nay, of as good strength as your naked affirmation.'[2] Why must 'substance' mean only 'matter'? Descartes spoke of 'Metaphysick-Matter', surely a different kind of substance from ordinary matter: and when we come to consider the nature of God, although we cannot speak of him as 'standing under' accidents, we can with certainty affirm that he has incorporeal attributes. It will not do, as Hobbes would have it, that all that we know of God is that he is, and that he is material, and that whatever else we say of him we say merely to honour him. If we know not also that he is true and good and just, then we cannot believe his revelations, we cannot love him with any height of affection, we cannot expect our hopes and our endeavours to come to any successful conclusions. It is true that the mind can frame no image of God which is derived from the senses; but the mind can have an Idea of God. Plato taught us (in the *Politicus*) 'that the greatest and most glorious objects have no Image attending on their perception'.[3] An idea is 'not meerly a corporeal similitude, but any notion without imagery'. It is 'the very form of cogitation, whereby I become conscious to myself that I have perceived'.[4] If this concept is difficult, consider, said Tenison, the nature of empty space, whose attributes we deduce from reason, not sense. Tenison did not agree with Henry More that space could be identified with God, or even that it could be considered analogous to the nature of God; he conceived of space as too 'dull and unactive' to have any of the moral perfections which are associated with God. But he was satisfied that the concept of space is a useful illustration of a being which has attributes but no body.

[1] *Ibid.* p. 23.   [2] *Ibid.* p. 25.   [3] Quoted by Tenison, p. 34.   [4] *Ibid.*

Tenison now moved to the heart of his argument—'the incapacity of Perception in meer matter'. First Hobbes rehearsed his doctrine of sensation; it consists in a process of motions arising from the pressure of external objects on the organs of sense, and proceeding, 'by the mediation of nerves, and other strings, and membranes of the body', to the brain and heart, where a counter-pressure or reaction is produced; this reaction is the image or 'fancie' of the object which started the process in the first place. But how, Tenison asked, does this process differ from the actions and reactions of any bodies in space? That is to say, if sensation is a mechanism of matter in motion, why ought we not to think that inert or lifeless matter in motion can also have sensations, 'that a Looking-glass saw, and a Lute heard?' Hobbes replied that it is perfectly conceivable that inanimate bodies have sensations, but the 'phantasms' so produced must vanish directly the object which produced them is removed. The property of sensations therefore which is unique for living animals is memory, and this depends on the possession of an organ—the brain—which is fit for the retaining of such motion as is made in it. Tenison was, however, not persuaded of the fitness of the brain or of any other organ to conserve motion:

I understand that there may remain a quivering in the Retina, Choroeides, and whole *Pia Mater* . . . after the Object of Sight is removed, whose presence occasioned a more stiff pressure. We see the like in extended and moved Nets and Ropes, and a thousand other examples in Art and Nature: but this trembling in them, as also in such Machines where the Motion may be more entirely and longer imprisoned, does soon vanish. [Glanvill repeated this argument in a more extreme form several years later when he said: 'Neither the *Brain* . . . nor any other *material* Substance, can for any considerable time conserve Motion. The *Brain* is such a *clammy* consistence that it can no more retain it than a *Quagmire*.']¹ Whereas the Re-action must remain extremely long, in such Men (for Instance), who at the seventieth year remember most perfectly, and will repeat with pleasure, the passages of their School-play, even those who retain not the things more newly passed. To tell how this can be explained by the meer mechanism of the Brain, which has received many millions of changes in it self, and Re-actions occasion'd from the Objects of every Hour, requires a more *skillful Oedipus* than has yet pretended to unriddle the Secrets of Humane Nature.²

¹ Joseph Glanvill, *Essays on Several Important Subjects* (London, 1676), p. 9.
² Tenison, pp. 92–3.

Memory cannot therefore be considered a property of matter in motion. Neither can reason.

For if two images cannot, as hath been prov'd, be aptly connected by Imagination and Memory, supposed Mechanical; Reason, surely, which ranketh all Beings into their distinct Orders and Dependencies; and connecteth myriads of such Idea's as have no Phantasm appertaining to them, must be Divine.[1]

Reason must be 'an immaterial faculty'. It apprehends relations between things, and it is inconceivable that this property of the mind can be the function of mere mechanical motions. Tenison suggested that Hobbes could learn a lesson from Ramus, a logician who was free of the Aristotelian taint and who therefore ought to be acceptable to Hobbes.

The Arguments in [Ramus's] first part of Logick, (that is, Topicks apt to argue or declare the relation of one thing to another . . .) such as are Cause, Effect, Subject, Adjunct, and the like; being used here not to find out the Nature of single Beings (which appertains to Natural Philosophy, Medicks, and other Sciences) nor to interpret names (which appertains to Grammar) but onely as places declaring the mutual . . . habitudes of one thing to another, which may be related divers ways; they cannot possibly arise from the single and absolute motions of sense.[2]

Reason also corrects sense. Tenison echoed Stillingfleet's argument about the size of the sun.

In Sense, Imagination, or Memory, one of the fixed Stars seems not bigger than that in the Badg of the Order of the Garter . . . and therefore Reason, which by consequences in Astronomy infers that it is bigger than the Earth, is something much superior to motion derived from the Object.[3]

Neither Tenison nor Stillingfleet was an original thinker; both used traditional arguments; both were derivative in their general philosophical outlook. Tenison, for example, was a Cartesian in his view of the universe as *plenum*, though he was

---

[1] *Ibid.* p. 104.
[2] *Ibid.* p. 103. Hobbes must have known the work of Ramus. His own redaction of Aristotle's *Rhetoric* was bound with a redaction of Ramus, under the general title *A Compendium of the Art of Logick and Rhetorick in the English Tongue, Containing All that Peter Ramus, Aristotle, and Others have writ thereon* (London, 1651). The redaction of Ramus was not actually by Hobbes, although it has usually been attributed to him. See Walter J. Ong, 'Hobbes and Talon's Ramist Rhetoric in English', *Transactions of the Cambridge Bibliographical Society*, 1 (1951), 260–9.
[3] Tenison, p. 105.

quite willing to argue about the idea of empty space as an example of immateriality. At other times he defended the notion of spirit on Platonic, and again, on scholastic grounds. He and Stillingfleet were alike also in their large erudition, which they displayed in frequent appeals to authority. What is interesting is that both writers considered the argument from authority to be essentially inferior to argument based upon reason. In this respect their work illustrates the rationalizing and secularizing tendency of English thought after the Restoration.

The merit of Stillingfleet and Tenison's arguments is that they exposed the weakness of Hobbes's theory of sensation. Hobbes asserted but never seriously attempted to prove that all mental experience is identical with corporeal motions. In the *Objectiones* to Descartes, Hobbes said that thinking was an act, and every act implies a subject or substance. 'Hence', he said, 'it follows that a thinking thing is of a corporeal nature; for the subjects of all acts seem to be intelligible *only* as corporeal or material.'[1] The fact that one set of corporeal motions, i.e. thought, has the capacity to prefigure or represent another set of corporeal motions, i.e. objects in the external world, was to Hobbes a source of perpetual wonder. 'Of all the phenomena or appearances which are near us, the most admirable is apparition itself το φαίνεσθαι; namely, that some natural bodies have in themselves the patterns almost of all things, and others of none at all.'[2] But Hobbes did not allow his usually speculative mind to deal with the problems which arise from a theory which equates mental activity with corporeal motion. Are thoughts the same as bodily motions, or are they merely accompanied by bodily motions? Or are thoughts qualitatively different from bodily motions, a view which ordinary experience would seem to suggest: Hobbes said they were the same as corporeal motions, and let the matter rest there.

Hobbes's treatment of the relation between 'phantasms' in the mind and external things was also cursory. He believed that all knowledge was rooted in sense-impressions. Where the senses are disordered, as in hallucinations or nightmares, the

[1] *The Philosophical Works of Descartes*, trans. Haldane and Ross (Cambridge, 1911), ii, 62.
[2] *De Corpore*, p. 389.

phantasms produced in the mind may bear no direct relation to things in nature, but they must be constructed, however fancifully, from sense data. Thus the phantasm of a centaur corresponds to nothing real, but is constructed out of such real (and material) things as a man and a horse. What however are the real things which correspond to *relations* and *proportions*? And if sense-impressions produce knowledge, can they also produce knowledge of knowledge? What are the sense-impressions which correspond to consciousness or reflection or reasoning? This is the heart of the objections raised by Stillingfleet and Tenison, and it cannot be said that Hobbes was able to offer a satisfactory reply. He said only that we know we know in the same way that we know, namely, by sense.

If the appearances be the principles by which we know all other things, we must needs acknowledge sense to be the principle by which we know those principles, and that the knowledge we have is derived from it. And as for the causes of sense, we cannot begin our search for them from any other phenomenon than that of sense itself.[1]

But of the nature of this 'meta-sense' from which we can discover the causes of sense, Hobbes says nothing at all.

[1] *Ibid.*

CHAPTER V

MATERIALISM: MORE, CUDWORTH, AND GLANVILL

I

The most systematic and rigorous refutation of Hobbist philosophy was made by the Cambridge Platonists Henry More and Ralph Cudworth. Hobbes was not polemically present in the minds of Whichcote, John Smith, and Culverwell, but he lay behind much of their work, just as he was implied in the works of all the writers who comprised the Cambridge School. Their criticism of Hobbes was written against the background of an idealist philosophy derived from Platonic and neo-Platonic sources; but 'while Platonism . . . may be said to have originated the [Cambridge] movement, Hobbism was the means of concentrating its thought and giving dogmatic direction to it. While the one was the positive the other was the negative influence which formed the school'.[1] Whether by implication or by direct attack, the Cambridge Platonists treated Hobbes as the opponent *sine qua non*.

This special relationship of the Cambridge Platonists to Hobbes emerges clearly from a review of some of the more familiar positions of the Cambridge school. As theologians, the Cambridge Platonists sought a *modus vivendi* between the extremes of sectarian controversy on the one hand and the dangers of atheism on the other. Although the majority of the Platonists had been trained in Puritan Emmanuel College, they reacted against dogmatic Calvinist theology, especially against the insistence on man's original sin and predestination. What they sought was a view of salvation which depended neither on arbitrary election into a state of grace, nor upon man's mere passive acceptance of so many articles of belief, but upon the probity and uprightness of man's moral life. They were thus able to free themselves from the sterile theological disputation

---

[1] John Tulloch, *Rational Theology and Christian Philosophy in the Seventeenth Century* (Edinburgh, 1874), II, 25–6.

of the sects. 'Non sum Christianus alicuius nominis,' Whichcote wrote,[1] and More said 'I am above all Sects whatsoever as Sects: For I am a true and free *Christian*. . . .'[2] Cudworth also declared that it was none of his purpose 'to contend for *this* or *that* Opinion; but onely to perswade men to the *Life of Christ* as the Pith and Kernel of all Religion'.[3] When the Cambridge Platonists discoursed about the differences which obtain *among* Christians their temper was equable, detached from the petty wranglings of the sects; they reserved what bitterness and wrath they could muster for atheists, for those, who, in their estimation, stood opposed to 'the Pith and Kernel of all Religion'.

Quite obviously Hobbes was their chief target. He was not the minor sectary, the special pleader for a particular article of Christian belief, the penny pamphleteer who defended a narrow creed. He was the adherent of no sect and the opponent of all, because, in the view of the Cambridge Platonists, his philosophy undermined the foundations of all religious belief. Everything he stood for cut athwart the favourite Cambridge Platonist positions. He believed in materialism, nominalism, determinism, ethical relativism, an egoistic psychology. The Cambridge Platonists believed in a spirit-world, in absolute ideas, free-will, an absolute and eternal morality, a psychology based upon the doctrine of innate goodness and selflessness. As the Platonists were Christian philosophers, they adopted all of these positions with a view towards clarifying and solidifying the essentials of Christian belief. The broad irenical tendencies of their programme led them to emphasize practical morality, that is to say, a truly Christian way of life, as the *unum necessarium* of a man's creed; it also led them to combat Hobbism as the greatest danger to that creed.

The danger was twofold: it lay in Hobbes's method as well as in his doctrines. The Cambridge Platonists opposed their own brand of 'rationalism' to Hobbes's rational method. This point

---

[1] 'Eight Letters of Dr Antony Tuckney and Dr Benjamin Whichcote', included in Benjamin Whichcote, *Aphorisms*, ed. S. Salter (London, 1753), p. 53.

[2] Cited by Richard Ward, *The Life of the Learned and Pious Dr Henry More* (London 1710), p. 188.

[3] Ralph Cudworth, *A Sermon Preached before the Honourable House of Commons . . . 31 March 1647*, reproduced by the Facsimile Text Society (New York, 1930), Dedication.

81

is sometimes obscured in Cambridge Platonist literature because the Platonists defined 'reason' in two ways, one of which is not so remote from Hobbes's use of the term. In the first place, 'reason', for the Platonists, referred to clear philosophical thinking, to a dialectical search for the truth, for the philosophically 'real', and to a sloughing-off of cant, preconceived notions, and the dead weight of mere authority. This is close to the Hobbesian sense, and indeed there is a curious Hobbesian ring in these words of Whichcote: '. . . I contradistinguish rational to conceited, impotent, affected CANTING; (as I may call it: when the Ear receeves wordes, which offer no matter to the Understanding; make no impression on the inward sense).'[1]

But the Cambridge Platonists also had a second and distinctly un-Hobbesian conception of reason. Reason, they said, does not merely perceive what is natural; it also receives what is supernatural. It is an inward illumination of the soul, attainable not through the adumbration of any particular creed, but through the practice of the Christian virtues. Human reason is but an 'imperfect copy' of divine reason, and the imperfection vanishes under the benign influence of Christian conduct. '. . . That which springs forth from true goodness . . . brings such a Divine light into the Soul, as is more clear and convincing than any Demonstration.'[2] The most truly virtuous man is at once the most rational and the most Godlike, because a virtuous life sharpens man's rational perceptions, and the sharpening of these perceptions brings man to a deeper understanding of, indeed almost to a participation in, the rational nature of God himself. The real presence of God in man is man's reason; hence whoever rejects reason rejects God.

[God's] commands are all rational; His word is the very pitch and marrow of reason; His law is the quickening and wakening of men's reason; His gospel is the flowing out of His own reason—the quintessence of wisdom from above; His spirit is a rational agent. By all this you see that God is the eternal Spring and Head of reason. . . .[3]

Hobbes could never follow the Platonists in this latter argument. He was by temperament impervious to mysticism: if

---

[1] Benjamin Whichcote, op. cit., p. 108.
[2] John Smith, Discourses (London, 1673), p. 4.
[3] Nathanael Culverwell, An Elegant and Learned Discourse of the Light of Nature (1652), reprinted by John Brown, ed. (Edinburgh, 1857), pp. 161–2.

reason is a light, then, he argued, it is a dry light, cold and clear. It is the reasoning mechanism, which any intelligent man can use. Moreover—and this is the point about reason which separates Hobbes most markedly from the Cambridge Platonic view —the knowledge which reason yields is in no way influenced by the moral conduct of the man who uses it: in matters pertaining to reason, a thief can be the equal of a saint. Hobbes believed that any man endowed with intelligence and knowledge of the laws of reasoning can reason correctly and discover the truth; whether a man is otherwise virtuous or not is without consequence.

When we come to consider the explicit refutation of Hobbes's doctrines by More and Cudworth we are at once confronted by a curious fact: in attacking Hobbes the Platonists never invoked their second and peculiarly Platonic view of reason. They never supported their argument with the claim that it was true because it had been put forward by virtuous men, or that Hobbes's position was false because it had been worked out by a mind not purified by Christian virtue and not in touch with the rational being of God. Cudworth, it is true, did on several occasions refer to Hobbes as a 'besotted Atheist', and I take this to be no mere vituperation but a criticism of Hobbes's atheism considered as the product of a mind which lacked the benefits that a Christian way of life must bestow upon it. Nevertheless, neither Cudworth nor More made their argument depend on this point. Instead they tried to refute Hobbes with Hobbes's own weapon, logical analysis, though they also relied frequently on the argument from authority, which they were able to supply out of the abundant resources of their own erudition. Primarily they adopted the rational method which Hobbes himself had perfected and which all of Hobbes's critics after Rosse and Vilvain had employed. The positive outlook of More and Cudworth was anti-rational, at least insofar as rationalism was understood by Hobbes; but when they argued explicitly against Hobbes they argued on his own ground, and thus gave further testimony of the growing importance which rationalism assumed in English thought during the latter part of the seventeenth century.

At the centre of More and Cudworth's quarrel with Hobbes was the doctrine of materialism. From this doctrine flowed al' of the evil consequences to religion which the Cambridge Platonists opposed by their general outlook and which More and Cudworth attacked with Hobbes specifically in mind. If one believes in materialism, More said, then one must also believe

That it is impossible there should be any God, or Soul, or Angel, Good or Bad; or any Immortality, or Life to come. That there is no Religion, no Piety nor Impiety, no Virtue nor Vice, Justice nor Injustice, but what it pleases him that has the longest sword to call so. That there is no Freedom of the Will, nor consequently any rational remorse of Conscience in any Being whatsoever, but that all that is, is nothing but Matter and Corporeal Motion; and that therefore every trace of man's life is as necessary as the tracts of Lightning, and the falling of Thunder, the blind impetus of the Matter breaking through or being stopt everywhere, with as certain and determinate necessity as the course of a Torrent after mighty storms and showers of Rain.[1]

To resist these implications of materialism, More and Cudworth struck at the core of the doctrine itself—the belief in the pervasiveness of matter.

II

More's explicit refutation of Hobbist materialism appeared in the *Antidote Against Atheism* (1653) and *The Immortality of the Soul* (1659); the arguments of both these books were slightly amplified but remained essentially unchanged in More's *Divine Dialogues* (1668) and *Enchiridion Metaphysicum* (1671), two works which were in fact largely directed against Descartes, with whom More had by that time become disenchanted. Descartes had declared that spirit is unextended, is nowhere; in More's view this was tantamount to saying that spirit did not exist at all. Whether or not Descartes himself placed such an interpretation on his doctrine was for More beside the point, since Descartes had in any case to bear the responsibility of inducing many unthinking persons to adopt the materialist-atheist position. It was however, not Descartes, but Hobbes who in the first place drew forth More's philosophic defence of spirit.

[1] Henry More, *Immortality of the Soul* in *A Collection of Several Philosophical Writings of Dr Henry More* (London, 1712), p. 33.

Even if he were to bring the existence of spirit 'only to a bare possibility', More felt that he would still have scored an important victory; for the strongest hold of the enemy Hobbes 'seems to be an unshaken Confidence, that the very Notion of a Spirit or Substance Immaterial is a perfect Incompossibility and Pure Non-scence'.[1] But how is the true notion of spirit to be established? By rational argument, said More, open to reasonable minds. For the most part More's arguments are traditional; they are based on one or another form of the ontological or teleological arguments for the existence of God; to these he added the arguments based upon witchcraft relations, and the argument based upon deductions drawn from the evidence of natural science.

To begin with, More believed that the human soul apprehends spirit directly without the intervention of sense. The soul is not *abrasa tabula*; it has 'actual' (i.e. innate) knowledge. How else does the soul receive 'a more accurate Idea of a Circle and Triangle than Matter can exhibit to her'?[2] The soul's knowledge of spirit is independent of sense-experience, and prior to it. Furthermore, spirit is demonstrated by the perfect design and orderliness of the universe.

Whether the Matter have any Sense or no, what is made out of it is nothing, but what results from the wild jumblings and knockings of one part therefor against another without any purpose, counsel, or direction. Wherefore the ordinary Phaenomena of Nature being guided according to the most Exquisite Wisdom imaginable, it is plain, that they are not the Effects of the mere motion of Matter, but of some Immaterial Principle.[3]

Against such well-tried arguments, what, asks More, does Hobbes offer? Only the feeble assertion that incorporeal substance is a contradiction in terms. To say that is 'to suppose what is to be proved, That the Universe is nothing else but an Aggregate of Bodies'.[4] The universe is more than that: it is an aggregate of bodies and souls, of matter and spirit. Human reason apprehends spirit directly and indirectly, from the analogy of perfect mathematical figures not found in nature. Reason is

---

[1] *Ibid.*
[2] *An Antidote Against Atheism* in *A Collection of Several Philosophical Writings of Dr Henry More*, p. 18.
[3] *Immortality of the Soul*, p. 46.   [4] *Ibid.* p. 36.

THE HUNTING OF LEVIATHAN

further apprised of the existence of spirit by the perfection and orderliness of the universe. And reason derives support for its conviction from the *consensus gentium* in all ages, ancient no less than modern, pagan no less than Christian. For instance, all educated men, including even the free thinker Vanini, agree and have agreed that apparitions exist. Apparitions are in fact a type of sense-evidence for the existence of spirit, and could be acceptable to Hobbes, were it not for his obstinacy in maintaining that apparitions, miracles and witch disturbances were nothing more than the product of dreams, fears, or superstitious fancies. But of the reality of ghosts and the power of witches reasonable men need have no doubt for these phenomena are confirmed by the most reliable witnesses, as well as by the authority of Scripture itself.

There was yet another way in which More deduced the existence of spirit—from the evidence of natural science. More had read with interest Boyle's *New Experiments Physico-Mechanical touching the Air* when that work appeared in 1660; because he was persuaded that Boyle had provided fresh evidence for the existence of spirit, More interpolated an account of three of Boyle's experiments on the vacuum into the third edition of *An Antidote Against Atheism* (1662).[1] In More's opinion Boyle's experiments exhibited more than the mere power of the vacuum-pump. They demonstrated the presence of an immaterial force which can only be equated with spirit. 'The ascending of the Sucker of the Air-pump with above an hundred pound weight at it' proves 'that there is a Principle transcending the nature and power of Matter.'

Wherefore it being so manifest, that there is a Principle in the world that does tug so stoutly and resolutely against the Mechanick Laws of Matter . . . this I say is a very sure Pledge to us, that when things are fitly done, though not with this seeming violence or peremptoriness, yet they are the Effects of the same *immaterial* Principle (call it the *Spirit of Nature*, or what you will) which is the Vicarious Power of God upon this great Automaton, the World.[2]

Boyle himself did not read any such conclusions into his work on the suction-pump, but he was not unwilling to lend his support to More in the controversy with Hobbes. Hobbes, writing

---

[1] This edition appeared as part of the first folio edition of More's collected works.
[2] *An Antidote Against Atheism*, pp. 46, 40.

as one who believes that matter is infinitely extended, had said in print that Boyle's experiments on vacuum were inconclusive.[1] Boyle replied in a tract entitled *An Examen of Mr T. Hobbes* (1662); in his preface he expressed the hope that his exposure of Hobbes's egregious errors in physics would serve also to diminish Hobbes's reputation as a philosopher of religion:

It was also suggested to me, that the dangerous Opinions about some important, if not fundamental Articles of Religion I had met with in his *Leviathan*, and some other of his Writings, having made but too great Impression upon divers persons (who, though said to be for the most part either of greater *Quality*, or of greater *Wit* then Learning, do yet divers of them deserve better Principles) those Errors being chiefly recommended by the Opinion they had of Mr *Hobbs's* demonstrative way of Philosophy; it might possibly prove some service to higher Truths than those in Controversie between him and me to shew that in Physicks themselves his Opinions, and even his Ratiocinations, have no such great advantage over those of some Orthodox Christian Naturalists.[2]

Boyle regarded himself as 'a 'Christian Virtuoso'. He was anxious to show that 'by being addicted to *Experimental Philosophy*, a man is rather Assisted, than Indisposed, to be a good Christian'.[3] But his interest in science (and the interest of the Royal Society as a whole) differed in one important respect from that of More and the Cambridge Platonists. For Boyle the primary function of science was the scrutiny of nature so as to unlock its mysteries, and, if possible, to control it. One consequence of the scientist's labours is the discovery of order in the universe, from which he deduces a divine presence. But this deduction, vitally important though it may be, is a by-product of science, not its main function.

More, on the other hand, regarded natural science as a vast laboratory for the confirmation of religious truths. The accumulation of natural knowledge for the sake of natural knowledge— the search, that is, into 'second causes'—was for More a negative procedure, except insofar as it defined the limits of natural knowledge, and by this means underlined the inescapable con-

---

[1] In the *Dialogus Physicus, sive De natura Aeris* (London, 1661).
[2] Robert Boyle, *An Examen of Mr T. Hobbes his Dialogus Physicus De Natura Aeris* (London, 1662), sig. a 2.
[3] R[obert] B[oyle], *The Christian Virtuoso* (London, 1690), t.p.

clusion that the ultimate forces which guide the universe are non-mechanical, immaterial, and divine. Science is useful because it exposes its own limitations, and leads finally to religious explanations. This is the sense in which More draws upon the evidence of science to refute Hobbes. Hobbes said that one of the seeds of religion is ignorance of second causes. More replied that one of the causes of atheism is 'ignorance of the scantness and insufficiency of second causes'.[1]

Ultimately, the differences between Hobbes and More are reducible to different theories of matter. For Hobbes all substance must have dimensions—that is, it must have spatial location, magnitude, and extension. Hence no two substances can occupy the same space at the same time. All substance (which by definition meant only body) is impenetrable. Hobbes scorned the scholastic doctrine that place *circumscribes* a body but only *defines* a spirit. 'Circumscription' and 'definition', when applied to place, were, in Hobbes's view, identical.[2] Similarly, Hobbes ridiculed the scholastic notion expressed in the proposition *totum in toto ac totum in qualibet parte.* Can anything be more absurd than to affirm that a man's soul is 'all of it in his little finger, and all of it in every other part, how small soever, of his body; and yet no more soul in the whole body, than in any one of those parts'?[3] Such nonsense is brought about by an inaccurate conception of matter, which is extended in space and impenetrable.

More replied that it 'is not the Characteristical of a Body to have Dimensions, but to be Impenetrable. All Substance has Dimensions. . . . But all has not Impenetrability'.[4] If Hobbes were not 'so frighted' by the 'mad Jingles' of the schools he might have found a true and settled meaning of spirit, which is 'that it is a Substance Penetrable and indiscerpible'.[5] Thus More posited two types of substance: matter, which is impenetrable, and spirit, which is penetrable but indiscerpible (i.e. indissoluble).

This theory was presented at large in More's most attractively-written book, *Divine Dialogues* (1668), in which a company of young and older men discourse on the vital philosophical problems of the day. One member of the company—Hylobares—

[1] *An Antidote Against Atheism*, p. 141.   [2] *Leviathan*, p. 443.   [3] *Ibid.*
[4] *Immortality of the Soul*, p. 37.   [5] *Ibid.* p. 39.

was a young and witty materialist,[1] but not a Hobbist, because he was 'well-moralized'. In the course of debating with Philotheus (who seems to speak for More), Hylobares is converted to a belief in spirit, but not before he expresses his profound misgivings on the subject:

I could wish [he said] the *nature* of a Spirit were more unknown to me than it is, that I might believe its *Existence* without meddling at all with its *Essence*. But I cannot but know this much of it, whether I will or no, that it is either extended, or not extended; I mean, it has either some *Amplitude* of *Essence*, or else none at all. If it has no *Amplitude* or Extension, the ridiculous Hypothesis of the Schools will get up again, and millions of Spirits, for aught I know, may dance on a Needle's point, or rather, they having no *Amplitude*, would be nothing. If they have any *Amplitude* or Extension, they will not be Spirits, but mere *Body* or *Matter*. For, as that admired Wit *Des-Cartes* solidly concludes, *Extension is the very essence of Matter*. This is one of the greatest Arguments that fatally bear me off from a chearfull closing with the belief of Spirits properly so called.[2]

Philotheus retorts that Descartes's assertion is 'weak and precarious . . . an upstart conceit of this present Age'. Matter and extension are not reciprocal, for we see that extension is 'intrinsicall' to motion, and yet motion is not matter. Hylobares protests that motion is not 'loose or *exemptitious*' from matter, but a mere mode of matter, having no other extension than that of matter itself. Philotheus has a reply. He means by motion 'not simply the *Translation*, but the *vis agitans* that pervades the whole body that is moved'.[3] And this is certainly '*Exemptitious* and loose', so that it may pass from one part of matter to another.

Hylobares is however not convinced, and Philotheus attacks the question from another point of view. Consider, he says, the motion of an arrow shot straight up into the air. 'This Arrow has described onely right Lines with its point, upwards and downwards, in the Air; but yet, holding the motion of the Earth, it must also have described in some sense a circular or

---

[1] A portrait of Sir Thomas Baines, More's pupil and the brother of Lady Conway. More wrote elsewhere of the 'low corporeall dispensation of T[homas] B[aines] that can phancy nothing but matter'. From an undated letter quoted in Archibald Malloch, *Finch and Baines: A Seventeenth Century Friendship* (Cambridge University Press, 1917), p. 43. See also Marjorie H. Nicolson, *Conway Letters*, p. 255.

[2] [Henry More], *Divine Dialogues* (London, 1668), p. 94.

[3] *Ibid.* p. 98.

curvilinear line.'[1] Here then is a type of circular extension without matter. Furthermore, space itself is both real and extended; but it is non-material. It is the perfect analogy to spirit; indeed it has some of the attributes of God and may almost be equated with God.

The idea of the spatial extension of God is More's most imaginative concept, and also—inasmuch as it was adopted by Newton[2]—his most influential. The idea is actually an ancient Jewish heritage,[3] and More may have originally come upon it in the course of his rabbinical and cabbalist readings; nevertheless he developed it primarily as a reaction to Descartes's distinction between *res extensae* and *res cogitans*, and he hoped that by refuting Descartes on this point he would effect a closer harmony between theology and the new science. We must remember however that behind More's dispute with Descartes over the nature of space lies the spectre of Hobbist materialism, since More believed that if Descartes were correct in affirming that spirit is unextended he would succeed in refining spirit out of existence altogether, and would thus play directly into the hands of Hobbes.

To avoid this possibility, to establish the reality of spirit, More urged upon Descartes the idea of spatial extension. He wrote to Descartes in 1647[4] that a vase emptied of air retains its shape not because it contained fine particles or vortices of matter, as Descartes suggested, but because its walls were supported by the 'divine extension', by space responding to the will of God. More amplified the idea in a second letter in which he stated that space is distinct from matter not by virtue of its extension, which is as true of matter as it is of space, but because space is infinitely extended and ubiquitous, whereas matter is finite and divisible. Afterwards, in the *Antidote*

[1] *Ibid.* pp. 101–2.
[2] '. . . there is a being incorporeal, living, intelligent, omnipresent, who in infinite space, as it were in his Sensory, sees the things themselves intimately . . . who being in all places, is more able by His will to move the bodies within His boundless sensorium, and thereby to form and reform the parts of the universe. . . .' Sir Isaac Newton, *Opticks* (3rd ed. London, 1721), pp. 345, 379. For an account of the mutual esteem in which More and Newton held each other, see Marjorie Nicolson, *Conway Letters*, pp. 471–2.
[3] Max Jammer, *Concepts of Space* (Cambridge, Mass., 1954), pp. 26–31.
[4] Correspondence with Descartes in *Oeuvres de Descartes*, ed. Cousin (Paris, 1825), tome 10, p. 184.

Against Atheism, he further refined his theory,[1] and in the *Divine Dialogues* he asserted that a plenitude of matter is logically impossible, because, although we can imagine a world empty of matter, we cannot 'dis-imagine' or think away the idea of space.[2] Finally More arrived at the conclusion in the *Enchiridion Metaphysicum* that the attributes of space are identical with those attributes of God which relate to his being, though not to his power or activity. He enumerated no fewer than twenty attributes which God and infinite space hold in common,[3] and though he hesitated on the question of whether space was to be absolutely identified with God or considered as analogous to God's being, he was persuaded nevertheless that spirit *has* spatial extension, that it was *somewhere*, that it was not a metaphysical abstraction, as Descartes would have it, but a real and extended being. In short, More felt assured that he had delivered Cartesianism from the pitfalls of materialism by making spirit as 'real' as Descartes had made matter.

A number of very able scholars have studied the implications of More's theory for the history of science.[4] They have shown how the doctrine of absolute space influenced Barrow's concept of absolute time, and how both theories were in turn assimilated by Newton in his speculations on the nature of space and time. More initiated a way of conceiving space which can be called peculiarly English because—except for Malebranche—it was widely opposed on the continent, while it dominated English speculations on the subject until the time of Berkeley.[5] Moreover, More's theory also had its repercussions in English literary history, as Professor Nicolson has demonstrated in her monograph *The Breaking of the Circle*.[6] By associating infinite space with God, More contributed to the growing sense of optimism

[1] *Antidote Against Atheism* in *A Collection*, pp. 199–201.   [2] *Divine Dialogues*, p. 104.
[3] *Enchiridion Metaphysicum* (London, 1671), Ch. 8, sec. 8.
[4] Robert Zimmerman, 'Henry More und die vierte Dimension des Raumes', *Sitzungsberichte der Philosophisch-Historischen Classe der Kaiserlichen Akademie der Wissenschaften* Bd. 98 (Vienna, 1881), pp. 403–48; Edwin Arthur Burtt, *The Metaphysical Foundations of Modern Physical Science* (rev. ed., New York, 1954), pp. 143–8; John Tull Baker, *An Historical and Critical Examination of English Space and Time Theories from Henry More to Bishop Berkeley* (Bronxville, N.Y., 1930), pp. 6–13, 15–17; Max Jammer, *Concepts of Space*, pp. 38–47.
[5] John Tull Baker, *op. cit.*, p. 13.
[6] Marjorie Hope Nicolson, *The Breaking of the Circle* (Evanston, 1950), pp. 139–45, 154.

with which some English poets responded to the vastly enlarged universe, in contrast to the pessimism of earlier poets such as Donne.

Hobbes played only a negative role in these developments. His doctrine of space had no effect on the progress of English science, nor did it serve to release the English poetic imagination in the way that More's had. In fact, unlike More, Hobbes did not make his doctrine a central feature of his metaphysics. He treated the question almost casually, whereas for More it was a subject of life-long interest.[1] When we contrast the two theories we notice that Hobbes's was a necessary consequence of his materialistic-nominalist outlook, but not a prop for that outlook, while More's theory lent vital and necessary support to his doctrine of spirit.

We have already noted Hobbes's definition of space as a 'phantasm of a thing existing without the mind simply'.[2] He meant by this that space is the subjective frame of reference for body. It is our awareness of body 'simply'—that is, of body having no other attribute except that it is located somewhere. But although body certainly exists outside our minds, the space which body occupies is a pure mental construction. 'Place is nothing out of the mind nor magnitude anything within it.'[3] Space is thus a 'phantasm', a mental abstraction, an imaginary extension—the system of coordinates or external locations which the mind constructs out of its experience of real extended things.[4]

Hobbes expressed this doctrine briefly in *De Corpore*, his mature work on the philosophy of matter. He did, however, leave an earlier and more detailed account of the question in a Latin manuscript recently discovered—the reply to Thomas White's *De Mundo*.[5] In this work Hobbes came closest to dealing with the problem of absolute space as understood by More. He began his discussion by affirming his belief in the absolute and independent existence of matter and from this position he pro-

[1] As late as 1684, More was still refining his space theory in a letter to John Norris. John Norris, *The Theory and Regulation of Love* (2nd ed. London, 1694), p. 128.
[2] *De Corpore* in *Works*, I, 94.
[3] *Ibid.* p. 105.
[4] For further discussion of this point, see R. Peters, *Hobbes* (London, 1956), p. 98.
[5] Described above, p. 9.

ceeded to argue that space, considered independently of body, is an 'imagination' or 'figment within us'.

Since imagination is born of the action of a certain agent, which we suppose to exist, or to have existed, and which, being supposed by us, we usually call a body or matter, it follows that bodies would subsist, even if there were no imagination at all. Nor is it possible for us to admit the existence of a certain body without at the same time thinking that it possesses dimensions, or spaces. That space is meant which can be called real, which is inherent in the body, as the accident in the subject, and would certainly exist, even if there were nothing that could imagine it. I define *real space* therefore as corporeity itself, or the essence of body simply, insofar as it is body; so that a body is to imaginary space what a thing is to the knowledge of that thing, for our knowledge of existing things is that imagination which is produced by the action of these things on our senses, and therefore imaginary space, which is the imagination of body, is the same as our knowledge of existing body. . . .[1]

So far Hobbes has said nothing which he was not to repeat later in *De Corpore*. But he appears in the next passage to have recognized some of the perplexing implications of his theory, as is evident when he asked the question: Does space exist when there is no person to imagine it?

Supposing no imagination existed, yet a certain finite body would exist which we shall call that in which all other bodies are not, but could be: for example, if the world were finite, and no being endowed with imagination existed, should we say or not say that space exists outside the world? Of course there is no real space outside the world, supposing the world to be finite, but there is no imaginary space either, on account of the exclusion of an imaginary being Then we must say that there is no space at all, and yet that there is a privation of body, and this is enough to make the existence of more bodies possible; for the *privation of body* is understood by means of the imagination of bodies themselves, and therefore it is the same as the space which we call imaginary. What privation really is in itself, and insofar as it is outside us, is a mere figment, and not a being, but these figments are something within us, namely, the movements of the mind, which are called imaginations.[2]

---

[1] MS., Bibliothèque Nationale, *Fonds latin*, 6566A, Ch. III, sect. 2, fols. 19–20. The translation of this passage and of the two following was made by Dr Jean Jacquot and is used by his kind permission.

[2] *Ibid.* fol. 21.

93

What then lies outside the finite world? It is not, said Hobbes, *real space*, because this refers only to our mental conception of the magnitude of a body, and of its position relative to other bodies. Neither can it be called *imaginary space*, because this consists of body mentally regarded as magnitude and position, but not as substance. Yet, Hobbes continued, if we consider the material world as finite, we are logically obliged to postulate some attribute or quality lying beyond the boundaries of the world. This attribute is *privation of body*. Hobbes was too much the materialist and nominalist to say that privation of body could be regarded as an attribute-in-itself, without reference to body. The meaning of privation depends in the first place on our knowledge of body, and refers only to the possibility of body coming into being. Considered by itself privation of body is a 'figment' or empty imagination—'the movements of the mind' within us, and nothing without.

How vastly different is this view of space from Henry More's. Nowhere does Hobbes admit the possibility of absolute space. 'Real' space is associated with body; all other space is imaginary. Hence there can be no question—in Hobbes's mind—of identifying space with God or with immaterial spirit. Nor can there be any question of viewing space as an infinitely extended and immobile vessel—a container filled with what More called the 'divine amplitude' and surrounding the moving bodies of the universe. '. . . Though what simple and ignorant men feel [about place],' Hobbes wrote in characteristic phrases,

is not of great importance to philosophers, yet shall I not concede that such men think that place is something environing and immobile, like a vessel. For this is a more learned error than one could believe to be in an ignorant man; to philosophers alone it is given to be learnedly ignorant. . . .[1]

In the *Divine Dialogues* Hylobares the materialist was converted to a belief in spirit by More's argument from spatial extension, and in particular by the argument, later repeated by Kant, that space cannot be 'dis-imagined'. Hylobares reasoned that 'though we should admit [spatial extension] to be imaginary, yet this at least will result therefrom, that extension being thus necessarily applicable as well to imaginary things as to real, it is rather a *Logicall* Motion than a *Physicall*, as well

[1] *Ibid.* fol. 25.

Metaphysicall as *Physicall*'.[1] Having thus accepted the idea that
space—as well as spirit—is extended, Hylobares was prepared
to receive More's final word on the nature of matter and spirit.
Matter is self-impenetrable; it is self-disunified, because it 'has
no *Vinculum* of its own to hold it together, so that of itself it
would be disunited into Congeries of mere *Physicall Monads*, that
is, into so little particles, that it implies a contradiction they
should be less';[2] and it is self-inactive, because it 'does not move
nor actuate, but is or has been alwaies excited by someother. . .'.
By contrast, spirit is self-penetrable, self-unified or indiscerpible, and self-active. It is an extended being, 'an essential
spissitude'; it belongs to a world which Hobbes never dreamt of
—an animate world, 'Spermaticall and Vital', a world which
has its own soul and which is populated by millions of other
souls and spiritual creatures.

More *felt* the presence of this world with so much intensity
that we are entitled to ask whether he did not believe in it before
he constructed its elaborate metaphysical supports. His meta-
physic affirms his belief, but does not prove it. As we follow his
ingenious argument we feel bound to agree with Basil Willey
that the dispute between Hobbes and More seems 'reducible
after all to a straight contest between one affirmation and its
opposite'.[3] More's bifurcation of substance into matter and
spirit is no less dogmatic than Hobbes's insistence on matter
alone. We can say of More's system what Hylobares said of it
before he was converted: 'Methinks I am, I know not how,
illaqueated, but not truly captivated into an assent. . . .'[4] Yet
it would be wrong to leave a negative impression of More. He
saw the dangers of Hobbes as clearly as anyone else, and if he
combated these dangers with arguments not always distinguished for their philosophical rigour, he fought them nevertheless with dignity and calmness and a real desire to test the issues
in a philosophical way. He was a philosopher by instinct, by his
very nature. Hobbes never replied directly to his criticisms, but
he paid More the ultimate compliment by saying that if he had
to choose a philosophical system different from his own he
would have chosen the system of Henry More.[5]

[1] *Divine Dialogues*, p. 111. [2] *Ibid.* pp. 119, 122.
[3] *The Seventeenth Century Background*, p. 155. [4] *Divine Dialogues*, p. 97.
[5] Richard Ward, *The Life of the Learned and Pious Dr Henry More*, p. 80. Ward
cites no authority for this attribution to Hobbes.

III

Cudworth is generally regarded as the theorist of the Cambridge School. Whichcote delivered his opinions aphoristically and with a certain diffidence; Smith and More had a mystical strain which upon occasion obscured the clear outlines of their thought; but Cudworth was the most tough-minded and lucid of them all. His work is however not easy to read. The difficulty is not that he was unsystematic, but that he was intolerably verbose. He was, as John Laird remarked, a 'book-glutton', and his *True Intellectual System* (1678) is 'monstrously obese'.[1] Into this 'vast and unwieldy fabric'[2] of almost a thousand folio pages Cudworth fused his immense learning, following a method of scholarly accretion set down by Ficino and going back to Plotinus.[3]

Part of the prolixity of the *True Intellectual System* results from Cudworth's attempt to show that atomism and dualism are perfectly compatible. Atomism, at least as taught in the school of Abdera, was normally associated with materialism and with atheism. It was Cudworth's design to show that this type of atomism was the decaying relic of an older dualistic and theistic variety. His demonstration of this point took the form of a long mythico-historical excursus; once that was out of the way he settled down to his real purpose—the refutation of atheism, and of its greatest living protagonist—Hobbes. Cudworth referred to Hobbes as 'the Atheist', 'the Atheistic Politician', 'a modern atheistic pretender to wit', etc.; he quoted and paraphrased Hobbes frequently, though not, it is to be feared, always accurately. Nevertheless he did communicate the sense of Hobbes's opinions, and understood perfectly what Hobbes was saying.[4]

Cudworth's theory of matter rested on one basic assumption: matter is inactive. He did not oppose More's view that matter is discerpible and impenetrable, but he laid no stress on these qualities. The essential point to grasp about matter, he thought,

[1] John Laird, *Hobbes*, p. 260.   [2] Basil Willey, *op. cit.* p. 157.
[3] J. A. Passmore, *Ralph Cudworth* (Cambridge University Press, 1951), p. 14.
[4] Oddly enough, in the whole of his immense book Cudworth never mentioned Hobbes by name, presumably because he felt he was writing *sub specie aeternitatis* and could not therefore scruple to notice so local a phenomenon as Hobbes. But Hobbes was never very far out of his mind.

is that it is passive, inactive, mere 'extended bulk', incapable of thought, feeling, or self-motion. If the world consisted entirely of 'this outside bulky extension and tumourous magnitude', if, as Hobbes said, 'the whole mass of all things that are is corporeal', then the world would be eternally at rest. 'There could be no motion or action at all in it; no life, cogitation, consciousness; no intellection, appetite, or volition (which things do yet make up the greatest part of the universe), but all would be a dead lump.'[1]

From this it follows that there must be another kind of entity beside matter, an entity whose essential attribute is 'life, self-activity, or cogitation'. This entity is Mind, an immaterial substance which activates matter from within, but is distinct from matter[2] and superior to it. Matter is 'the lowest of all being, and next to nothing'. Mind, on the other hand, 'hath a higher degree of entity or perfection in it, and is a greater reality in nature, than mere senseless matter'.[3] Cudworth was outraged by Hobbes's rejection of the chain of being.

He that does not perceive any higher degree of perfection in a man than in an oyster, nay, than in a clod of earth or lump of ice, in a piece of paste or piecrust, hath not the reason or understanding of a man in him. There is unquestionably a scale or ladder of nature, and degrees of perfection and entity one above another, as of life, sense, and cogitation, above dead, senseless, and unthinking matter; of reason and understanding above sense, etc. . . . A perfect understanding Being is the beginning and head of the scale of entity; from whence things gradually descend downward, lower and lower, till they end in senseless matter.[4]

Mind is 'senior to the world, and the architect thereof'. If Mind is 'proleptical' to matter it is seen at once to exist independently of matter, and Hobbes's assumption that '*knowledge* and *understanding* [are] nothing else, but a tumult of the

---

[1] Ralph Cudworth, *The True Intellectual System of the Universe*, ed. J. L. Mosheim (London, 1845), III, 394. (All references will be to this edition.)
[2] Cudworth was not only opposed to 'Democritic' and Hobbist atheism, in which thought is equated with some 'internal motions in the head', but also to 'hylozoism', in which thought and matter are regarded as two aspects of the same substance. He attributes this latter doctrine to the peripatetic philosopher Straton, but he may also have been thinking of Spinoza, whose *Tractatus Theologico-Politicus* appeared in 1670, one year before *The True Intellectual System* received its imprimatur.
[3] *True Intellectual System*, III, 434.   [4] *Ibid.* III, 434–5.

mind, raised by external things that press the organical parts of man's body'[1] becomes untenable. Furthermore, if thought is nothing but a process of corporeal motions, 'then would every thing that suffered and reacted motion, especially polite bodies, as looking-glasses, have something both of sense and of understanding in them';[2] or, as Tenison put it, the looking-glass would see and the lute would hear. We can escape from such absurdities only by affirming the independent existence of Mind, and this is established by recognizing the fact (or what was a fact for Cudworth) that Mind existed before body came into being.

Again, by considering Mind as independent of body, Cudworth laid the ground for a comprehensive criticism of Hobbes's doctrine of sensation. He agreed with Hobbes that sense-perception begins as a mechanical process, but its end product—the sense percept—is an immaterial entity, a function of Mind. For no object in nature can correspond to our awareness of that object; but the 'awareness' is in nature as much as the object. 'Awareness', in fact, represents a higher reality than the material motions involved in sensation, because 'awareness' is an immaterial entity and hence belongs to a higher link in the chain of being, while material motions are mere 'passions' (i.e. passive movements); they are matter in motion, but senseless matter, belonging to the lowest link in the great chain of being, lacking in the self-activity and 'internal energy' which are the attributes of Mind. It is Hobbes's 'sottishness' which leads him to identify these material motions of sensation with Mind itself.

The 'fancies', 'awarenesses', and 'seemings' in us are thus immaterial attributes of Mind, not simply the 'several contextures of matter, or combinations of magnitudes, figures, sites, and motions' with which Hobbes identified mental activity. And if sensation is more than mere local motion, how much more significant are cogitation and judgment, in which Mind is not merely producing an image of an object in nature, but reflecting on its meaning. In some instances Mind reflects on the meaning of objects not revealed to us through the senses at all,

[1] *Leviathan*, p. 238. Cudworth quoted this passage (with some slight inaccuracies) in the *True Intellectual System*, III, 60.
[2] *True Intellectual System*, III, 422.

but known *a priori*. Such abstractions as 'life', 'sense', 'reason', 'knowledge' and the like

do not at all fall under sense; which therefore could never possibly be impressed upon us from singular bodies by local motion; and again some such, as though they belong to corporeal and sensible things, yet, as their accuracy cannot be reached to by sense, so neither did they ever exist in that matter of this lower world which here encompasseth us, and therefore could not be stamped upon us from without: as for example, the ideas of a perfect straight line, and a plain superficies, or of an exact triangle, circle, sphere, or cube; no material thing here amongst us being terminated in so straight lines but that even by microscopes there may be discovered much irregularity and deformity in them; and very probable it is, that there are no perfectly straight lines, no such triangles, circles, spheres, or cubes as answer to the exactness of our conceptions in any part of the whole material universe, nor never will be.[1]

The argument for the existence of spirit deduced from the apprehension of perfect mathematical figures had already been used in similar form by Seth Ward, Stillingfleet, Tenison, and More; Cudworth, however, made a further deduction from it. A perfect mathematical figure, he said, is a universal, and its apprehension exposes the falsity of Hobbes's nominalism.

It is a ridiculous conceit of a modern atheistic writer, that universals are nothing else but names, attributed to many singular bodies, because whatsoever *is*, is singular. For though whatsoever exists without [i.e. outside] the mind be singular, yet it is plain, that there are conceptions in our minds objectively universal. . . . When from the universal idea of a triangle, which is neither here nor there, nor anywhere, without our mind, but yet hath an intelligible entity, we see a plain necessity, that its three angles must be equal to two right, then do we know the truth of this universal theorem, and not before; as also we understand, that every singular triangle (so far as it is true) hath this property in it. Wherefore the knowledge of this, and the like truths, is not derived from singulars. . . .[2]

It is plain for Cudworth that the human mind has other conceptions in it besides what Hobbes called the 'phantasms of singular things'; it has also 'the ideas of the intelligible natures and essences of things, which are universal, and by and under which it understands singulars'.[3] Universal knowledge is the criterion of absolute truth; sensible knowledge is merely 'fan-

[1] *Ibid.* III, 63. [2] *Ibid.* III, 62–3. [3] *Ibid.* III, 62.

99

THE HUNTING OF LEVIATHAN

tastical and relative to the sentient'. Hobbes affirmed that all knowledge is relative to the sentient; against this view Cudworth reasserted the Platonic-idealist tradition of absolute ideas.

In the middle years of the seventeenth century this idealist tradition was upheld eloquently by the Cambridge Platonists, but it had still to make its way against the rising currents of materialism and scepticism. What is immaterial, self-active, absolute and universal Mind? Is it an occult force, a linguistic fiction bequeathed to us by the schoolmen, a vain belief such as men indulge in when they believe in hobgoblins and fairies? Or is it the rational being of God, the divine creative principle in the universe? The Cambridge Platonists denied that Mind was an occult force. They were as anxious as Hobbes was to reject the occult qualities of scholastic philosophy. 'He that asserts an occult quality for the cause of any phenomenon,' wrote Cudworth, 'does indeed assign no cause at all of it, but only declare his own ignorance of the cause.'[1] Nevertheless the Platonists refused to be daunted by the mistakes of the schoolmen. Mind is real, immaterial, and absolute; but its operations are not occult.

Is Mind then to be identified with the Divine Spirit? This question posed a genuine dilemma for the Cambridge Platonists, because if Mind is identified with God, then the operations of Mind have the same perfections as God; and yet the universe, animated though it be by Mind, and perfect though it be in its larger cosmic proportions, has still imperfections in it, 'errors and bungles' which are incompatible with the divine character. There are monstrous births, flies, gnats, noxious vapours, etc., which would appear either to be directly created by God, or else (in Hobbes's scheme) to be the products of mechanical second causes. Is there then no alternative between Hobbesian mechanism and a type of vitalism in which the universe is created and guided in its minute details by God? The answer, said the Platonists, lies in the recognition of a subdivision of immaterial Mind, a subordinate agency of God which performs the more mundane tasks of creation, and which is responsible, through its own occasional lapses, for the imperfections in the universe.

More called this subordinate agency of Mind the 'Spirit of

[1] *Ibid.* I, 234.

the World', a 'hylarchic principle'; Cudworth called it 'plastic nature'.[1] To Cudworth the doctrine of plastic nature provided a more certain refutation of Hobbesian mechanism than the theory of Occasionalism, according to which mind actuated matter through the direct and continuous intervention of God, as though all the processes of nature were a perpetual miracle. Such a view 'would render divine Providence operose, solicitous, and distractious',[2] whereas plastic nature 'takes God off' from the necessity of doing 'all the meanest and triflingest things' himself, and at the same time rejects Hobbes's strictly mechanical view of nature.

Wherefore since neither all things are produced fortuitously, or by the unguided mechanism of matter, nor God himself may be thought to do all things immediately and miraculously; it may well be concluded, that there is a plastic nature under him, which, as an inferior and subordinate instrument, doth drudgingly execute that part of his providence, which consists in the regular and orderly motion of matter. . . . In this way it will appear . . . to human reason, that all things are disposed and ordered by the Deity, without any solicitous çare or distractious providence.[3]

Plastic nature derives its power from God, but it is not to be equated with God. It is 'ectypal' rather than 'archtypal'. God has, as it were, delegated to plastic nature certain powers which it would be unworthy of him to reserve for himself. These powers operate unconsciously, but they are not governed by chance; they are teleological; they are the (occasionally imperfect) medium through which God imparts his sense of purpose to the non-human parts of the universe. In this way, Cudworth avoids the determinism of Hobbes's mechanical view of nature. The universe for Cudworth is instinct with God's purpose, which when God chooses, he carries out through the agency of subordinate Mind—plastic nature. The perfections of plastic nature are thus attributable to the will of God, while the imperfections—the creation of flies, the raising of noxious

---

[1] Both More and Cudworth derived the concept from a variety of Renaissance and classical sources, most notably from Agrippa, Plotinus, and Plato. The idea continued to have a sort of underground existence in the seventeenth century, appearing in the work of Richard Burthogge, John Ray, and Nehemiah Grew. For the later history of the idea, see Joseph Warren Beach, *The Concept of Nature in Nineteenth-Century English Poetry* (New York, 1936), pp. 70–109.
[2] *True Intellectual System*, i, 222. See also ii, 606. [3] *Ibid.* i, 223–4.

THE HUNTING OF LEVIATHAN

vapours—are due to the incapacity of plastic nature to reflect, and hence to perform its God-given functions intelligently.

This spirit-world of Cudworth and More is the background against which their criticism of Hobbes must be understood. Their world is animate with spirit, Hobbes's is uniformly material. Their world has creativity, novelty, vitality; Hobbes's is an automaton governed by the strict laws of motion. Their world is possessed of universal truth, absolute value, and qualitative distinctions according to which senseless matter is placed at the bottom of a scale of value and immaterial Mind at the top; Hobbes's world is a collocation of singulars, differing only in magnitude, spatial location, and velocity, and value has meaning only by reference to the will of the individual. The world as conceived by Hobbes was to Cudworth and More pallid and insignificant.

> Onely that vitality,
> That doth extend this great Universall,
> And move th'inert Materiality
> Of great and little worlds, that keep in memory.[1]

IV

The world of the Cambridge Platonists was also populated by devils. These, like the plastic powers, could actuate matter in a purposive, non-mechanical way; but the purposes of devils were wholly nefarious. Of the reality of devils and of the power of witches, the Cambridge Platonists entertained no doubts whatsoever. They insisted that belief in witchcraft must be upheld against the attacks of Hobbes and other sceptical minds. The issue as Henry More saw it was simply this: if one believed in spirits, then he must also believe in evil spirits; and if one denies evil spirits, then he will be led to deny all spirits, and ultimately to deny the Godhead itself.

And forasmuch as such coarse grain'd Philosophers as those *Hobbians* and *Spinozians*, and the rest of that Rabble, slight Religion and the

---

[1] Henry More, *Psychothanasia*, Bk. II, canto 1, in *Philosophical Poems* (Cambridge, 1647), p. 108.

Scriptures, because there is such express mention of Spirits and Angels in them, Things that their dull Souls are so inclinable to conceit to be impossible; I look upon it as a special Piece of Providence, that there are ever and anon such fresh Examples of Apparitions and Witchcrafts, as may rub up and awaken their benumm'd and lethargick Minds, into a Suspicion at least, if not Assurance, that there are other intelligent Beings, besides those that are clad in heavy Earth or Clay; in this, I say, methinks the Divine Providence does plainly outwit the Powers of the dark Kingdom, in permitting wicked Men and Women, and vagrant spirits of that Kingdom, to make Leagues or Covenants one with another; the Confession of Witches against their own Lives, being so palpable an Evidence, besides the Miraculous Feats they play, that there are bad Spirits, which will necessarily open a Door to the Belief that there are good Ones; and, lastly, that there is a God.[1]

The argument that disbelief in witchcraft leads to atheism was not new: it was employed on the continent as early as 1605,[2] and in England as early as 1617,[3] and the corollary argument— that belief in psychic phenomena provides support for theism— has been used by spiritualists in our own day.[4] The fullest elaboration of the argument was made by Joseph Glanvill, More's friend and ally, who wrote in reaction to the strictures of Hobbes.

Hobbes left no doubt about his opinion of witchcraft. The belief in it, he said, is a superstition, and the practice of it a fraud which deserves to be punished. 'As for witches, I think not that their witchcraft is any real power; but yet that they are justly punished, for the false belief they have that they can do

<hr>

[1] A letter from Henry More to Joseph Glanvill, 25 May 1678, printed in Glanvill, *Sadducismus Triumphatus* (4th ed. London, 1681), pp. 9–10.
[2] Pierre le Loyer, *Discours et histoires des spectres* (Paris, 1605), pp. 7–31. I have not seen this book, which is cited by Moody E. Prior, in 'Joseph Glanvill, Witchcraft, and Seventeenth-Century Science', *MP*, 30 (1932), 178.
[3] Thomas Cooper, *The Mystery of Witchcraft* (London, 1617), p. 22. In 1642 Thomas Browne wrote: 'For my part, I have ever believed, and do now know, that there are witches. They that doubt of these do not only deny them, but spirits: and are obliquely, and upon consequence, a sort, not of infidels, but atheists'. Browne, *Religio Medici* in *Works*, ed. S. Wilkin (London, 1901), II, 366. [Bohn Library reprint.]
[4] Cf. a recent statement: 'These [poltergeist] phenomena seem to me to have their value as a proof of the existence of spiritual agencies, not cognoscible directly by our sense-perceptions'. Herbert Thurston, S.J., *Ghosts and Poltergeists* (Chicago, 1953), p. 202.

such mischief, joined with their purpose to do it if they can.'[1] In this Hobbes followed closely the views of his friend Selden, who wrote in the *Table Talk* that 'the Law against Witches does not prove there be any; but it punishes the Malice of those people that use such means to take away mens Lives'.[2] Selden wrote as a lawyer, Hobbes as a philosopher; both were less than humane in declaring for the punishment of witches, but Hobbes at least was consistent to his philosophical principles. He believed that the security of the state depends on civil obedience, and civil obedience is relaxed when 'crafty ambitious persons abuse the simple people' by playing on their 'superstitious fear of spirits'.[3] Hobbes may also have been remembering the class of professional conjurors who, during the reign of Elizabeth, seem to have been involved in seditious plots against the Crown.[4] While Hobbes's legal argument for the punishment of false witches may therefore have been inspired by something less than humane motives, it had nevertheless the force of a philosophic creed behind it.

Similarly, Hobbes's denial of the power of witches was a direct consequence of his materialism. In chapter xlvii of *Leviathan*, on demonology, Hobbes reviewed his mechanico-materialist theory of sensation in order to show that a man may have hallucinations from purely natural and material causes, which may be called demons by unsophisticated minds.[5] When to ignorance of second causes is added the 'juggling and confederate knavery' of charlatans, one can form some impression of how the belief in witchcraft takes hold. The moving force is

[1] *Leviathan*, p. 12, Cf. also the statement in *A Dialogue Between a Philosopher and a Student of the Common-Laws, Works*, VI, 96: '. . . though without doubt there is some great wickedness signified by those crimes [of witches] yet have I ever found myself too dull to conceive the nature of them, or how the Devil hath power to do many things which Witches have been accused of.'

[2] John Selden, *Table Talk* (London, 1689), *vide* 'Witches'. It is not certain that Selden preceded Hobbes in this opinion; *Table Talk* is thought to have been composed between 1634 and 1654. Selden's opinion is quoted with comment by Aldous Huxley, *The Devils of Loudon* (New York, 1953), pp. 131–2.

[3] *Leviathan*, pp. 12, 13.

[4] For an account of how the seditious acts of the conjurors hardened public and legal opinion against them, and thus contributed to the spread of witch-persecutions in England, see the brilliant monograph by Wallace Notestein, *A History of Witchcraft in England* (Washington, 1911), pp. 18–27.

[5] '. . . . as if the dead of whom they dreamed, were not inhabitants of their own brain, but of the air, or of heaven, or hell; not phantasms, but ghosts.' *Leviathan*, p. 419.

superstitious fear. Fear, said Hobbes, is contagious, and when it is provoked by ignorance or by practised fraud it can produce extraordinary mass-delusions, causing people to think that they have seen apparitions, or that the devil has earthly minions, or that there are immaterial spirits, or that the devil leaves his mark on witches's bodies, or that witches can fly, or have evil glances, etc. In short Hobbes rejected the whole apparatus of witchcraft as either deliberate fraud or large-scale delusion.

An attack on witchcraft on these grounds alone would not have disturbed the faith of most believers, since Hobbes also had to contend with the widespread doctrine that a belief in witchcraft was sanctioned by the Bible. Did not the Witch of Endor raise the dead? Did not Jesus cast out devils? When in 1664 Sir Matthew Hale charged the jury in a celebrated witch-trial at Bury St Edmunds he told them that he 'made no doubt at all' that 'there were such creatures as witches' and the first reason he gave for the strength of his conviction was: 'the *Scriptures* had affirmed so much'.[1] But Hobbes denied that the belief in witchcraft had Scriptural sanction. He acknowledged that there 'be some texts of Scripture, that seem to attribute the power of working wonders . . . to certain arts of magic and incantation'.[2] But these texts 'must needs have another sense, than at first sight they seem to bear'.[3] There is no place in Scripture that tells us what an enchantment is, and we are not entitled to believe that it is anything more than a deception effected by natural means to deceive a gullible audience. The raising of Samuel by the Witch of Endor was undoubtedly an 'imposture' designed to induce terror in Saul and thereby contribute to his downfall.[4] And though Christ is said to have cast out devils, yet is there 'nothing at all in the Scripture, that requireth a belief, that demoniacs were any other thing but madmen'.[5] Where the devils are said to confess Christ, 'it is not necessary to interpret those places otherwise, than that those madmen confessed him'.[6] Possession is a tumult of the brain, a type of mental disease. The Bible supports no other interpretation.

[1] [Anon.] *A Tryal of Witches at . . . Bury St Edmunds* (London, 1682), p. 102. (Sir Thomas Browne was an expert witness for the prosecution at this trial. See Jeremiah S. Finch, *Sir Thomas Browne* (New York, 1950), pp. 214–18.)

[2] *Leviathan*, p. 288. [3] *Ibid.* p. 289. [4] *Ibid.* p. 277. [5] *Ibid.* p. 51.

[6] *Ibid.* See also pp. 420–1.

Hobbes's views on witchcraft have so distinctly a modern ring that it is interesting to know in what respect they are in advance of their time. The fullest attack before Hobbes was also probably the first written in England: Reginald Scot's *Discoverie of Witchcraft* (1584). Scot anticipated many of Hobbes's arguments. The Witch of Endor, he said, was a sham who practised ventriloquism.[1] Demoniac possession was a kind of disease.[2] Witches can be classified in two ways—'couseners', frauds, knaves; or 'poor doting women' who were honestly self-deluded. Of the latter Scot wrote:

The witch . . . seeing things sometimes come to passe according to hir wishes . . . being called before a Justice . . . confesseth that she hath brought such things to passe. Wherein, not onlie she, but the accuser, and also the Justice are fowlie deceived and abused.[3]

But Scot was appalled by the severity with which witches were punished, and by the vindictiveness of the public and the courts towards 'old, lame, bleare-eied, pale, fowle . . . leane and deformed . . . doting'[4] but obviously harmless women. Scot was no materialist: he believed devils are immaterial spirits, and that matter and spirit are incontrovertible; indeed, this is how he refuted the popular belief that devils have carnal relations with witches.

Powerful though Scot's scepticism was, it was not so complete as Hobbes's. Hobbes's rejection of the belief was unqualified; in this respect his scepticism was more radical than Scot's or than Scot's successors George Gifford and Francis Osborne, or even than John Selden. Certainly, Hobbes was more thorough than the non-conformist clergyman John Webster, whose much-discussed *Displaying of Supposed Witchcraft* (1677) nibbled away at the outworks of the superstition, but left the centre of the creed intact. Although Hobbes's direct utterances on witchcraft were few and characteristically concise, they represented the most forthright and modern assault on the dogma until Francis Hutcheson's *Historical Essay on Witchcraft* (1718) delivered the final blow.

But the sceptics were in the minority. Opinion generally, and

---

[1] A woman who bore false witness at a witch-trial in Kent was exposed as a ventriloquist. See Reginald Scot, *Discoverie of Witchcraft*, ed. Brinsley Nicholson (London, 1886), p. 130.

[2] Scot, *Discoverie*, p. 512.   [3] *Ibid.* p. 8.   [4] *Ibid.*

this included most educated opinion, was favourable to the belief in witches. Such eminent men as Baxter, Boyle and Sir Matthew Hale (all of whom, it will be recalled, had written against Hobbes on other grounds) believed in the power of witches. So did Sir Thomas Browne. Robert Vilvain expressed his own opinion and attacked Hobbes's by saying that

those that hold Hel to be no real place, and Devils meer Metaphors, must of cours deny Witchcraft: yea many who pretend to be wise pious professors, are too incredulous of Witches; contrary to the faith of all Gods People (both Jews and Christians) who will not suffer a Witch to liv as God commanded. The best is, only privat persons deny it: but al public Princes and Christian Commonwealths make strict laws against it....[1]

The most indefatigable supporter of the belief was Joseph Glanvill.[2] His first treatise on the subject was *A Philosophical Endeavour towards the Defence of the Being of Witches and Apparitions*, published in 1666, and then revised, enlarged and reissued under various titles until it took its final form as *Sadducismus Triumphatus* (1681).[3] Glanvill's point was the same as More's: Sadducism—the denial of immaterial spirits—was a first step towards the denial of God. 'There is a *latent Atheism* at the root of SADDUCEAN Principle: for too many deny *Witches*, because they believe there are no *Spirits*; and they are so perswaded because they own no Being in the world, but *matter*, and the results of *motion*, and consequently, can acknowledge *nothing* of a *God*.'[4]

Glanvill was anxious to put the whole question of witches on a scientific footing. It did not occur to him that such an approach might engender scepticism of witchcraft, because he considered witchcraft to be an indispensible prop for theism, and science the faithful ally of religion. This chain of reasoning,

[1] Robert Vilvain, *Theoremata Theologica*, p. 239r.
[2] The best account of Glanvill's witchcraft researches is by Moody E. Prior, 'Joseph Glanvill, Witchcraft, and Seventeenth-Century Science', *MP*, 30 (Nov. 1932), 167–93. A fuller study, treating also Glanvill's Platonist and ecclesiastical interests, is Jackson I. Cope, *Joseph Glanvill: Anglican Apologist* (St Louis, 1956).
[3] The work was immensely popular, having achieved no fewer than eight editions by 1726. Its complicated bibliographical history may be studied in Ferris Greenslet, *Joseph Glanvill: A Study in English Thought and Letters of the Seventeenth Century* (New York, 1900), pp. 224–6.
[4] [Joseph Glanvill], *A Whip for the Droll, Fiddler to the Atheist: Being Reflections on Drollery & Atheism* (London, 1668), pp. 176–7.

not remarkable for its acuity, can be put in the following way: witchcraft is true because it supports religion; science supports religion; science supports the belief in witchcraft, or can, if the techniques of science can be refined enough to discover the truth. Glanvill prided himself on his scepticism, but it was a type of scepticism which doubted dogmatic *unbelief* as much as it doubted vain belief. Glanvill argued that our ignorance of 'how the Foetus is form'd in the *Womb*' or 'how a *Plant* springs from the *Earth* we tread on' should not lead us to deny the reality of foetus or plant.

What sort of evidence did Glanvill expect science to provide in support of the witch-belief? Not experimental evidence certainly, but evidence based on the direct observation of unimpeachable witnesses. He suggested to the Royal Society that it 'direct some of its *wary*, and *luciferous* enquiries towards the *World* of *Spirits*' by making 'a *Cautious*, and *Faithful* History . . . of those *certain and uncommon appearances*'[1] of witchcraft. The Royal Society did not act on this suggestion; indeed it took no official position on the entire question. Glanvill therefore undertook to write the 'Cautious and Faithful History' himself. He collected and published witch-relations, some of which he personally investigated. For the most part his treatment of these stories displayed a mood of credulity and of crusading zeal, inspired probably by his 'philosophical' bias in favour of spirits.

One of the cases he investigated attracted wide public interest. It concerned an itinerant drummer who was expelled from a village in Wiltshire for disturbing the peace, and who (so it was alleged) returned to haunt the house in Tedworth of the man who had expelled him. Drumming noises were heard on the roof; levitation phenomena were observed; children were thrown about in bed, etc. When Glanvill came to the house the spirit or spirits were quiet, but not quiet enough to escape his detection. According to Henry More 'some Hobbians' also came, presumably to mock, but they too were convinced.[2] On the other hand a Royal investigating committee

[1] Joseph Glanvill, *A Blow at Modern Sadducism* (London, 1668), pp. 115–17.
[2] Henry More to Lady Conway, 11 August 1663, in *Conway Letters*, p. 216. See also George Edelen, 'Joseph Glanvill, Henry More, and the Phantom Drummer of Tedworth', *Harvard Library Bulletin*, (1956), 192.

found nothing conclusive, and the best available evidence indicates that the affair was a hoax perpetrated by the injured drummer and certain accomplices.[1] Nevertheless, Glanvill clung to this story and to others like it as the best evidence for the reality of witches. If people will not believe these stories, 'if they will believe in *Scott, Hobbes,* and *Osborne,* and think them more infallible, than the Sacred Oracles, the *History* of all Ages, and the full Experience of our *own,* who can help it'?[2]

Glanvill thought that his defence of witchcraft was an effective rebuttal of Hobbesian materialism. He saw very clearly that Hobbes wrote against witchcraft from the standpoint of a materialist and a mechanist. But belief in witchcraft depends upon the assumption that there *are* immaterial spirits and that diabolically-inspired supernatural events *do* occur. To uphold these beliefs against the corroding scepticism of Hobbes and Hobbists was the peculiar task which Glanvill set for himself. He thought it was a necessary task because he felt that the belief in witchcraft and the belief in spirit and the belief in God were all inextricably linked together, and that to give up any one of them would amount to giving up all. When we view Glanvill's defence of witchcraft in this light we see that it is part of the general reaction to Hobbesian materialism. '*No Spirit,*' said Henry More, '*no God.*' This was the motto of all the critics of Hobbes's materialism.

---

[1] See Notestein, *A History of Witchcraft,* p. 275. Glanvill gives his side of the story in *Sadducismus Triumphatus* (4th ed. London, 1681), pt. ii, preface, and Relation I.
[2] *Sadducismus Triumphatus,* sig. A5.

CHAPTER VI

THE FREE-WILL CONTROVERSY:
BRAMHALL AND CUDWORTH

I

From materialism Hobbes passed easily to determinism. The two doctrines were closely linked: if everything that is, is material, then all causes, or at least all second causes, are material; and what then becomes of free-will?

Hobbes's treatise *Of Liberty and Necessity* was published, without its author's permission, in 1654. It had been written in Rouen eight years earlier, in reply to a manuscript treatise on the same subject by Bishop Bramhall.[1] Bramhall printed his own manuscript and reprinted Hobbes's in 1655, and Hobbes replied in the following year in *The Questions Concerning Liberty, Necessity, and Chance*, which contained both Bramhall's treatise and Hobbes's own detailed rejoinders. Of this whole controversy John Laird has written that it is 'worthy to be compared with Locke's correspondence with Stillingfleet, Arnauld's with Malebranche, or Clarke's with Leibniz' as 'one of the best of all philosophical duels'.[2] Such praise is well-deserved. Both Hobbes and Bramhall wrote clearly and reasoned acutely on a vexed philosophical subject; both employed a minimum of the heavy irony so characteristic of seventeenth-century dispute; each adversary respected his opponent's intelligence, and each gave the other a fair hearing. Hobbes's *Of Liberty and Necessity* in particular was written with exceptional clarity and dialectical rigour, and its position in the history of scientific determinism is, according to Croom Robertson, unsurpassed.[3]

Hobbes's argument was essentially this: all human actions are strictly determined or 'necessitated'. A man is 'free' to do anything he desires if there are no obstacles in his way, but his

[1] For the circumstances of the controversy between Bramhall and Hobbes, see above, pp. 11–12.
[2] Laird, *Hobbes*, p. 189 and 189 n. [3] Robertson, *Hobbes*, p. 134.

desire to do anything has necessary and material causes. Freedom in this view means the 'absence of the lets and hindrances of motion';[1] if a man wants to do something, and there are no impediments to his action, then he is 'free' to act; but both his action and his will to act are predetermined. Hobbes was fond of paradox, and nothing seems more paradoxical than the statement that an act can be simultaneously free and determined. The paradox disappears when we remember Hobbes's definition of freedom as the 'privation' of obstacles to any act that a man desires to perform.

According to this meaning of freedom, only the man who has the will, and not the will itself, can be called free. Hobbes derided Bramhall's notion that the will is a separate faculty or entity. If this were true then one could say that 'to will is an act allured or drawn out of the power to will', which is as absurd as saying that 'to dance is an act allured or drawn by fair means out of the ability to dance'.[2] The will is the last desire or appetite in a process of deliberation. When a man deliberates over whether to act in a certain way, what he is really doing is weighing the good or evil consequences to himself of the act; which is the same as to say that there is within him an alternating succession of hopes or desires and fears or aversions, and that the last member of this succession before he acts, or before he finally chooses not to act, is called the will. Here we see Hobbes's egoistical psychology brought into play, but even if he had attributed other motives to the actions of men than desire or fear he would still have insisted—and this is the important point in his doctrine of the will—that the last dictate of the judgment in the deliberative process *necessarily* produces the effect which follows, 'in such manner as the last feather may be said to break a horse's back, when there were so many laid on before as there wanted but that one to do it'.[3] Thus Hobbes makes 'not only the *effect*, but also the *election*, of that particular effect *necessary*, inasmuch as the will itself, and each propension of a man during his deliberation, is as much necessitated, and depends on a sufficient cause, as any thing else whatsoever'.[4]

Hobbes was aware that most people *feel* they are free. 'Sir, we know our will is free, and there's an end on't!' said Dr

[1] *De Cive*, in *Works*, ii, 120. [2] *Of Liberty and Necessity*, in *Works*, iv, 266.
[3] *Ibid.* p. 247. [4] *Ibid.*

Johnson.[1] Such an attitude, claimed Hobbes, arises from the fact that most people are ignorant of the causes of things, and it is a simple matter to pass from the ignorance of causes to the belief that there are none.

A wooden top that is lashed by the boys, and runs about sometimes to one wall, sometimes to another, sometimes spinning, sometimes hitting men on the shins, if it were sensible of its own motion, would think it proceeded from its own will, unless it felt what lashed it. And is a man any wiser, when he runs to one place for a benefice, to another for a bargain . . . because he thinks he doth it without other cause than his own will, and seeth not what are the lashings that cause his will?[2]

All acts are caused, even if the causes are unknown. To say that an act is contingent is merely to acknowledge that we are ignorant of its causes. Of course, we may say that the ultimate cause of all things is God Almighty as the prime mover. But this will tell us nothing about second causes, and these frequently baffle us by their elusiveness. Nevertheless we must not assume that second causes are absent just because they are unknown. They are there, and they produce their effects necessarily, even in those instances which are commonly ascribed to contingency or to chance. Thus, if we think that the statement *'Either it will rain tomorrow or it will not rain'* proves contingency, what we are really showing is that 'one of them is true, but we know not which, and so the necessity remains, though we know it not'.[3] And if we think that the casting of dice illustrates the operation of chance, we are only acknowledging our ignorance of the true and necessary causes of the event, such as the contours of the dice, 'the posture of the parts of the *hand*, the measure of *force* applied by the caster, the posture of the parts of the table',[4] etc.

It is easy to see how this radical determinism proceeded from Hobbes's materialist and mechanist positions. In a world consisting wholly of matter and governed by the laws of motion, every event—even the 'nimble local motion' of Bramhall's fingers when he wrote against Hobbes—was physically and antecedently and externally caused.

We can therefore say that Bramhall's attack on Hobbes's

[1] James Boswell, *Life of Johnson*, ed. G. Birbeck Hill (Oxford, 1887), II, 82.
[2] *The Questions Concerning Liberty, Necessity, and Chance*, in *Works*, v, 55.
[3] *Works*, IV, 277. [4] *Ibid.* pp. 276-7.

determinism was also by implication an attack on the materialism; but only by implication, because Bramhall addressed himself primarily to what he called the logical 'inconsistencies' and
ethical 'inconveniences' of the doctrine of necessity.

On the score of logic his argument was this: there are four
classes of action—'natural', actions extrinsically caused, 'as the
throwing of a stone upwards'; 'natural' actions intrinsically
caused, 'as the falling of a stone downwards'; 'voluntary' or
'spontaneous' acts intrinsically caused, but performed without
deliberation or election, 'as the acts of fools, children, beasts';
and 'voluntary' or 'spontaneous' acts intrinsically caused, but
elected upon deliberation, 'with a more perfect knowledge of
the end'.[1] These distinctions were all drawn from the Schoolmen, with whom Bramhall was always willing to 'consult
awhile', and from whom he derived, in large part, both the
method and the content of his reasoning. His object in putting
forward this classification was to show that whereas the actions
belonging to the first three classes were all 'necessitated', the
actions of the fourth class—voluntary acts performed after
deliberation—were free. Hobbes on the other hand had reduced all four classes of action to the first of them—that is, to
natural acts extrinsically caused. According to Bramhall
voluntary acts which proceeded from deliberation were 'intrinsically caused' by a separate faculty of the soul called the
'will', and the will was free.

At issue was the nature of the will. Hobbes said that the will
was the last act of the judgment in a conflict between fear and
hope. A 'voluntary' act is therefore strictly determined by the
individual's assessment of his own best interest. Bramhall denied
this. A man's self-interest may be involved in his deliberation,
but his final judgment as to what is best for him is determined
not by his self-interest, but by the 'will' itself, which is a self-
moved or self-determined rational faculty. A horse may be
moved out of fear, but he does not deliberate, and hence his
'voluntary' acts cannot be called free.[2] 'Deliberation implyeth
the actual use of reason,'[3] and reason is a self-moved faculty, an
aspect of the soul. Thus self-interest may provide the *issues* of the

<hr>

[1] John Bramhall, *A Defence of True Liberty From Antecedent and Extrinsicall Necessity*
(1655), reprinted in Hobbes, *Works*, v, 84, and hereafter referred to as *Works*, v.
[2] *Works*, v, 87.   [3] *Ibid.* p. 84.

mental debate which precedes a voluntary action, but it cannot provide the *decision*. This is determined by the will, that is to say, by the rational faculty. Bramhall may have overloaded his argument with scholastic vocabulary, but he went to the very heart of the question. Either everything in the deliberative process is strictly determined, or it is not. Bramhall insisted that it is not.

I shall not presume to say which side in this controversy was right. Hobbes put the case for scientific determinism as clearly as it could be put; Bramhall, though perhaps not always so lucid, was an able opponent.[1] In the seventeenth century his performance in this dispute was widely applauded by his Anglican contemporaries. Jeremy Taylor said that

it is known everywhere with what Piety and acumen he wrote against the Manichean doctrine of fatal necessity, which a late witty Man had pretended to adorn with a new vizor; but this excellent person washed off the ceruse and the meretricious paintings, rarely well asserted the Oeconomy of the Divine Providence, and having once more triumph'd over his adversary, *plenus victoriarum & trophaerum*, betook himself to the more agreeable attendance upon sacred offices.[2]

Taylor, it will be noticed, spoke of Hobbes's doctrine as a revived heresy, and paid tribute to Bramhall's 'Piety'. He was impressed by Bramhall's skill in exposing the ethical and theological 'inconveniences' of Hobbes's doctrine; and it was, indeed, the ethical and religious side of the controversy which claimed Bramhall's greatest attention and brought forth his purest flights of rhetoric:

[1] It is sometimes argued that the issues in this dispute have been finally settled in Bramhall's favour by the discovery of the indeterminacy principle in modern physics. Perhaps this is so as regards the behaviour of particles, but at least one eminent physicist—Schrödinger—has objected that 'whether or no this physical indeterminacy plays any relevant role in organic life, we must, I think, sternly refuse to make it the physical counterpart of voluntary actions of living beings. . . . Quantum physics has nothing to do with the free-will problem. If there is such a problem it is not furthered a whit by the latest developments in physics'. Erwin Schrödinger, *Science and Humanism* (Cambridge University Press, 1952), p. 67. Kathleen Nott, *inter alia*, makes the same point as Schrödinger, and cites also contrary opinions in *The Emperor's Clothes* (Bloomington, 1954), pp. 17–19, 63–4, 87, 270.
[2] Jeremy Taylor, *A Sermon Preached in Christ-Church, Dublin: at the Funeral of the most Reverend . . . John, Late Lord Archbishop of Armagh, and Primate of all Ireland* (London, 1663), p. 29.

Though I honour T.H. for his person and for his learning, yet I must confess ingenuously, I hate [his] doctrine from my heart. And I believe both I have reason so to do, and all others who shall seriously ponder the horrid consequences which flow from it. It destroys liberty, and dishonours the nature of man. It makes the second causes and outward objects to be the rackets, and men to be but the tennis-balls of destiny. It makes the first cause, that is, God Almighty, to be the introducer of all evil and sin into the world, as much as man, yea, more than man. . . . Excuse me if I hate this doctrine with a perfect hatred, which is so dishonourable both to God and man; which makes men to blaspheme of necessity, to steal of necessity, to be hanged of necessity, and to be damned of necessity. And therefore I must say and say again, *quicquid ostendes mihi sic, incredulus odi.* It were better to be a Manichee, to believe two gods, a God of good and a God of evil; or with the heathens to believe thirty thousand Gods: than thus to charge the true God to be the proper cause and the true author of all the sins and evils which are in the world.[1]

Bramhall amplified this general point of view in three ways: by arguing, first, from Scripture; second, from the attributes of God; third, from the moral 'inconveniences' inherent in Hobbes's doctrine.

The Scriptural argument consisted of quotations from both Testaments which in Bramhall's opinion demonstrated a clear Scriptural preference for free-will. One such text is Numbers 30.13: *If a wife make a vow it is left to her husband's choice, either to establish it or make it void.* Here, said Bramhall, is clear evidence that men have 'liberty of election', and additional evidence is provided by 2 Samuel 24.12: *I offer thee three things, choose thee which of them I shall do.* 'If one of these things was necessarily determined, and the other two impossible, how was it left to him to choose what should be done? Therefore we have true liberty.'[2]

Hobbes had no difficulty in showing that these and all the other texts adduced by Bramhall simply proved that men may make choices, but not that their choices were freed from necessity. Whether the husband in Numbers 30.13 establishes or whether he abrogates the vow of his wife, his choice will be strictly determined.

[1] *Works*, v, 110–12. [2] *Ibid.* p. 66.

For if there come into the husband's mind greater good by establishing than abrogating such a vow, the establishing will follow necessarily; and if the evil that will follow in the husband's opinion outweigh the good, the contrary must needs follow: and yet in this following of one's *hopes* and *fears*, consisteth the nature of *election*. So that a man may both choose this, and cannot but choose this, and consequently *choosing* and *necessity* are joined together.[1]

Hobbes also paid his respects to the Scriptural method of argument by offering counter-quotations in support of his position. God's words *I will harden Pharoah's heart* must mean that although the Pharoah *thought* his hostility towards the Hebrews was freely elected, it was in fact predetermined. But Hobbes had no particular reverence for Scripture *qua* Scripture. He conceded that certain texts 'make equally for the Bishop and me',[2] but he insisted that no text is better than the rational interpretation placed upon it. We may therefore conclude that he used the scriptural method because that method might still, in 1656, commend itself to his readers, and because he wanted to show (what was true) that he knew as much Scripture as did the Bishop.

On points of theology he was also the Bishop's equal, even though Bramhall spoke with the authority of a High-Churchman and Arminian. Arminianism was in fact the subject which initiated the entire debate between them.[3] The term 'Arminianism' was variously used in the seventeenth century. In its original sense it referred, of course, to the creed which the Dutch theologian Jacob Arminius opposed to Calvinism, and particularly to the doctrine of free-grace opposed to predestination; but even in Holland the theological meaning was quickly complicated by diverse political considerations, and in England the political complications multiplied when Archbishop Laud made the doctrine of free-will an official article of belief. By the middle years of the century the term became a loose appellation for everything that was bad—or good, depending on the speaker's political and religious persuasion—in Laud's relentless policy towards conformism. And even this characterization of the term will not account for the position of certain individual spirits like Milton, who rejected episcopacy

[1] *Works*, IV, 242. [2] *Works*, V, 9. [3] *Ibid.* p. 2.

THE FREE-WILL CONTROVERSY

and kingship but believed in free-will, or of certain Royalists who believed in episcopacy but rejected free-will.[1]

When his political enemies called Bramhall an 'Arminian', (they called him also 'Bishop Bramble'), they were referring to his Laudian zeal in administering the diocese of Derry and later the see of Armagh. When Hobbes used the term it retained still some of its political opprobrium. Hobbes's description of Arminianism as 'the readiest way to ecclesiastical promotion'[2] is an echo of the famous epigram which Bishop Morley of Winchester made in reply to the question, 'What do the Arminians hold?' They hold, he said, all the best bishoprics and deaneries in England.[3] For the most part, however, Hobbes used the word in its theological sense, and the issue between him and Bramhall turned on the implications of God's foreknowledge.

Both men agreed that God had absolute foreknowledge. For Hobbes this implied that all things are necessary, since if they were not, some of the things which God foreknew might not come to pass, and 'the prescience of God is quite taken away'.[4] Hobbes perceived very rightly that God's foreknowledge is not the *cause* of the things foreknown, because foreknowledge is a type of knowledge, 'and knowledge depends on the existence of the things known, and not they on it'.[5] But, though God's foreknowledge does not cause all events foreknown to come to pass, it implies that they must come to pass, for if they did not they would not be foreknown, since foreknowledge means knowing that which cannot be otherwise, and necessary means 'that which cannot possibly be otherwise'.[6] The problem therefore which confronted the Arminian theologian was: how is God's foreknowledge consistent with man's freedom?

Bramhall's reply was based on his conception of God's foreknowledge. 'The knowledge of God comprehends all times in a point, by reason of the eminence and virtue of its infinite perfection.'[7] From man's vantage point this type of knowledge must be called foreknowledge, but for God it is actually a

[1] For an excellent survey of English Arminianism and its Dutch antecedents, see Rosalie L. Colie, *Light and Enlightenment* (Cambridge University Press, 1957). Other useful information will be found in G. R. Cragg, *From Puritanism to the Age of Reason* (Cambridge University Press, 1950), pp. 4, 14–36 and *passim*, and A. W. Harrison, *Arminianism* (London, 1937).
[2] *Works*, v, 2. [3] Cited by Clarendon, *Life of . . . Himself* (Oxford, 1827), I, 56.
[4] *Works*, v, 17–18. [5] *Works*, IV, 246. [6] *Works*, v, 19. [7] *Ibid.* p. 430.

knowledge of past, present and future comprehended simultaneously. This means that God's knowledge of any future event does not depend on his knowledge of that event's antecedent causes, and hence necessity cannot be inferred from foreknowledge. 'God did know that Judas should betray Christ; but Judas was not necessitated to be a traitor by God's knowledge. If Judas had not betrayed Christ, then God had not foreknown that Judas should betray him.'[1] God foreknows every thing, but in matters affecting human volition, the determining agent is man's own unfettered will. God knows what choices man will make, but he has left man free to choose. As God, in Milton's words, said, the fallen angels themselves decreed

> Their own revolt, not I: if I foreknew,
> Foreknowledge had no influence on their fault,
> Which had no less prov'd certain unforeknown.
> So without least impulse or shadow of Fate,
> Or aught by me immutably foreseen,
> They trespass, Authors to themselves in all
> Both what they judge and what they choose; for so
> I form'd them free, and free they must remain,
> Till they enthrall themselves. . . .[2]

It was one of the ironies of English religious history that Milton should have been in complete agreement with the Royalist Bishop on this and other points of Arminian theology. Some of Milton's arguments in *The Christian Doctrine* closely resemble Bramhall's, and sound as though they were directed against Hobbes:

I allow that future events which God has foreseen, will happen certainly, but not of necessity. They will happen certainly, because the divine prescience cannot be deceived, but they will not happen necessarily, because prescience can have no influence on the object foreknown, inasmuch as it is only an intransitive action. What therefore is to happen according to contingency and the free will of men, is not the effect of God's prescience, but is produced by the free agency of its own natural causes, the future spontaneous inclination of which is perfectly known to God. Thus God foreknew that Adam would fall of his own free will; his fall was therefore certain, but not necessary, since it proceeded from his own free will, which is incompatible with necessity.[3]

[1] *Ibid.* p. 431. [2] *Paradise Lost*, III, 116–25.
[3] *The Christian Doctrine* (trans. Bishop Sumner) in *The Works of John Milton* (Columbia edition, New York, 1933), XIV, 85–7.

Milton and Bramhall also claimed that if all human acts followed necessarily from the absolute decrees of God, God would be unjust in blaming men for their sins; the blame must in each case attach to God himself, who was the author of the sin. Bramhall developed this argument into a number of ethical 'inconveniences' implicit in the doctrine of necessity. These may be summarized as follows:

1. That laws which prohibit any action will (if all actions are externally determined) be unjust.
2. That all consultations are vain.
3. That admonitions to men of understanding are of no more use, than to children, fools, and madmen.
4. That praise, dispraise, reward and punishment, are in vain.
5. That counsels, arts, arms, books, instruments, study, tutors, medicines, are in vain.[1]

Hobbes entered a general denial to these particulars, and then repudiated each one separately. The first 'inconvenience' drew from him a clear statement of his theory of capital punishment.[2] Suppose, he said, there is a man who is executed for a capital crime. We do not punish him because he was *necessitated* 'by strength of temptation' to commit his crime, but rather because we believe that his execution will deter others from committing the same crime, and because we are anxious to prevent him, effectively and absolutely, from committing the same crime again. But, it will be asked, 'how is it just to kill one man to amend another, if what were done were *necessary*?' To this Hobbes answered that the transgressor was killed not because his actions were necessitated but because they were noxious, and society has the right to kill within the law for its own self-preservation as much as men in the state of nature before there was law had the right to kill for the same reason. Thus the exercise of law is just, because it deters future crimes, and in the case of capital law, because it has the added function of destroying what is noxious.

Consultations are equally effectual because 'it is the *consultation* that *causeth* a man, and *necessitateth* him to choose to do one thing rather than another'.

[1] See *Works*, IV, 252, where Hobbes thus accurately summarizes Bramhall's arguments.
[2] *Works*, IV, 253-4.

119

I

But it seemeth his Lordship reasons thus: If I must do this rather than that, I shall do this rather than that, though I consult not at all; which is a false proposition and a false consequence, and no better than this: If I shall live till tomorrow, I shall live till tomorrow, though I run myself through with a sword today.[1]

Consultations are necessary causes of an action, and the same may be said for admonitions (the third 'inconvenience'), and for counsels, arts, arms, instruments, books, study, medicines, and the like (the fifth 'inconvenience').

In dealing with the problem of praise and dispraise Hobbes invoked his doctrine of ethical relativism. What do we mean when we say a thing is good? We mean that we like it, or that someone else likes it, or that it is approved by the state or commonwealth. 'Does my Lord think that no action can please me, or him, or the commonwealth that should proceed from *necessity*? Things may be therefore *necessary*, and yet *praiseworthy*, as also necessary, and yet *dispraised*.'[2] Of course, we cannot influence a completed course of action by expressing our attitude towards it; but this does not mean that our praise and dispraise, or our rewards and punishments, are in vain. They have the effect of influencing future actions by 'framing the will' to good and evil. In short, as regards the thing praised, praise is no more than the expression of a personal (or a public, but still subjective) attitude; as regards future actions praise is a causal link in the chain of necessary effects. Hobbes thought it was a very great praise that Velleius Paterculus gave Cato, 'where he says that he was good by *nature, et quia aliter esse non potuit*'.[3]

But, asks Bramhall, what is to become of piety, if 'this opinion be once radicated in the minds of men, that there is no true liberty, and that all things come to pass inevitably'?[4] What is the use of prayer? 'We indeed know not what good or evil shall happen to us: but this we know, that if all things be necessary, our devotions and endeavours cannot alter that which must be.'[5] And what meaning can we assign to repentance? And how can we exempt God from blame in the production of evil and sin? And how exempt him from injustice in venting his wrath on sinners? We must either 'allow liberty, or destroy Church as well as commonwealth, religion as well as policy'.[6]

[1] *Ibid.* pp. 254–5. [2] *Ibid.* pp. 255–6. [3] *Ibid.* p. 256. [4] *Works*, v, 197–8.
[5] *Ibid.* p. 198. [6] *Ibid.*

We will not be surprised to learn that Hobbes had ready answers to these questions; even so, he trod delicately when considering the subject of piety He admitted that there are many men so deficient in their reasoning powers 'that the dispute of this question will rather hurt than help their piety'. Nevertheless it was the Bishop who raised this question; and 'truth is truth'; so Hobbes will not be silent.

The *necessity* of events [he asserted] does not of itself draw with it any *impiety* at all. For *piety* consisteth only in two things; one, that we honour God in our hearts, which is, that we think as highly of his *power* as we can, for to honour anything is nothing else but to think it to be of great power; the other is, that we signify that honour and esteem by our words and actions, which is called *cultus*, or *worship of God*.[1]

Thus, if a man accepts the doctrine of necessity he is rather more than less pious, because he is acknowledging God's omnipotence, which is the same as to say he is honouring God's power, and hence is performing an essential act of piety. Again, the inner conviction that God is omnipotent leads in turn to certain outward acts and signs of this conviction. These acts consist of our verbal acknowledgment of God's power, and this acknowledgment is what we mean by worship. So that we must conclude that necessity, which leads us to believe in God's power, promotes piety, which is our inner and outward recognition of that power.

One form of worship is prayer. It is true that prayer cannot move God's will, 'his will being unchangeable'; Hobbes did not shrink from this consequence of determinism. But he maintained that the 'end of prayer is not to *move* but to *honour* God Almighty, in acknowledging that what we ask can be effected by him only'.[2] When we pray we are not petitioning God for some redress of a wrong or other future benefit to ourselves; rather we are giving thanks for God's blessings in general, for all those benefits to ourselves which have been preordained and rendered immutable by the power of God. It is manifest that prayer is no *cause* of God's blessings, and in that sense it can be called futile; but it is still a pious act, because piety consists in just such recognition of God's power as can be found in prayer.

As for repentance, it is 'nothing else but a glad returning into the right way, after the grief of being out of the way'.[3]

[1] *Works*, IV, 257. [2] *Ibid.* p. 258. [3] *Ibid.* p. 257.

It is the name we give to our 'grief for the error, and joy for returning'. And though the cause of the error and the cause of returning are both necessary, we will still grieve and rejoice. 'The *necessity* of the actions taketh away neither of those parts of repentance.'

The same relentless kind of analysis was applied to the problem of sin. With perfect audacity Hobbes admitted that God was the cause (that is to say, the first cause) of sin. Does this make God unjust? No, because '*power irresistible justifies all actions, really and properly*'.[1] That which God does is made just by his doing it whether or not his actions conform to the notions of justice which 'men make amongst themselves here by pacts and covenants'. Why then did God cause sin? Because it pleased him to do so, and because he had the power to do so. Did he not imply as much in the Book of Job—Hobbes's favourite book of Scripture—where he justified his afflicting of Job 'by telling him of his *power*: (Job xl.9): *Hast thou, saith God, an arm like mine?* (Job xxviii.4): *Where wert thou when I laid the foundations of the earth?* and the like'.[2] But does this doctrine destroy the goodness of God? Does it, as Bramhall put it, make him 'to be a hater of mankind, and to delight in the torments of his creatures; whereas the very dogs licked the sores of Lazarus, in pity and commiseration of him'?[3] It does not.

Health, sickness, ease, torments, life and death, are without all passions in [God] dispensed by him; and he putteth an end to them when they end, and a beginning when they begin, according to his eternal purpose, which cannot be resisted. That the necessity argueth a delight of God in the torments of his creatures, is even as true as that it was pity and commiseration in the dogs that made them lick the sores of Lazarus.[4]

What then becomes of God's mercy? Is he not tyrannical and merciless if he makes millions to burn eternally for sins which they could not prevent and for which they are blameless? Perhaps, Hobbes replied, God can be called merciless for doing these things, but he would have been no less merciless if man had free-will; for even then God could have delivered men from punishment by preventing them from choosing evil. 'How can the Bishop praise God for his goodness, who thinks he hath created millions of millions to burn eternally when he could

---

[1] *Ibid.* p. 250.   [2] *Ibid.* p. 249.   [3] *Works*, v, 202.   [4] *Ibid.* p. 213.

have kept them so easily from committing any faults?'[1] In any case Hobbes did not believe that punishment after death was eternal; he interpreted the phrase 'second death' in Revelation xx:13, 14 to mean that the damned will suffer some kind of mental anguish for a limited period, after which they will be annihilated altogether.[2]

It need hardly be pointed out that Hobbes's views on piety were profoundly offensive to Bramhall. They were 'destructive to true godliness'.[3] They made worship a mere matter of politeness in esteeming God's power. They made power the only attribute of God worthy of esteem. They reduced prayer and repentance to bloodless abstractions. They denied God's mercy and goodness, and they deprived man of love, faith, and hope. But piety, Bramhall retorted, is more than the recognition of power. God is good as well as strong. '*Magnos facile laudamus, bonos lubenter.*'[4] Man is free to sin, and free to repent, free to be saved, and free to be damned through all eternity. Whoever denies this makes a mockery of piety and is himself impious.

And there the matter rested. In his prefatory remarks to the whole controversy Bramhall said that he had proved his point simply by *planning* to write against Hobbes. Apparently he did not consider this argument conclusive, because he wrote his treatise anyway. And we are to be grateful that he did. It is a good treatise—clear, forceful, well-argued, not infrequently eloquent, only infrequently vituperative. It deserves to be praised for these reasons, but it is by no means certain that, as T. S. Eliot will have it, Bramhall had raised unanswerable objections, or that Bramhall's opponent was 'the most eminent example in his age of a particularly lazy type of thinker'— 'one of those extraordinary little upstarts whom the chaotic motions of the Renaissance tossed into an eminence which they hardly deserved and have never lost'.[5] Mr Eliot, it must be observed, wrote with less detachment and smaller understanding of the issues at stake in the controversy than did Bramhall.

After Bramhall, three other writers—Philip Tanny, Benjamin Laney, and Cudworth—attacked Hobbes's determinism in separate treatises.

[1] *Ibid.* p. 216.   [2] *Leviathan*, p. 300.   [3] *Works*, v, 201.   [4] *Ibid.*
[5] T. S. Eliot, 'John Bramhall', in *Selected Essays*, 3rd ed. (London, 1951), pp. 359, 355.

Tanny was a Londoner, perhaps a clergyman, who flourished in the 1650's.[1] He wrote against Hobbes in 1656, only a few months after Hobbes had published his reply to Bramhall. Tanny's treatise was unpublished and is now lost, but we can gather something of its nature from two surviving letters which he sent to Hobbes. 'I do not,' he wrote in the first letter, 'conceive my selfe bound to defend the Bishop of Derry, but to Looke after the evinceing of truth.'[2] What this 'truth' was we cannot with certainty tell, but it was more than likely a type of 'religious' truth. Tanny wrote to Hobbes that it 'had been well notwithstanding, you had silenced your Judgment [of Bramhall] until your affection had bin more sweately carryed forth to glorify Jesus Christ and not your own wit, which doth much abound in diverse parts of your Little booke'.[3]

In his second letter Tanny put a number of questions to Hobbes about free-will and at the same time revealed something of his own pathetic situation:

Sr.

I am soe poore, that I cannot fetch my things from the presse, I pray you Excuse mee that I send to you noe sooner: my troubles are many, as well as your occasions. Excuse mee withall, that I have put the transactions in printeing, I confesse I had this thought, that by this meanes I should the more clearly gaine an an'swere from you to my Questions. Which are in short these.

1. Whether doe you not suppose that every man hath a will to doe, or to forbeare a thing, wrought in him by such strong influences which he cannot resist.

2. Whether doe you make freedome to consist eyther

1. In the not being hindred in the doing of things which we have a wish to doe, or

2ndly. In the willingness of the will freely chusing to doe that which it is wrought to wish for else

3rd. In any third thing, which I yet cannot imagine.

I did propound a third question for your selfe to ask yourselfe, but being satisfyed in it I expect noe answere. Sr I am heartily yours, what ever you thinke of mee. Let me heare from you, as soon as you

---

[1] I have not been able to discover more about him. He might have been the Philip Tandy who is entered in the British Museum Catalogue as the author of *Christ Knocking at the Doore* (London, 1655).

[2] Philip Tanny to Hobbes, 13 May, 1656. British Museum, *Additional Manuscripts*, 32, 553, fol. 2 r.

[3] *Ibid.* fol. 1.

can, and then I shall goe about that publique satisfaction to you, which I hope will not bee grievous. Excuse mee, in every thing, which you suspect me in, I am a riddle, and you may bee mistaken in mee. Doe as charitably, as I shall doe with you, and doe desire God to doe with my owne soule. I am, Sr, whatever you surmise.

Your affectionately humble servt

Philip Tanny.[1]

What Hobbes thought of this eccentric mixture of humility and intellectual curiosity is not known. If he replied to Tanny he must have answered 'yes' to question one, though he might have quarrelled about its language. To question two he would have assented only to the first part. There is no reason to think that Hobbes would have had any difficulty in meeting Tanny's arguments, however those may have been developed in the treatise which was never 'fetched from the presse'.

Nor is there reason to believe that Hobbes was at all disturbed by Bishop Laney's animadversions. Laney was successively Bishop of Peterborough, Lincoln, and Ely. He was a Cambridge man, educated at Christ's, and afterwards Master of Pembroke Hall. As a Bishop his policies were Laudian, and he was denounced by Prynne as 'one of the professed Arminians, Laud's creatures to prosecute his designs in the university of Cambridge'.[2] His treatise against Hobbes (1677) was in the form of a commentary appended to a reprint of Hobbes's *Of Liberty and Necessity*. Laney offered no substantial argument against determinism, contenting himself merely with affirming that the will is free. He was more interested in what he thought were the immoral and irreligious consequences of Hobbes's doctrine.

If M. *Hobbes* had vented his new Speculations upon making Faces and Distortions, turning and tossing the poor Figures up and down, and then guessing at some Reasons of them, which he merrily calls his Opticks; I say, if Mr. *Hobbes* had spent his Time and Philosophy upon these onely, he had onely disturbed the Common-wealth of Images and Representations, which are nothing, and therefore ought not to have been disturbed by any in those his pleasant Speculations. But when (against mine and every bodies Interest) he

---

[1] Tanny to Hobbes, 2 July, 1656. British Museum, *Additional Manuscripts* 32, 553, fol. 3.

[2] Quoted in the *DNB* from William Prynne, *Canterburies Doome* (London, 1646), p. 177.

labours to introduce a Necessity into all mens Actions, that they have no power to do more or less than they do, he takes away the nature of Vertues and Vices, and so their relation to Reward and Punishment; and by consequence leaves no place for Hope or Fear: which must needs shake not onely the Foundation of all Religion, but even of humane Society. It is such a pernicious piece of Philosophy, as a Wise man would not, and a Fool should not be suffered to vent; fitter indeed for a Beadle's, than a Scholar's Whip; and to him I leave him.[1]

II

No one in the seventeenth century wrestled more strenuously with the problem of free-will than Cudworth. He wrote and revised and wrote again until he completed an enormous treatise entitled *A Discourse of Liberty and Necessity*. Of this work, which was seen in its entirety by Cudworth's eighteenth-century editor Thomas Birch, 945 folio pages comprising four fragmentary treatises survive.[2] A fifth fragment (British Museum, *Additional Manuscripts* 4978) was published by the Reverend John Allen in 1838 as *A Treatise of Free-Will*. The rest of the large *Discourse* is lost, as indeed are the majority of Cudworth's manuscripts, including one seen by Birch and called 'An explanation of Hobbes's notion of God and of the extension of spirits'.

In the free-will manuscripts Cudworth directed his fire against two types of determinism—the Hobbist and Calvinist varieties. His recognition that these were separate types constituted an advance over the criticism of some of his Anglican contempo-

[1] Benjamin Laney, 'Observations' appended to Thomas Hobbes, *A Letter About Liberty & Necessity* (London, 1677), pp. 102–4.

[2] British Museum, *Additional Manuscripts* 4979–82. These will henceforth be referred to by their manuscript and folio numbers, as thus: 4979, fol. 1. For the provenance of these manuscripts, and for some plausible conjecture, based on handwriting and internal evidence, of their order of composition, see J. A. Passmore, *Ralph Cudworth*, 'Appendix', pp. 107–13. Microfilm copies of the manuscripts are available at the Columbia University Library. The manuscripts are discussed by Passmore, *passim*, from whose discussion I have learned much; by John Muirhead, *The Platonic Tradition in Anglo-Saxon Philosophy* (London, 1931), Appendix; and by Marilyn Meyer, *The Philosophy of Ralph Cudworth* (unpublished doctoral dissertation, Columbia University, 1952), *passim*. Dr Meyer has also provided summaries of 4979–4952 as well as a reprint of 'Liberum Arbitrium', Cudworth's appendix summary to 4981.

raries who preferred to see in Hobbes's determinism another instance of Calvinist predestinarianism. The Calvinists themselves disavowed any such connection, but their protests were of no avail. To the assertion made by the Calvinist William Barlee that he would 'as soon own the Devil for his Master, as Mr Hobbs', Thomas Pierce replied that Barlee 'doth but write like one of the lowest of [Hobbes's] Disciples. . . . The *monstrous Leviathan Hobbs* hath assisted Barlee's party . . . in asserting their Doctrins of Gods Decrees'.[1] But Cudworth distinguished between Hobbist and Calvinist determinism. Hobbes believed that God's role in causation was to *initiate* the course of events, after which all events proceeded from natural, second causes, whereas the Calvinists held that all events proceeded directly from God's arbitrary decrees. Of course man is not 'free' in either view, but Cudworth saw clearly enough that Hobbes's doctrine had less need of God, was in fact more secular and 'scientific' and less obsessed with the notions of divine election, sin, and damnation than the Calvinist doctrine was. Cudworth, with his love of scholarship and his passion for classifying ideas, traced Hobbes's brand of determinism to the Stoics, and called it 'Divine Fatalism Natural', though he added that the purely divine element in Hobbes's system was spurious, since it represented a material deity incompatible with the true notion of God. The Calvinist variety of determinism he called 'Divine Fatalism Arbitrary'. He hated both types with a perfect hatred.

To refute Hobbes, Cudworth felt it was only necessary to show that spirit exists. If it does not, if, that is, everything in the universe is material, and is moved by external pressure only, then every event in the universe must be strictly determined. Hobbes therefore denied free-will because he 'denied all spirituality and immateriality and made all cogitation, intellection and volition to be nothing but mechanical motion and passion from objects without. . . . Wherefore it is a sufficient confutation of [Hobbes] to show that there is another substance in the world besides body',[2] and this, said Cudworth, he had already done in *The True Intellectual System of the Universe*.

[1] Thomas Pierce, *EAYTONTIMΩPOYMENOΣ, or the Self-Revenger Exemplified in Mr William Barlee* (London, 1658), p. 71. Barlee's statement is quoted by Pierce from William Barlee, *A Necessary Vindication*, a work which appears to be no longer extant.
[2] 4979, fol. 61.

According to Cudworth, this vital connection between materialism and determinism was missed by Bramhall. Bramhall, he said, wrote against Hobbes 'like a Scholastick Divine'; he dwelt on small points of logic and failed to grasp the essential materialistic assumptions of Hobbes's doctrine. He did not perceive that 'physickall fatalism is really one and the same thing with Saddiceism and Atheism'.[1] Moreover, Cudworth maintained that Bramhall's criticism of Hobbes was vitiated by a faulty psychology according to which the will is regarded as a separate entity or faculty, as though one could say that 'the will and not the man willeth'. Bramhall, in short, approached Hobbes from the wrong end of the stick, and though he reached a correct conclusion he did not really prove his case. The only way to refute 'materialist fatalists' such as Hobbes is to show that self-moving spirit does exist.

But if Cudworth rejected Bramhall's method, he did repeat with approval a number of Bramhall's logical arguments, and even, on occasion, quoted Bramhall's words, though without acknowledgment. For instance, he agreed with Bramhall that the disjunctive proposition '*Either it will rain tomorrow or it will not rain*' demonstrates the possibility of contingency. Hobbes's argument that the proposition was untrue unless either of its members was necessary represented to Cudworth a confusion between logical necessity and physical necessity. A proposition, Cudworth said, may be true even when both of its members are untrue, or even when both are impossible. The proposition $2 \times 2 = 10$, therefore $4 \times 2 = 20$ shows that the whole may be necessary, but not either of its parts. The truth of the proposition lies in the disjunction itself and not in its members, a point which Aristotle made clear, and which Hobbes, 'not well versed in Aristotle',[2] failed to understand.

Similarly, Bramhall was right and Hobbes was wrong on the question of God's foreknowledge. Cudworth said that if he thought foreknowledge were incompatible with free-will he would give up his belief in foreknowledge and save free-will, for without free-will there could be no praise or blame, no moral responsibility, no right or wrong. But foreknowledge and free-will are perfectly compatible. 'The truth of a proposition concerning the future is its relation or conformity with the event

[1] 4979, fol. 60. [2] 4980, fol. 267.

itself and not the knowableness of the thing conceived a priori by antecedent necessary causes.'[1] All is *present* to God in eternity. 'Though there be future contingents that are not foreknowable by antecedent causes, yet they are all foreknown by God to speak respectively to our time "by anticipation of futurity" but to speak respectively to God's eternity ... by looking down from a higher watch.'[2] Man sees the future as the culmination of past and present events; God sees all events simultaneously, and hence his foreknowledge does not depend on antecedent causes, and is freed from necessity.

These logical arguments in favour of free-will were, in Cudworth's opinion, confirmed by human experience. We know that we are free. We act as if we are free. We praise and blame the free acts of others. Our moral life is meaningful only within the context of freedom. Without free-will there would be no 'measure or norma in nature'. The 'naturality' (i.e. the absolute character) of a moral act would be destroyed, and with it the whole order of being. Free-will is 'agreeable to the phenomena', it is a part of our experience and it is supported by logic.

But experience and logic can only tell us 'that it is'. It does not tell us 'what it is'. To tell us 'what it is' was the major task Cudworth set for himself in the manuscripts. The theory he developed in pursuit of this aim—and not the minor polemical skirmishes in which he engaged along the way—must represent his true answer to Hobbes and the Calvinists. It is a theory of high philosophical interest, though it is not without its difficulties. Cudworth perfected it over several decades during a period when both his public doctrines and his personal character were under attack;[3] but he persevered, and as we follow the development of the theory we cannot fail to be impressed by its seriousness of purpose, by the magnitude of Cudworth's labours, and by his feeling, everywhere implied, that if the notion of free-will is not finally established, the whole fabric of morality and religion must crumble beneath the onslaughts of Hobbism.

All men, said Cudworth, have the power in themselves to

[1] 4980, fol. 293. [2] 4981, fol. 69.
[3] For an account of these reactions, and especially for the attack on Cudworth's liberal theology which Ralph Widdrington made under the guise of an attack on Cudworth's administration at Christ's, see Marjorie H. Nicolson, 'Christ's College and the Latitude-Men', *MP*, xxvii (1929), 35–53.

cleave to virtue. On this point all the libertarians were agreed. To More and to John Smith a 'Power in our selves' to do good was a further proof of the existence of spirit.[1] For Cudworth there were two important questions—what is the nature of this power, and what is its scope?

It is, said Cudworth, a very small power; but it is uniquely human. God does not have it because he can do only good. Animals do not have it because they are indifferent to good and evil and can do only what their appetites and instincts dictate. Man alone possesses the power to choose freely. Where does this power reside? It is certainly not an attribute of passion, because passion is moved by the 'mere Swinges & Impetuocitys of Nature that have no internal self-flexibility in them'.[2] Beasts are ruled entirely by passion and Cudworth agreed with 'ye Author of ye Booke *De Homine*' that the liberty of beasts consists only in the absence of external impediments.[3] Is the power of free-choice then a function of human reason, as Bramhall thought it was? Cudworth did not believe so. He divided reason into two types—inferior reason, which comprehends an individual's private utility, and superior reason, which dictates a man's sense of 'honesty' or moral excellence. As both types of reason are attributes of spirit and not inert matter they 'contribute something of their own'—that is, they are self-moving. But they are not self-directing or 'self-conscious'. They are not above their own activity. They cannot change or direct or act. Hence they are not the same as the Will.

Nor is Will the result of rational understanding, the last act necessarily following a process of judgment. If it were 'it would be nothing else but the Understanding it self Extended outwards towards action. And so there would be as little Liberty and self power in it as there is in Brutish Appetites themselves' —a view which would 'again destroy the Nature of Sinne'.[4] Cudworth therefore insisted that the Will must be separate from Reason. But separate in a special way. Reason and Will are not separate substances, because both comprise the same soul. Neither are they separate faculties of the soul, because to divide

[1] Henry More, *Enchiridion Metaphysicum*, xxv, 7, and John Smith, *Select Discourses*, p. 83.
[2] 4981, fol. 1 of Appendix Summary.   [3] 4979, fol. 2.
[4] 4981, fol. 3 of Appendix Summary.

the soul in this way would be to revive the occult categories of scholasticism, and would moreover make it impossible for one faculty to influence another. Reason is the whole soul and Will is the whole soul. How then do they differ? In this, that Will is the soul redoubled upon itself. In modern parlance we might describe it as a type of *Gestalt* equal to and at the same time greater than the sum of its parts. Cudworth himself resorted to metaphor to make this difficult docrtine intelligible. He compared the redoubled soul to a 'resounding Echo', an echo of an echo. It is not, he said, 'a straight line but a Circle, a thing collected into itself—within itself and superior to itselfe'.[1] It is the soul 'holding it Selfe as it were in its own hand'.[2] It can weild, steere, guide ye whole Soul, and exercise a power and dominion over it, arbitrate all Difference and determine all Strife & Discord in it; . . . this can be no other than ye whole Soule Redoubled upon it Selfe, which being as it were with in it Selfe, and comprehending it Selfe . . . hath a Sui potestas over it Selfe, and can command it Selfe or turne it Selfe this way and yt way.[3]

What is the scope of this power? Does the reduplicated soul exert itself arbitrarily? In short, is the will free to act in any way it pleases? Cudworth replied emphatically that it is not. He rejected the doctrine of 'indifferency' as vehemently as he rejected material fatalism. His argument was that if the will is indifferent to good and evil, then a man is no more deserving of blame for choosing evil than he would be if his act were strictly necessitated. If the moral life consists of *activa indifferentia* then there is no moral responsibility; no one can be praised or blamed for doing what the will has elected to do gratuitously.[4] The self-determination of the will is always a self-determination 'for the sake of some good'.

This redoubled self-active life of the Soul which is really the same thing with that which is called Will must needs have some naturall and necessary inclination upon it. For we do not will merely because we will but it is always for the sake of some good. Nemo eligit ut eligat, Nemo vult ut velit, Nemo facit ut faciat, the end of all motion and action is something that is not moved but standing.[5]

By taking the position that the Will is necessarily inclined towards the good, Cudworth gave much ground to the deter-

[1] 4981, fol. 4 of Appendix Summary. [2] 4979, fol. 5. [3] 4979, fol. 5.
[4] 4982, fol. 15. [5] 4981, fol. 4.

minists, but he believed that there is a large range of behaviour in which the Will is free. This results from the fact that although the Will is inclined towards good in general, and is averse to evil in general, it cannot always distinguish between the two. In the ordinary choices which confront the individual, good and evil are commonly mixed together. They 'grow up together almost inseparably', said Milton; they are 'two twins cleaving together . . .'.[1] The individual, said Cudworth, is confronted with choices which he cannot always decide on the basis of his habitual disposition towards good; hence he is free. In the mixture of good and evil 'is a great compasse for the will or redoubled self-active life to exercise contingent liberty in and actively to determine itself to this or that particular good, that is either to the good of honesty or to the good of utility and Jucundity, to the Divine or Animal life.'[2]

The attempt to avoid the pitfalls of determinism on the one hand and 'indifferency' on the other involved Cudworth in a serious dilemma. He rejected 'indifferency' by asserting that the Will, far from being indifferent to good and evil, was naturally inclined towards the good. This however placed him in a determinist position from which he extricated himself by declaring that the Will is free to choose in those cases—actually the majority of cases—in which the distinction between good and evil is obscured. Freedom is then a choice between two not very clear alternatives. But how is the choice made? If it is not determined, in the Hobbesian sense, by external antecedent causes, and if it is not a natural inclination towards the good, then it must be an arbitrary choice, indifferent to good and evil; and if it is arbitrary it cannot be praised or blamed. This was Cudworth's dilemma. He insisted that praise and blame must form the basis of any intelligible doctrine of free-will, but he was finally left with a type of freedom to which praise and blame could not be applied. Nor was he able to obviate this difficulty by defining evil as a privation of good, 'a discongruity to our nature', the failure of the Will or redoubled soul to exert itself towards good, and the 'sluggish remission' of the Will 'sinking down to the lower'.[3] It remains impossible to apportion blame whether the Will actively chooses evil or passively fails to exert

[1] *Areopagitica* in *The Works of John Milton* (Columbia edition), IV, 310.
[2] 4981, fol. 7. [3] 4980, fol. 141.

itself toward some higher good. The failure of the Will to receive the good must be accounted for in some way. If the failure was not 'necessitated' by antecedent causes then it was 'indifferent'.

In the end Cudworth accepted 'indifferency'. He did so with a noticeable lack of enthusiasm and after what must have been an agony of doubt, if we are to judge from the very large number of manuscript revisions, corrections and interpolations which marked his treatment of this question.[1] It is true that he may have altered his opinion in the completed treatise now lost to us, but I think this is doubtful; the whole tendency of his analysis led him to the conclusion that there is an 'indifferent Voluntaneity' which makes a man free to neglect the good life. It is a strange conclusion. It meant that freedom is arbitrary, that we cannot justifiably blame a man for an immoral act, that praise and blame cannot support the theory of free-will. Cudworth was defeated in his attempt to replace Hobbist and Calvinist determinism with a type of freedom that preserved the absolute character of morality. Of this absolute character he was never in any doubt; but he could find no way to unite it with his theory of freedom. Yet we cannot say that his defeat was inglorious. His tenacity of purpose, his high seriousness, his ability to lay bare aspects of the problem which Bramhall ignored or misunderstood—these qualities command our respect and even our admiration. He carried out his endeavours on a heroic scale, and it is always fascinating to watch his mind, like the 'redoubled Soul' itself, 'turning this way and that way' in its quest for a solution.

[1] See 4982, fol. 20 ff.

CHAPTER VII

HOBBES AND LIBERTINISM

After the Restoration a new type of criticism emerged. The high philosophical tone maintained in the polemics against Hobbes's materialism and determinism gave way to an eruption of popular feeling against 'Hobbists' and 'libertines'. Materialism and determinism were after all relatively abstruse subjects, requiring of their opponents at least some degree of philosophical training; but in matters affecting public conduct, in questions of practical morality, every clergyman considered himself an expert. When the indecent behaviour of courtiers and wits became a national scandal, an outraged clergy looked for the cause. They found it, or thought they found it, in the 'libertine' principles of Hobbes.

The word 'libertinism' was used in England as early as 1563.[1] At first it referred to free-thinking or antinomian opinion. Within a few decades it acquired a second meaning— the disregard of moral restraint, especially in relations between the sexes. Gabriel Harvey spoke in 1593 of the 'whole brood of venerous Libertines, that knowe no reason but appetite, no Lawe but Luste'.[2] Both meanings of the term continued to be used throughout the seventeenth century, though they were kept more or less distinct until after the Restoration, when they were combined in the attacks on Hobbes. Hobbes was a 'libertine' because he denied religion; the courtiers and wits were 'libertines' because they led dissolute, immoral lives. What Hobbes's critics tried to show was that the second type of libertinism resulted from the first, that the immoral conduct of the courtiers was inspired by the free-thinking opinions of Hobbes.

Irreligion 'tis true in its practice hath been still the companion of every Age, but its open and publick defence seems the peculiar of this; 'Tis but of late that men come to defend ill living and secure themselves against their own guilt, by an open defyance to all the

[1] O.E.D., 'libertinism'. [2] Ibid.

great maxims of Piety and Virtue . . . and most of the bad Principles of this Age are of no earlier a date then [sic] one very ill Book, are indeed but the spawn of the Leviathan.[1]

By arguing in this way the critics paid only the slightest attention to what Hobbes actually taught; they ignored the fact that his whole outlook told against licence and absolute egoism and that the commonwealth which he envisioned was intended to deliver men from the *bellum omnium contra omnes* of the state of nature. They might have pointed out that Hobbes's objections to licence rested on strictly utilitarian, not on Christian grounds. Hobbes contended that licence ought to be suppressed not because it is 'immoral' or 'unjust', but because it frustrates the search for human felicity. To this point the critics surprisingly did not address themselves; they preferred instead to make large generalizations about Hobbes's enormous 'share in the debauchery of his generation'.[2] Bishop Parker assaulted those 'Apes of Wit'—

a sorte of Creatures that study nothing but Folly and Extravagance, that aspire to no higher Accomplishments than fine Phrases, terse Oaths, and gay Plumes, that pretend to no other stock of Learning but a few shavings of Wit gather'd out of Plays and Comedies; and these they abuse too, and labour to pervert their chaste Expressions to Obscene and Irreligious Purposes; and *Johnson* and *Fletcher* are prophaned, as well as Holy Scripture. . . . With what a greedy Confidence do they swallow down the Principles of the *Malmsbury Philosophy*, without any chewing or consideration? How huffingly will they assert . . . that Power is Right, and justifies all actions whatsoever, whether good or bad . . . and that the Laws of Nature are nothing but Maxims and Principles of meer self-interest! How boldly do they take up with these and other resembling Principles of Baseness and Irreligion, upon the bare Authority and proofless Assertions of one proud and haughty Philosopher?[3]

Robert Sharrock added a number of other 'Principles of Baseness' which he derived from Hobbes:

Fill yourselves with costly Wine and Oyntments and let none of you go without some part of his voluptuousnesse . . . oppresse the poor righteous man, spare not

---

[1] Charles Wolseley, *The Reasonableness of Scripture-Belief* (London, 1672), sigs. A3–4.

[2] John Vesey, 'The Life of primate Bramhall' in Bramhall, *Works* (Dublin, 1677), sig. nv.

[3] Samuel Parker, *A Discourse of Ecclesiastical Politie* (London, 1670), pp. xxii–xxiii, xxxv–xxxv..

the Widow and (which is perfect Hobbisme) *Let your strength be the Law of Justice and what is feeble count it little worth. Lay wait for the Righteous Man . . . . Examine him with Despitefullnesse . . . know his meeknesse . . . prove his Patience.* Do not only make your scoffs at Vertue, but which are acts worthy a *perfect Brave*; destroy it and root it out and then fear not to venture upon any acts of Impiety or Insolence.[1]

Principles such as these, which are a perversion or at best a parody of Hobbes's teaching, were nevertheless attributed to him by the majority of his critics, and were said to have inspired not only the widespread scepticism and naturalistic temper of the age, but also its immorality.

A smaller group of Restoration critics appears to have drawn a distinction between what Hobbes actually said and the way in which his doctrines were received by his readers. According to these critics, Hobbes was certainly immoral and anti-Christian, but it is questionable whether he actually planted the seeds of immorality in his readers; what is more likely, they argued, is that Hobbes's principles harmonized easily with the outlook of men who had already been corrupted before they came to read his work. John Eachard addressed the following remarks to Hobbes in his *Mr Hobbs's State of Nature Considered:*

For most of those that talk over those places of your *Books*, wherein you are singular, do it either out of *humour*, or because they are already *debauch'd*, or intend to be so, as soon as they can shake off all *modesty* and good *nature*, and can furnish themselves with some of your little *slender Philosophical pretences* to be wicked.[2]

And an anonymous writer who in 1705 made 'an inquiry into the causes of the late growth of infidelity' said that at the Restoration

the humour of being witty grew so much in vogue that to be thought so Men made a jest of the most serious business and even of Religion itself. It was the prevalence of this scoffing humour that made Mr Hobbs' writing so well received in the World, and so much applauded by the advocates of Irreligion and Libertinism.

Hobbes's 'Notions . . . fell in with the Capricious and Licentious Humour of the Age'.[3]

---

[1] R[obert] S[harrock], *De Finibus Virtutis Christianae* (Oxford, 1673), pp. 195–6.
[2] Eachard, p. 9.
[3] Quoted in R. H. Syfret, 'Some Early Reactions to the Royal Society', *Notes and Records of the Royal Society*, VII (April, 1950), 237.

This latter view, which seems much the sounder of the two opinions about Hobbes's influence, is largely ignored by modern writers on the subject. According to Macaulay, 'Hobbism soon became an almost essential part of the character of the fine gentleman', and was welcomed by thousands because it 'degraded religion into a mere affair of the state'.[1] Taine says that Hobbes 'erigeait le manuel de leur [the courtiers] conduite, et redigeat d'avance les axiomes qu'ils allaient traduire en actions'.[2] But the evidence for such positive statements is inconclusive. It rests upon the continued demand for Hobbes's work throughout the Restoration period; on the general outlook expressed in Restoration drama, where the 'Hobbist' is depicted as unprincipled and irreligious; and on the self-avowed Hobbism of the most famous of the English libertines, Rochester.

There is no doubt that Hobbes was widely read; the printing history of the *Leviathan* attests to this, and there are, moreover, copious extracts from Hobbes's works in commonplace books of the period.[3] Hobbes was also widely talked about. An anonymous *Character of a Town Gallant* mentions 'the Rattle of [the *Leviathan*] at *Coffee-houses*'[4] and another tract, which gives the 'symptomes of a town wit', says that the 'two *Poles* whereon all his discourses turn are *Atheism* and *Bawdry*' and that he 'boasts aloud that he holds his Gospel from the *Apostle of Malmesbury*'. But the writer adds 'it is more than probable he ne'r read, at least understood *ten* leaves of that unlucky *Author*'.[5]

In the heroic drama of the period the Hobbist was presented as a rebel, usurper, tyrant, or Machiavellian, and he expressed,

[1] Macaulay, *The History of England from the Accession of James II* (New York, 1855), I, 135.

[2] Taine, *Histoire de la Littérature Anglaise* (10th ed. Paris, 1899), III, 34. Other similar views are expressed in W. J. Courthope, *History of English Poetry* (London, 1903), III, 459; Johannes Prinz, *John Wilmot, Earl of Rochester* (Leipzig, 1927), pp. 16–18; R. G. Ham, *Otway and Lee* (New Haven, 1931), pp. 46–9; and (with reservations) Thomas H. Fujimura, *The Restoration Comedy of Wit* (Princeton, 1952), pp. 43–50.

[3] British Museum, *Sloan MSS.* 1458, 8888. The extracts from Hobbes appear alongside a mock 'Credo of Mr Hobbes' taken from Thomas Tenison's *Creed of Mr Hobbes Examined*. Also included in these commonplace books are profane satires, erotica, and quotations from contemporary plays.

[4] [Anon.] *Character of a Town Gallant* (London, 1675), p. 7.

[5] [Anon.] *The Character of a Coffee House, with the Symptomes of a Town Wit* (London, 1673), pp. 4–5.

either by word or deed, a point of view loosely adopted from the *Leviathan*, and largely distorted. Tyrants justified their conduct by claiming the prerogatives of a 'mortal god', Hobbes's absolute sovereign. Thus in Dryden's *Tyrannic Love* Maximum boasts:

> Who can do all things, can do nothing ill.
> Ill is rebellion 'gainst some higher power:
> The world may sin, but not its emperor.[1]

When in John Crowne's *Caligula* the virtuous Julia resists her emperor with these words: 'Sir, for the world I'd not my honour lose,' Caligula's retort is Hobbist in the extreme.

> Oh! I'm the fountain whence all honour flows.
> Yes, Madam; sure you are not to be told . . .
> I can make virtue scorn'd and vice esteem'd,
> I can make hell ador'd, and Heav'n blasphemed,
> Success, dominion, and the longest sword,
> Make any creeds believ'd, or gods ador'd.[2]

And in Elkanah Settle's *Empress of Morocco* (1673) the tyrant Crimalhaz endows Hobbes's conception of the state of nature with a historical context, and uses it to justify his own career in regicide, usurpation, and murder:

> This work, which we so roughly do begin,
> Zeal and Religion may perhaps call Sin.
> No; the more Barb'rous garb our Deeds assume,
> We nearer to our First perfection come,
> Since Nature first made Man wild, savage, strong,
> And his Blood hot, then when the world was young:
> If Infant-times such Rising valours bore,
> Why should not Riper Ages now do more.
> But whilst our Souls wax Tame, and Spirits Cold,
> We Only show th'unactive World grows Old.[3]

---

[1] Act V, scene i, in John Dryden, *Works*, ed. Scott and Saintsbury, III, 456. For a full discussion of Hobbes's influence on Dryden, see Louis Bredvold, 'Dryden, Hobbes and the Royal Society', *Modern Philology*, XXV (1928), 431 ff., and *The Intellectual Milieu of John Dryden* (Ann Arbor, 1934), *passim*. Bredvold concluded that although Dryden had read Hobbes with some care, and had attacked the concept of free will in a Hobbist way, his sceptical outlook was inconsistent with Hobbist dogmatism, and can instead be attributed to the influence of Pyrrhonism and the teachings of Sextus Empiricus.

[2] Act III, scene i, in John Crowne, *Works*, ed. Maidment and Logan, IV, 402.

[3] Elkanah Settle, *The Empress of Morocco* (London, 1673), Act III, scene ii.

The role which Hobbes played in Restoration heroic drama
was, in the words of a modern observer, 'much the same role as
that played by Machiavelli before him'.[1] The Hobbist was a
stage villain, his ideas a blend of ill-digested Machiavellian and
Hobbesian principles. But he is never presented sympathetically;
he is indeed held up to obloquy; so that we may justly conclude
that Hobbes's influence in this area was negative, and the uses
to which his ideas were put in the heroic drama can hardly be
said to have inspired the sort of conduct which the critics were
attacking.

In Restoration comedy, however, Hobbes's positive influence is more marked. The attitude towards life displayed in
the comedies of Dryden, Etherege, Wycherley and Congreve
may be described as roughly analogous to Hobbes's view of the
state of nature, at least insofar as the rakes who move through
the plays are licentious, predatory and rapacious. Such charac-
ters as Dorimant in Etherege's *The Man of Mode*, Jack Horner in
Wycherley's *The Country Wife*, and Mirabel in Congreve's *The
Way of the World* are types of wits who show no trace of moral
scruple; they pursue pleasure uninhibitedly, for its own sake,
and without regard to the feelings of others. If it serves their
purpose, which is the purpose of gratifying their senses, they
will break trusts and betray friendships. Their egoism is absolute,
and they look upon this as 'natural', as closer to the spirit of
human nature than conventional morality will ever bring them.
In the prologue to *The Plain Dealer* (1676), Wycherley announced that he will 'follow Life and Nature only', and so he

> makes his fine woman
> A mercenary Jilt, and true to no Man; . . .
> He draws a Friend only to Custom just,
> And makes him naturally break his trust.[2]

Thus, if the gallants in these plays attempted to justify their
conduct at all, it was by reference to what man is, not what he
ought to be. And what man is in these plays is a dramatized and
highly stylized version of what man is in Hobbes's state of
nature, with added touches furnished from popular mis-

[1] Louis Teeter, 'The Dramatic Use of Hobbes's Political Ideas', *ELH*, III
(June 1936), 154.
[2] William Wycherley, *The Complete Works*, ed. Montague Summers (London,
1924), II, 101–2.

139

conceptions of Epicurean philosophy. 'In matter of Women,' says Merryman in Sedley's *Bellamira*, 'we are all in the State of Nature, every man's hand against every man, whatever we pretend.'[1]

The stage wits, then (and in varying degrees the playwrights and courtiers themselves) exploited Hobbes's synthetic and 'low' view of human nature for their own purposes; but they ignored his *caveat* against the uninhibited exercise of 'natural right'. They behaved in an unprincipled way, on principle; the principle can be fairly described as only half-Hobbist—a cynical and brutalized view of human nature unrelieved by Hobbes's remedy for it. A remark which Hobbes himself made about some of the wits may be apposite here: he objected, in a letter, to the works of some 'comique' writers who 'by conversation with ill People have been able to present Vices upon the Stage more ridiculously and immodestly, by which they take their Rabble'.[2]

The case of Rochester is the most spectacular, and the evidence which it provides the most tantalizing. Rochester was a gifted lyric poet and satirist, and a member of the circle of court wits which included Buckingham, Dorset, Sedley, Etherege, Henry Savile and Thomas Killigrew. Rochester's personality was complex and contradictory; he refused to squander his wife's personal wealth, and he appears (to judge from his letters) to have been a genuinely affectionate husband;

[1] Act III, scene iv, in Sir Charles Sedley, *The Poetical and Dramatic Works*, ed. V. De Sola Pinto (London, 1928), II, 54. Other allusions to Hobbes and Hobbism in Restoration comedy have been collected by Samuel Weiss, *Hobbism and Restoration Comedy* (unpublished doctoral dissertation, Columbia University, 1953), q.v.

[2] A letter to the Duchess of Newcastle, 9 February 1661, in Margaret Cavendish, *A Collection of Letters and Poems* (London, 1678), p. 67. It is also worth recording that Hobbes's opponents, with one exception, did not charge him with personal misconduct. The exception is Bishop Kennet, who asserted that Hobbes had a natural daughter whom he cherished (*Athenae Oxonienses*, III, 1218). Kennet's charge has no apparent foundation. In 1904 Professor Tönnies unearthed an early letter from Hobbes to his pupil Cavendish giving advice on love matters. 'Lastly I think it no ill counsell, that you profess no love to any woman which you hope not to marry or otherwise to enjoy. For an action without design is that which all the world calls vanity'. 22 August 1638, printed in Ferdinand Tönnies, 'Hobbes-Analekten', *Archiv für Philosophie*, XVII (1904), 291–317. Tönnies speculated learnedly on the seventeenth-century meaning of the word 'enjoy' and then concluded with regret that Hobbes probably had in mind 'die gröbere Deutung' *to conquer*. The evidence from all contemporary sources however is that Hobbes's personal conduct was exemplary.

also, he had a true if fitful sense of his obligations as a landlord. At the same time he was guilty of numerous sexual infidelities, and he acquired the reputation, some small portion of it no doubt spurious, of being the wittiest scapegrace and most aggressive libertine of his time. He died at the age of thirty-three, in 1670, worn out by venereal disease, and 'tir'd with the noysom Follies of the Age'. In the year before his death Rochester sought out Gilbert Burnet, a churchman of latitudinarian principles and a notable enemy of Hobbes.[1] Together the rake and the Bishop debated the great issues of religion and morality; Burnet was able to persuade Rochester that a good man must not only renounce a life of sensual pleasure, but must also be 'internally regenerated and changed by a higher principle'.[2] During his final illness Rochester was attended regularly by two other of Hobbes's opponents, Dr John Fell and Dr Thomas Pierce, author of $AYTOKATAKPI\Sigma I\Sigma$, or Self-Condemnation Exemplified . . . Especially [in] Master Hobbs [1658]. Shortly before he died Rochester confessed all his sins and confided to his mother's chaplain that 'that absurd and foolish Philosophy, which the world so much admired, propagated by the late Mr Hobbs, and others, had undone him, and many more of the best parts in the Nation'.[3] The story of the death-bed conversion very soon became a popular subject for hortatory literature. In one contemporary elegy we learn that Rochester

> Himself his *looser lines* to Flames bequeaths
> And *Hobbs' creed* with Detestation leaves.[4]

Later the story was embellished with what appear to be apocryphal details: 'During his last illness he [Rochester] often exclaimed, "Mr Hobbes and the philosophers have been my ruin": then putting his hand upon a large bible which lay beside him, he cried out with great rapture, "This, this is the

[1] See Burnet's *History of his Own Times* (London, 1818), I, 108, 207–8, where Hobbes is pilloried for his atheism.

[2] Gilbert Burnet, *Some Passages in the Life and Death of John Earl of Rochester* (London, 1810), p. 40. The first edition was at London, 1680. Dr Johnson, in his *Life of Rochester*, said of this book that 'the critic ought to read it for its elegance, the philosopher for its arguments, and the saint for its piety'.

[3] Robert Parsons, *A Sermon Preached at the Funeral of the Rt Honorable John Earl of Rochester* (Oxford, 1680), p. 26.

[4] Samuel Holland, *An Elegie . . .to the Memory of . . . Rochester who most Piously exchanged Earthly Honour for Never-fading Glory the 26th Day of July, 1680.* [Broadside.]

true philosophy!" '[1] Even as late as the nineteenth century the dramatic conversion furnished material for thousands of pious exhortations distributed by the Society for the Propagation of Christian Knowledge.[2]

So we have it on the authority of Rochester himself that Hobbes had led him into sin. But the authority of a man *in extremis* is not the most reliable, and is in this instance rendered more suspect by the fact that the dying man was ministered to by three of Hobbes's opponents, one of them—Dr Fell—a bigot and a zealot. There is sufficient evidence to show that Rochester's conversion was not insincere. Also, it is certain that Rochester had read and admired Hobbes, and that, like the other wits, he had adopted certain of Hobbes's opinions for his own literary purposes, though the part played by Hobbist principles in shaping his intellectual outlook is small when contrasted with the influence of Seneca and Lucretius. But it does not follow from this, or from the conversion, that Rochester's libertinism was inspired by Hobbes. What seems most likely is that Rochester's amoral conduct and sceptical outlook proceeded from a complex of causes of which the influence of Hobbes is only a small contributing factor. Rochester and his fellow wits had borrowed from Hobbes those ideas which satisfied their own conception of court life. It was a conception which derived in part from French *libertin* principles, in part from the loose standard of conduct set by their king, in part from the feeling they had that the moral code of the Puritans whom they replaced was stultifying, and in part from the peculiar needs of their own volatile personalities. By responding to these underlying causes (and possibly to others as well) the wits were able to find in Hobbes a set of ideas which when torn from its context answered their own idealized conception of the 'natural man', of the individual who is freed from all social and moral restraint.

The attacks on Hobbes's influence on Restoration conduct were accompanied by a repudiation of his egoistic psychology. The view emerged, gradually at first, and then more rapidly in the last quarter of the century, that man is essentially altruistic,

[1] William Seward, *Biographiana* (London, 1799), II, 509.
[2] See John Hayward, ed., *Collected Works of John Wilmot Earl of Rochester* (London, 1926), Introduction, p. xliii.

a creature of sensiblity radically different in his 'nature' from Hobbes's arch-egoist.[1] Shaftesbury's 'man of feeling' was foreshadowed by Hobbes's critics.

One of the most interesting features of this development is the rational, secular, and extra-theological tone of the argument. Less and less frequently do we hear such terms as Original Sin, Sub- and Supralapsarianism, natural depravity, etc. Instead the critics conducted their argument on the basis of rational belief and empirical evidence. They referred to an inward belief in the natural goodness of man, and they supported this belief with the evidence of common experience, frequently, as they claimed, their own experience. To refute Hobbes's belief that fear of death is the fundamental motive and self-preservation the fundamental law of human nature, Bishop Lucy of St David's produced the following pathetic anecdote:

A Child of mine own, somewhat above four years old, being sickly, I put out to a neighbours house, in whose care I confided, to attend her; she grew weaker and weaker unto *death*, and almost immediately before her *death* the man of the house coming home from his business, she called the woman, whom she usually called *old Mother*: *old Mother*, said she, *goe give the* old Man *his breakfast, he will be angry else; and leave such a boy to rock me in my Cradle*, and so straightway *dyed*. This is my Collection, if *death* had been so *painfull*, this Child could not have had so much leasure from the *anguish* of it, as to have attended . . . that kindness to the *old Man*.[2]

We have only to look around us, Bishop Lucy said, to see that people are sociable creatures, more often than not selfless and kind.

When Hobbes looked about him what he saw was men motivated by fear, arming themselves against future calamities. 'They who go to sleep, shut their doors; they who travel, carry their swords with them, because they fear thieves. Kingdoms guard their coasts and frontiers with forts and castles; cities are compact with walls; and all for fear of neighbouring kingdoms and towns.'[3] The critics, however, refused to generalize these observations into the conclusion that *all* human behaviour is

[1] See Ronald S. Crane, 'Suggestions Toward a Genealogy of the "Man of Feeling"', *ELH*, I (1934), 205–30.
[2] William Lucy, *Observations, Censures and Confutations of Notorious Errors in Mr Hobbes His Leviathan and other of his Bookes* (London, 1663), pp. 171–2.
[3] Hobbes, *Works*, II, 6 n.

motivated by the urge for self-preservation. Lucy, Clarendon, and John Eachard insisted that Hobbes was charging the many with the faults of the few. Eachard, the Master of St Catharine's College, Cambridge, is particularly quotable on this point because he employed a racy, colloquial style, richly deserving of Dryden's praise as 'Lucianic':[1]

We see indeed Castles, Walks, Drawbridges, Guards, Swords, Doors, Locks, and the like. But surely it is not absolutely necessary to say that all this Care is taken and these Defences made, because Human Nature at first was, and in general still is a *Whore*, a *Bitch*, a *Crab*, a *Cut-purse*, etc. But because there be *Dogs, Foxes, Hogs, Children, Fools, Madmen, Drunkards, Thieves, Pyrats* and *Philantians* [i.e. Hobbists]. And upon that account (considering the wickedness of the *World*) it is a most dangerous and frightful thing to leave the *Dairy-door* open; for who knows, but on a suddain the Sow, having some small Scruples about *meum* and *tuum*, may rush in with her Train of Little Thoughts, and *invading* the *Milk-bowls*, should rejoice in the Confusion? . . . I would have you call to mind, that there be such things in the World as . . . *Quakers* and *Fifth Monarchymen*, whose Religious Frenzy may disturb the Peace; and there be also such things, which in the Morning were true *lawful Men*, who by night with *Intemperance* have lost that *Priviledge;* and lastly, there may be here and there some besides, called *Pilferers* and *Thieves*, who count it a piece of dull Pedantry to live by any *set Form* or *Profession*, or to be guided by any *Reason*, or to stand to any *Laws*. And for you to conclude from hence, that *Humane* Nature in general is a *shirking, rooking, pilfering, padding Nature* is as extravagant, as to say that the chief of Mankind are perfectly distracted, and that the true *state of Nature* is a state of perpetual *Drunkenness*.[2]

What then is the true state of human nature? It is certainly not summed up by what Isaac Barrow called 'the monstrous paradox . . . that all men naturally are enemies one to another'.[3] It is not egoism, self-love, an immutable law of self-preservation.

[1] John Dryden, *Works*, ed. Walter Scot, rev. G. Saintsbury (London, 1893), xviii, 76–7: '. . . the reverend, ingenious, and learned Dr Eachard . . . has more baffled the philosopher of Malmesbury, than those who assaulted him with blunt heavy arguments drawn from orthodox divinity; for Hobbes foresaw where those strokes would fall, and leaped aside before they could descend; but he could not avoid those nimble passes, which were made on him by a wit more active than his own, and which were within his body, before he could provide for his defence.'
[2] John Eachard, *Mr Hobbs's State of Nature Considered*, 4th ed. (London, 1696), p. 87.
[3] Isaac Barrow, *Theological Works*, vol. IV, Sermon XXVIII (Oxford, 1830), p. 79.

Rather, the critics declared, it is love directed outwards, it is selflessness, it is a principle of natural goodness inhering in all men. Lady Conway noted that although there are wicked parents, even the most wicked love their children.[1] It may, said Thomas Traherne, come as 'a surprise to an Atheistical fool, that it should be ones interest to love another better than ones self; yet Bears, Dogs, Hens, Bees, Lions, Ants do it; they die for their young-ones. Nurses, Fathers, Mothers do it. Brides and Bridegrooms frequently do it; and so do Friends.'[2] In fact, observed John Shafto, if we submit the doctrine of self preservation 'to the judgment and dictates of right reason', we will find that 'each man's private happiness [is] linked together with, knit and united to the happiness and felicity of the rest of his Fellows, as to this life; the greatest pleasures whereof . . . consist in Society, and the benefits we have by the mutual commerce, company and enjoyment of one another.'[3] 'So far then,' said John Norris, 'is the State of Nature from being (according to the Elements of the *Leviathan*) a state of Hostility and War, that there is no one thing that makes more apparently for the Interest of Mankind, than Universal Charity and Benevolence.'[4]

The view that man is naturally good was most fully developed by Richard Cumberland, the Bishop of Peterborough. In his *De Legibus Naturae* (1672) he defended the proposition 'that the happiness of each Individual . . . is deriv'd from the best State of the whole System';[5] 'the common Good,' he said, 'is the supreme Law of Nature,'[6] and all the laws of nature may be summed up by the term 'benevolence'. In some few places Cumberland anticipated the nineteenth-century utilitarians; but he returned always to a distinctly Platonic conception of morality. There is, he said, an independent and absolute good. Knowing this, we are enjoined to seek it, and we can find it only

[1] [Anne Conway], *The Principles of the most Ancient and Modern Philosophy* (London, 1692), p. 98.
[2] Thomas Traherne, *Christian Ethicks* (London, 1675), p. 520.
[3] [John Shafto], *The Great Law of Nature, or Self-Preservation, Examined, Asserted, and Vindicated from Mr Hobbes his Abuses* (London, 1673), pp. 36–7.
[4] John Norris, 'The Christian Law Asserted and Vindicated'; *A Collection of Miscellanies* (4th ed. London, 1706), p. 190.
[5] Richard Cumberland, *A Treatise of the Laws of Nature*, trans. John Maxwell (London, 1727), p. 21.
[6] *Ibid.* p. 41.

when we promote the common good. The predatory Hobbesian man can never be happy, because 'that inward *Peace* . . . which arises in a benevolent Mind, from a sense of the Felicity of others . . . is wanting'.[1] Cumberland's 'proof' is perhaps not so impressive, but his conviction that altruism is useful is extremely interesting; moreover, he worked it out in a marvellously philosophical spirit. His method was not unlike Hobbes's in its insistence on reason and experience. 'I have altogether *abstained from Theological Questions*,' he wrote. 'Nor have I consider'd how much the Faculties of Mankind have been impair'd by the *Transgressions of our first Parents* . . . but I have endeavour'd to prove the *Law of Nature*, only from that *Reason* we find ourselves at present possess'd of, and from *Experience*.'[2]

It was, however, Cudworth who had the last word. In his free-will manuscripts as well as in *The Treatise Concerning Eternal and Immutable Morality*, Cudworth assailed Hobbes's doctrine that human choices are determined by self-interest only. He asserted that self-interest is an 'inferior' and minor motive in human behaviour. He proclaimed the natural goodness of man. He believed that all men aspire towards the good, though they may be remiss along the way when their conception of the good is blurred by difficult choices. And he held that good is an absolute entity, eternal and immutable. The contrary view—that 'moral good and evil, just and unjust, honest and dishonest' are '. . . mere names without any signification, or names for nothing else, but willed and commanded',[3] was to him simply inconceivable. There is, he said, 'an absolut Emparshall and Super-selfish good which ought to be the mesure of all our axans [actions] both to our Selfe & other men.'[4]

---

[1] *Ibid.* p. 44.
[2] *Ibid.* p. 34. A. M. Kyle has called Cumberland's treatise 'the first attempt in England at philosophic ethics'. See A. M. Kyle, 'British Ethical Theories: The Intuitionist Reaction Against Hobbes', *The Australasian Journal of Psychology and Philosophy*, v (1927), 114. For further discussion of Cumberland, see Marjorie Nicolson, 'Milton and Hobbes', *SP*, 23 (1926), 425, and W. C. De Pauley, *The Candle of the Lord* (New York, 1937), pp. 151–9.
[3] Ralph Cudworth, *A Treatise Concerning Eternal and Immutable Morality*, ed. L. Mosheim as Vol. III of *The True Intellectual System* (London, 1845), p. 530–1.
[4] Ralph Cudworth, British Museum, *Additional Manuscript* 4979, fol. 39.

CHAPTER VIII

CONCLUSION

'There is nothing in this whole discourse,' Hobbes wrote at the end of *Leviathan*, 'nor in that I writ before of the same subject in Latin, as far as I can perceive, contrary either to the Word of God, or to good manners; or to the disturbance of the public tranquility. Therefore I think it may be profitably printed, and more profitably taught in the Universities. . . .'[1] Hobbes's optimism was misplaced. The calm self-assurance expressed in this passage, the confidence in the usefulness as well as in the innocuousness of *Leviathan*, the hope that *Leviathan* would become a university text—none of these moods corresponded with the facts concerning Hobbes's reputation in the seventeenth century. The *Leviathan* was printed, but it was quickly suppressed; and far from being taught in the universities, it drew some of its sharpest opposition from Cambridge and Oxford. The truth is that Hobbes's influence on his countrymen during his own lifetime and for almost a century after was negative. He left no disciples. He founded no school. He made no such impact on English thought as did Bacon, whose memory was revered by the Royal Society, or as did Newton and Locke, whose influence was felt throughout the eighteenth century. There were, of course, the putative Hobbists—the Cambridge don Scargill, who publicly abjured his 'contamination' by Hobbes; a Fellow of Merton who took his own life because, as was alleged, he suffered remorse over his Hobbist principles;[2] another suicide, Charles Blount, a hack journalist, who plagiarized from Hobbes and many others on behalf of his own

[1] *Leviathan*, p. 467.
[2] Humphrey Prideaux, *Letters to John Ellis* (Camden Society, London, 1875), p. 116. The Fellow of Merton was Cardonnel, who hanged himself in 1681. Prideaux wrote to Ellis: 'It seems [Cardonnel] had lived with the Earle of Devonshire as praeceptor to his grandson, where, having been poisoned by Hobbes, on his return hither, blasphemy and atheism was his most frequent talke; of the guilt of which being at last sensible, this, 'tis supposed, praecipitated him into despair.'

147

ill-formulated Deist principles[1]—but none of these was a disciple in the strict sense, none had absorbed, accepted, and promoted Hobbes's doctrines. Much the same can be said of the courtier-libertines, of Rochester, Sedley, Wycherley and that whole tribe of rakes and wits who pursued pleasure for its own sake, but who had never really assimilated Hobbes's principles into their thought or their way of life.

One friend of Hobbes did publish a book in the philosopher's defence, but then only on a matter of the smallest importance. Henry Stubbe's *Clamor, Rixa, Joci, Mendacia, Furta, Cachini*[2] was published in 1657 in support of Hobbes against Wallis in the dispute concerning points of Latin and Greek grammar. Stubbe cited Cicero, Vossius, Emanuel Alvarus, Scaliger, and other authorities to prove *inter alia* that Hobbes was correct in using the preposition 'cum' for the ablative of manner in the construction 'occidere cum gladio'; but on matters concerning Hobbes's politics, religion, or general philosophy, Stubbe—who was Hobbes's friend,[3] and who was besides a professional controversialist of proven ability, having in his lifetime contended with some of the very best opponents, including Wallis, Sprat, Glanvill, and Andrew Marvell—Stubbe on the question of Hobbism was wary and discreet. There are those, he said

who would not stick to entitle me to all of [Hobbes's] Heterodoxyes because I agree with him in some few inconsiderable points of Critical Learning, and make me guilty of his sentiments, because I excuse his Latine. With such as think all manner of correspondence

---

[1] See [Charles Blount], *Miracles, No Violations of the Laws of Nature* (London, 1683), and Charles Blount, *The Oracles of Reason: In Several Letters to Mr Hobbs and other Persons of Eminent Quality, and Learning* (London, 1693). The latter work is a farrago of letters, papers, and deistic polemic, with much unacknowledged borrowing from Hobbes, Boyle, Sprat and others. A MS note by a contemporary in the McAlpin Collection copy of *Miracles, No Violations* makes it clear that Blount's suicide resulted from his frustration over ecclesiastical opposition to a marriage he contemplated, and not from remorse over his alleged Hobbist principles.

[2] Henry Stubbe, *Clamor, Rixa, Joci, Mendacia, Furta, Cachini, or, A Severe Enquiry into the late Oneirocritica* (London, 1657). This work is extremely rare. A MS note in the volume of the Keynes Collection at King's College, Cambridge, states that Molesworth had the greatest difficulty in obtaining a copy. The book can claim our attention for other reasons besides its relevance to Hobbes: it makes three enthusiastic and hitherto unnoted allusions to Milton, 'that glory of our English nation!' (p. 45. See also pp. 13 and 16.)

[3] Five letters from Stubbe to Hobbes, written between 7 July 1656 and December 1656, are preserved in the British Museum, *Additional Manuscripts*, 32, 553.

CONCLUSION

(which cannot be denyed without incivility) with him to be scandalous; all agreement even in Philology transcendently [*sic*] heretical; what can I hope for but they repute it apostasy to appear for him in publick?[1]

Because he defended Hobbes's grammar Stubbe was obliged to defend his own reputation as a Christian gentleman; but he made it clear that he was defending only Hobbes's 'Philology', not his doctrines, 'to which I am so great a stranger that I know no more of them than common talk hath acquainted me with, having never had leisure to examine his books.'[2]

Are we therefore to suppose that Hobbes was wholly without influence upon his fellow countrymen, that in the great debate between him and his critics he was—at least in the eyes of his contemporaries—the undoubted loser? Must we conclude that out of the vast intellectual ferment which characterized seventeenth-century thought Hobbes emerged as an isolated figure, distinguished only for the cries of shock and dismay which he wrung from his opponents? We must not. Hobbes exerted a subtle but powerful influence on his critics: he imposed upon them his own strict, rational standards of argument. He obliged them to meet him on his own grounds, to combat him with his own weapons of logical exactitude and severe reasoning. He caused them, for the purposes of argument, to lay aside their theological presuppositions and moral predilections, and to try the issues on their own merits. Thus, by his very provocation, Hobbes endowed the thought of his critics with a strong rationalist impulse, in much the same way that Père Simon imposed his logical standards on his critic Bossuet.[3] The critics were satisfied that they had cut Hobbes down to size; in fact they had yielded, slowly and imperceptibly but also very surely, to the force of his rationalist method.

In the earliest critics this influence is not yet apparent. Ross, Vilvain and Lucy[4] wrote against Hobbes in the middle years of the century, but they belonged to an earlier generation; their outlook was conservative; they were insensitive to the new currents of thought. Vilvain committed all the questions raised by Hobbes to the authority of Scripture, and found Hobbes

[1] Stubbe, *Clamor, Rixa*, p. 1. [2] *Ibid.*
[3] See Paul Hazard, *The European Mind* (London, 1953), pp. 198–216.
[4] Discussed below, pp. 65, 67–9.

149

wanting. His was the method adopted by Sir Simonds D'Ewes when that gentleman was assailed by atheistic doubts in the year 1624. 'I found,' Sir Simonds wrote, 'that those unruly thoughts of atheism were the devil's engines and the fruits of infidelity, not to be dallied withall or *disputed*, but to be avoided, prayed against, and resisted by a strong and lively faith.'[1] Ross and Lucy on the other hand were Aristotelians, trained in the scholastic method at Oxford. Their real interest lay in their conservatism; having retained the essential doctrines of the schools, they showed how the schools felt about Hobbes.[2] Both Ross and Lucy were aware of Hobbes's originality—Lucy in fact said in one place that Hobbes's 'opinions do confute that saying, *Nihil dictum quod non fuit dictum prius*'. But the novelty in Hobbes's thought appeared to them merely senseless. Their method of refuting a new doctrine was simply to cite an old one, and then to list the numerous authorities in the schools who upheld the earlier position.

By the end of the century the whole mental climate had been altered. The claims of rationalism in the Hobbesian sense of logical exactitude were everywhere put forward. Religious truths were now subjected to mathematical and logical 'demonstrations', as may be seen in the theological writings of John Wallis, or somewhat later, in the arguments of the Boyle lecturers. To prove that the 'Holy Trinity is also a Unity', Wallis eschewed Patristic argument and asked his readers instead to imagine a cube having infinitely extended dimensions and which, though it had three distinct dimensions, was nevertheless a single cube.[3] And since we 'have no Notions in our Mind, other than what we derive, Mediately or Immediately, from Sensible Impressions of Finite Corporeal Beings'[4]—a

[1] Sir Simonds D'Ewes, *Autobiography and Correspondence during the Reigns of James I and Charles I*, ed. J. O. Halliwell, (2 vols. London, 1845), I, 253. (Italics mine.)

[2] 'Lucy was three years at Oxford, where he graduated B.A. in 1613, some five years after Hobbes, and later he spent four years at Cambridge. Scholasticism reigned at both Universities, and his philosophy was learned once for all. Fifty years later it remained almost untouched by the advance of contemporary thought. In theology we learn that he leaned to Arminianism, but Descartes did not exist for him, and if he knew any of the work of the earlier Cambridge Platonists, their influence upon him was slight.' T. Loveday, 'An Early Criticism of Hobbes', *Mind*, XVII (1908), 494.

[3] John Wallis, *The Doctrine of the Blessed Trinity Briefly Explained* (London, 1690), pp. 11–14.

[4] John Wallis, *A Seventh Letter, Concerning the Sacred Trinity* (London, 1691), p. 15.

CONCLUSION

doctrine palpably Hobbist—Wallis shared Hobbes's scepticism about reaching any certain knowledge of God's attributes. Wallis is in fact a good example of the critic who, though he had opposed Hobbes's metaphysics all of his life, had nevertheless assimilated Hobbes's method, and by means of this method, some of Hobbes's doctrine as well.

It must be understood that the spread of rationalism is not chargeable to Hobbes alone. What Hobbes had done was to give fresh impetus to the movement, and, in the case of his critics, to penetrate their defences by obliging them to adopt the rationalist approach. For the Cambridge Platonists this meant that in refuting Hobbes they softened the neo-Platonic overtones of their thought and concentrated on logical arguments for the existence of God and spirit. The Cambridge Platonist conception of reason was typically mediating: from the dissenting Puritan sectaries, the Platonists inherited a view of Right Reason as an illumination of the soul, an intuitive, extralogical grasp of the truth; from the rationalist movement, and particularly from Descartes and Hobbes, they had acquired a much more 'secular' rationalist outlook. But their final position was a fusion of both attitudes, and they viewed with the most profound hostility any attempt to establish reason as one or the other of the two extremes. From their point of view the 'inner light' of the Quakers and the philosophical rigour of Hobbes were equally perversions of Right Reason, since neither the Quakers nor Hobbes had apprehended each other's positions, and only a mixture of both in the right proportions could lay a just claim to the truth. In Henry More's opinion the writings of Henry Nicholas, the sixteenth-century mystic whom More erroneously believed to be the founder of Quakerism, were no different in their ultimate effect from the works of Hobbes. 'I think Hobbs has wrote as many books to promote Atheisme as H.N. has to promote infidelity.'[1] The point is however that whereas More railed against the Quakers for their 'insincerity' or 'hypocrisy', he *reasoned* with Hobbes.

The critics' arguments thus assumed a Hobbist form; but their conclusions were as far from Hobbist as it was possible to be. With varying degrees of philosophical acumen, they reviewed his materialist doctrine, his scepticism of witchcraft, his

[1] Henry More to Lady Conway, 15 September 1670, in the *Conway Letters*, p. 307.

determinism, his ethical relativism, his 'low', pessimistic view of human nature. In everything they found him a prime example of the philosopher whose doctrines are wrong in themselves and dangerous to the public welfare.

His materialism was wrong because in the first place it could not support a theory of consciousness. If we accept Hobbes's view of mind as a mere mechanism, not animated by spirit, how, the critics asked, can we account for memory and reasoning and awareness? If mind is matter in motion, why are inanimate objects mindless? Why are we to suppose, asked Tenison (echoing Seth Ward, and in turn echoed by Cudworth), 'that a Looking-glass saw, and a Lute heard?' And how does the material mind, asked Stillingfleet, apprehend things not conveyed to it by the senses? How, unless it is ruled by an immaterial principle, can it apprehend relations and distances and proportions? Only a mind in touch with the reality of spirit, said Cudworth, can comprehend a perfect mathematical figure such as does not exist and never has existed in material nature.

As a counter-theory to Hobbes's materialism, Cudworth and More worked out an elaborate doctrine of spirit, which they furnished with the elements of classical and Renaissance Platonism. Mind, they said, was an absolute and independent spirit, 'Senior to the world, and proleptical to it', as superior in the scale of being to dull, inert matter as the angels are superior to men, or men to beasts. God, the highest and most perfect example of spirit, gave to the world a spirit of its own, a plastic nature which performs the menial tasks of God's creation. Spiritual substance is immaterial, circumscribed, penetrable, indestructible. Only the spirit of God is boundless, and to Henry More, whose imagination was stirred by the newest discoveries in astronomy, the vast ocean of infinite space was analogous to, perhaps even identical with, the divine being itself.

How was the doctrine of spirit to be confirmed? It was supported by scriptural authority, by the testimony of centuries of philosophers, by the consensus of educated persons. But More felt that these were not enough. He invoked the discoveries of natural science; he confronted Hobbes with Boyle's experiments on the vacuum, and argued that only an immaterial force could account for the power necessary to operate a vacuum-pump. He argued in short that natural science exposed the limitations of mechanical theory and brought all thinking persons to a belief in spirit.

Abetted by More, Joseph Glanvill embarked on his own peculiar defence of spirit. For him spirit was manifested in the presence of witches, warlocks, demons, and ghosts. He construed Hobbes's scepticism of witchcraft as one more sin committed in the name of materialism. Let the unbelievers mock; let them quote Scot and Hobbes. He at any rate had investigated many witch tales, and collected many more. To the weight of scriptural proof he added the testimony of dozens of men and women who had seen witches, of women who had confessed to being witches, of children haunted by a ghostly drummer. He knew the truth about evil and hence he was satisfied that he knew the truth about good. You cannot, he argued, deny the existence of witches and still believe in spirit. Give up witches and you give up all spirit, and you give up God. Prove that there are witches and you prove spirit and you uphold the belief in God.

To uphold the belief in God. That was the fundamental motive behind all the attacks on Hobbes's materialism. The question was not merely philosophical; it was a matter of faith and public morals. Materialism was a dangerous doctrine as well as an invalid one, because it undermined the spiritual basis of religious belief. It led naturally to a determinist position, and determinism made a mockery of moral responsibility. Robbed of his freedom to choose between good and evil, man would deserve neither reward nor punishment; his piety, his prayers, the whole apparatus of worship would then become meaningless; justice, heaven, hell would then be empty words; and the whole edifice of religion must tumble down. So argued Bramhall. Cudworth looked more deeply into the philosophical side of the free-will problem, and he found himself lost in a sea of perplexities. But if he never discovered a solution to the problem, he never wavered in his belief that a solution must be found, a solution which establishes for once and all the truth of human freedom, and by so doing preserves the fabric of religion and morality.

In Hobbes's ethical relativism the critics saw the same corroding, anti-religious influence at work. Short of saying bluntly that there is no God, can anything, they asked, be more destructive of religion than Hobbes's doctrine that 'good' and 'evil' are mere names, without 'signification' except as they represent the will of the sovereign; that all law, moral as well as civil, is positive law; that natural law is a rational method for attaining civil peace, rather than a divine decree engraved by God in the hearts of men? Are there no absolute and immutable values? 'If Cain had lain with his Mother, there being no positive law to prohibit it at that time, that we know of, had it been no sin?'[1] Is not the sovereign bound by the same moral laws that oblige us all? 'Where the Good or Evil of an Action is Determined by the Law of Nature, no Positive Humane Law can take off its Morality.'[2] Where our moral conduct is at issue, the critics said, we are subject to God, not to men.

Moreover, the critics maintained that man is essentially decent, that he is motivated by disinterested love at least as often as he is motivated by self-interest. He can be as magnanimous in his nature as Hobbes thinks he is cruel. The critics refused to view the world *sub specie potestatis*. They said that it was a mistake to deduce human nature from its aberrations, to observe that because one man plunders, all men want to. Against Hobbes's egoistic psychology they set the picture of a selfless, benevolent human nature. In effect they substituted one hypothesis for another, and considering the rudimentary state of psychology as a science in the seventeenth century, it is hard to see whether they made any surer contribution to the subject than Hobbes had. But they recognized, or at least the most perceptive among them recognized, that Hobbes's premise about human nature gave to his system a logical coherence which only a contrary premise could disturb. Furthermore, they believed in the principle of Christian love. One of them, Bishop Cumberland, developed this principle in a utilitarian fashion that is not entirely remote from Hobbes: he agreed that we are moved by self-interest, but he said that the promotion of the common good was the surest guarantee of personal well-being. In a certain sense Cumberland and all those critics of Hobbes who believed so passionately in the 'man of good feeling' added weight to a very acute remark made by John Dewey: 'Progress beyond [Hobbes] comes not from a hostile attitude

[1] John Whitehall, *The Leviathan Found Out* (London, 1679), p. 23.
[2] [Samuel Parker], *Discourse of Ecclesiastical Politie* (London, 1670), p. 113.

CONCLUSION

to his conceptions, but from an improved knowledge of human nature.'[1]

Yet the hostility continued after Hobbes's death, after his century closed, and, though with diminishing intensity, through most of the eighteenth century. In the nineteenth century Hobbes was admired by the Utilitarians and the legal positivists, and in the twentieth century he has found a host of sympathetic commentators. Nevertheless the storm he raised in his own time has not wholly abated. There is only the slightest difference between Bishop Vesey's remark, made in 1677, that Hobbes was a 'pandor to bestiality', and George Catlin's comment of 1922 that Hobbes was a 'moral defective',[2] or between Samuel Strimesius' judgment of 1677 that Hobbes was 'Diabolus Incarnatus'[3] and the opinion offered in 1956 by the Roman Catholic author Papini that the *Leviathan* was 'diabolically inspired'.[4] Such opinions about Hobbes are rare in our own time, probably because in a very real sense Hobbes's secular approach to philosophy has prevailed. But the occasional outbursts of indignation which are still heard today take us back to the seventeenth century when scorn and abuse of Hobbes were the rule, not the exception, when the problem of free-will engaged men's emotions as well as their minds, when the threat which Hobbes presented to traditional belief was felt with an immediacy and a depth of feeling that only a conscious act of the historical imagination can hope to recapture.

The effort to see Hobbes against the background of his own time is worth while: it adds a dimension to his thought which a study of his ideas seen *in vacuo* cannot match. His boldness and originality are set in high relief by the intense opposition which they provoked. And the opposition is fascinating in itself, being nothing less than the absorbing spectacle of men's minds nurtured on old ideas and caught in the grip of new ones. Moreover, reading Hobbes's critics imparts to us some of the delight which they themselves obviously took in the play of

[1] John Dewey, 'The Motivation of Hobbes's Political Philosophy', *Studies in the History of Ideas*, Vol. 1 (New York, 1918), p. 114.
[2] George Catlin, *Thomas Hobbes as Philosopher, Publicist and Man of Letters* (Oxford, 1922), p. 14.
[3] Samuel Strimesius, *Praxiologia Apodictica Seu Philosophia Moralis Demonstrativa Pythanologiae Hobbesianae Opposita* (Frankfurti ad Oderam, 1677), sig.)(.
[4] Giovanni Papini, *The Devil* (New York, 1954), p. 150.

155

ideas. Their pages breathe an air of intellectual excitement. In the seventeenth century old ideas were revived and new ones sprang up in dizzying profusion. Hobbes's critics fought their battles in this element of rapid intellectual change; and for all that they debated great and solemn issues, they had a rousing good time. They must have endorsed Hobbes's passionate defence of the intellectual life. 'I would very fain commend philosophy to you,' Hobbes wrote. Those who neglect it 'know not how great a pleasure it is to the mind of man to be ravished in the vigorous and perpetual embraces of the most beauteous world.'[1]

---

[1] *De Corpore*, 'The Author's Epistle to the Reader', in *Works*, I, xiv.

APPENDIX: CHECKLIST OF ANTI-HOBBES LITERATURE AND ALLUSION IN ENGLAND, 1650-1700

(*Note:* Works written against Hobbes having exclusively mathematical interest have been omitted. The greater number of these were written by John Wallis, whose bibliography is recorded in J. F. Scott, *The Mathematical Work of John Wallis,* London, 1938.)

1650   Nedham, Marchamont. *Case of the Common-Wealth . . . Stated.*
       Scot, Philip. *A Treatise of the Schism.*
1652   Culverwell, Nathanael. *Discourse of the Light of Nature.*
       [Fawn, Luke]. *A Beacon Set on Fire.*
       [Filmer, Robert]. *Observations . . . Upon Mr Hobs Leviathan.*
1653   More, Henry. *Antidote to Atheism.*
       Ross, Alexander. *Leviathan drawn out with a Hook.*
1654   [Fawn, Luke]. *A Second Beacon Fired.*
       Vilvain, Robert. *Theoremata Theologica.*
       Ward, Seth. *Vindiciae Academiarum.*
1655   Baxter, Richard. *Humble Advice.*
       Ward, Seth. *A Philosophicall Essay.*
1656   Harrington, James. *The Common-wealth of Oceana.*
       Tanny, Philip. 'Letters on Free Will'. B.M. Add. MSS., 32, 553.
       Ward, Seth. *In Thomae Hobbii Philosophiam.*
1657   Saye and Sele to Wharton, 29 December 1657. A Letter printed by Firth.
1658   Bramhall, John. *Castigations of Mr Hobbes.*
       Bramhall, John. *The Catching of the Leviathan.*
       Pierce, Thomas. *The Self-Avenger Exemplified.*
       Pierce, Thomas. *Self-Condemnation Exemplified.*
1659   Baxter, Richard. *A Holy Commonwealth.*
       More, Henry. *Immortality of the Soul.*
       Thorndike, Herbert. *An Epilogue to the Tragedy.*
       Wren, Matthew. *Monarchy Asserted.*

1660   Thorndike, Herbert. *The Due Way of Composing the Differences*.
        Worthington, John. Letter to Samuel Hartlib. 11 March, 1660, in *Diary and Correspondence*.
1661   Rust, George. *A Letter of Resolution*.
        Stillingfleet, Edward. *Irenicum*.
        Ward, Seth. *Against Resistance of Lawful Powers*.
1662   Boyle, Robert. *An Examen of Mr T. Hobbes*.
        Clark, Gilbert. *Tractatus de restitutione Corporum*.
        Coke, Roger. *Survey of the Politicks*.
        Stillingfleet, Edward. *Origines Sacrae*.
        Thorndike, Herbert. *Just Weights and Measures*.
        Wallis, John. *Hobbius Heauton-timorumenos*.
1663   Lucy, William. *Observations, Censures, and Confutations*.
        Newcastle, Margaret Cavendish. *Philosophical and Physical Opinions*.
        Taylor, Jeremy. *A Sermon Preached . . . at the Funeral of . . . John* [Bramhall].
1664   Newcastle, Margaret Cavendish. *Philosophical Letters*.
1665   Boyle, Robert. *New Experiments . . . touching Cold*.
1667   More, Henry. *Enchiridion Ethicum*.
1668   [Glanvill, Joseph]. *A Blow to Modern Sadducism*.
        [Glanvill, Joseph]. *A Whip for the Droll*.
1669   *Insolence and Impudence triumphant*.
        Owen, John. *Truth and Innocence Vindicated*.
        Scargill, Daniel. *The Recantation*.
        Wolseley, Sir Charles. *Unreasonablenesse of Atheism*.
1670   [Parker, Samuel]. *Discourse of Ecclesiastical Politie*.
        Tenison, Thomas. *The Creed of Mr Hobbes Examined*.
        Thorndike, Herbert. *A Discourse of the Forbearance*.
1671   Burthogge, Richard. *Divine Goodness Explicated*.
        More, Henry. *Enchiridion Metaphysicum*.
        [Parker, Samuel]. *Defence . . . of the Ecclesiastical Politie*.
1672   Cumberland, Richard. *De Legibus Naturae*.
        Eachard, John. *Mr Hobbs's State of Nature Considered*.
        Wolseley, Sir Charles. *Reasonableness of Scripture-Belief*.
1673   *Character of a Coffee-House*.
        Eachard, John. *Some Opinions of Mr Hobbs Considered*.
        Ferguson, Robert. *A Sober Enquiry*.
        Lucy, William. *An Answer to Mr Hobbs His Leviathan*.

Settle, Elkanah. *The Empress of Morocco.*
[Shafto, John]. *The Great Law of Naturé.*
S[harrock], R[obert]. *De Finibus Virtutis.*
Templer, John. *Idea Theologiae Leviathanis.*
1675 Addison, Lancelot. *The Present State of the Jews.*
Character of a Town Gallant.
Traherne, Thomas. *Christian Ethicks.*
1676 Clarendon, Edward, Earl of. *Brief View and Survey.*
Glanvill, Joseph. *Essays on Several Important Subjects.*
Glanvill, Joseph. *Seasonable Reflections.*
Laney, Benjamin. 'Observations' on *Liberty and Necessity.*
South, Robert. Sermon, 'Of the Wisdom of this World',
    preached at Westminster-Abbey, 30 April 1676.
1677 Bramhall, John. *Collected Works.*
1678 Cudworth, Ralph. *The True Intellectual System.*
Long, Thomas. *Mr Hale's Treatise of Schism Examined.*
1679 *Elegie upon Mr Thomas Hobbes.*
Falkner, William. *Christian Loyalty.*
H[owell], W[illiam]. *Spirit of Prophecie.*
Pierce, Thomas. *A Decad of Caveats.*
Whitehall, John. *The Leviathan Found out.*
1680 Baxter, Richard. *Defence of the Nonconformist's Plea for*
    Peace.
Elegy upon Mr Hobbes.
Molyneux, William. Introduction to his translation of
    Descartes's *Six Metaphysical Meditations.*
Parsons, Robert. *A Sermon . . . at the Funeral of Rochester.*
True Effigies of the Monster of Malmesbury.
1681 Glanvill, Joseph. *Sadducismus Triumphatus.*
Parker, Samuel. *Demonstration of the Divine Authority.*
1682 [Glanvill, Joseph]. *Lux Orientalis.*
1683 [Browne, Rev. Thomas]. *Miracles Work's Above and*
    Contrary to Nature.
Crowne, John. *City Politiques.*
Dowel, John. *The Leviathan Heretical.*
Judgment and Decree of the University of Oxford.
1686 South, Robert. Sermon, 'Of the Fatal Imposture of
    Words', Preached at Whitehall, 9 May, 1686.
1688 Norris, John. *Theory and Regulation of Love.*
Scarisbrike, Edward. *Catholic Loyalty.*

1690   B[oyle], R[obert]. *The Christian Virtuoso.*
1691   Sherlock, William. *Their Present Majesties Government Prov'd.*
1692   [Conway, Anne]. *The Principles of the most Ancient and Modern Philosophy.*
1694   Lowde, James. *Discourse Concerning the Nature of Man.*
1696   Eachard, John. *Some Observations Upon the Answer.*
        Edwards, John. *Socinianism Unmask'd.*
1698   Crowne, John. *Caligula.*
        Sidney, Algernon. *Discourses Concerning Government.*
1700   Collier, Jeremy. 'Upon General Kindness', in *Essays Upon Several Moral Subjects.*

Undated:

Barrow, Isaac. Sermon delivered at Cambridge alluding to 'a monstrous paradox' of Hobbes.

Cudworth, Ralph. 'Free-Will Manuscripts', B.M. Add. MSS. 4979–4982.

Hale, Sir Matthew. 'Reflections by the Lord Cheife [*sic*] Justice.' B.M. Harleian MSS. 711. [c. 1675].

BIBLIOGRAPHY

I. CONTEMPORARY SOURCES

A. Manuscripts

CUDWORTH, RALPH. 'Free-Will Manuscripts', British Museum, Additional MSS. 4979–4982.

HALE, SIR MATTHEW. 'Reflections by the Lord Cheife [*sic*] Justice Hale on Mr Hobbes his Dialogue of the Lawe', British Museum, Harleian MSS. 711.

HOBBES, THOMAS. 'Reply to Thomas White's *De mundo dialogi tres quibus materia*', Bibliothèque Nationale, Fonds Latin MSS. 6566A.

'Career of Daniel Scargill', Corpus Christi College Library, Cambridge, Corpus Christi Chapter Books, 1660–1670.

'Proceedings Against Daniel Scargill at Cambridge', Cambridge University Library, Baker MSS. Mn. 1. 38.

'Late Seventeenth-Century Commonplace Books', British Museum, Sloan MSS. 1458 and 8888.

SHELDON, GILBERT, Archbishop. 'Letter-Book', British Museum, Harleian MSS. 7377.

STUBBE, HENRY. 'Five Letters to Hobbes, July–December, 1656', British Museum, Additional MSS. 32553.

TANNY, PHILIP. 'Two Letters to Hobbes on Free-Will: May 13, 1656; July 2, 1656', British Museum, Additional MSS. 32553.

B. Printed Matter

ADDISON, LANCELOT. *The Present State of the Jews.* London: Printed by J. C. for William Crooke, and to be sold by John Courtney in Sarum, 1675.

Advice from the Shades-Below. Or; a Letter From Thomas Hobbs of Malmsbury, To His Brother B—n H—dly. In Imitation of Mr Brown's Letters from the Dead to the Living. 2nd ed. London: Printed, and are to be Sold, by the Booksellers of London, and Westminster, 1710.

ATTERBURY, FRANCIS. *Sermons and Discourses On Several Occasions.* 2 vols. London: Printed by J. Aris for Jonah Bowyer, at the Rose in St Paul's Church-Yard, 1723.

AUBREY, JOHN. *'Brief Lives', chiefly of Contemporaries, set down by John Aubrey, between the years 1669 & 1696.* Edited by Andrew Clark. 2 vols. Oxford: The Clarendon Press, 1898.

BAILLIE, ROBERT. *The Letters and Journals of Robert Baillie.* Edited by David Laing. 3 vols. Edinborough [*sic*]: The Bannatyne Club, 1841–1842.

BARLOW, THOMAS. *The Genuine Remains of That Learned Prelate Dr Thomas Barlow.* London: Printed and Sold by Randal Taylor, near Stationers-Hall, 1693.

BARROW, ISAAC. *Theological Works.* Vol. IV. *Sermons on Several Occasions.* Oxford: Oxford University Press, 1830.

BATES, WILLIAM. *Considerations of the Existence of God, and the Immortality of the Soul, with The Recompences of the future state.* 2nd ed. London: Printed by J.D. for Brabazon Aylmer, at the three Pigeons, over against the Royal Exchange in Cornhill, 1677.

BAXTER, RICHARD. *The Defence of the Nonconformist's Plea for Peace.* London: Printed for Benj. Alsop, 1680.

―― *A Holy Commonwealth, or Political Aphorisms, Opening The True Principles of Government: For the Healing of the Mistakes, and Resolving the Doubts, that most endanger and trouble England at this time: (if yet there may be hope).* London: Printed for Thomas Underhill and Francis Tyton, and are to be sold at the Sign of the Anchor and Bible in Pauls Churchyard, and at the Three Daggers in Fleetstreet, 1659.

―― *Humble Advice: Or the Heads of those things which were offered to many Honourable Members of Parliament.* London: Printed for Thomas Underhill and Francis Tyton, 1655.

―― *The Practical Works of The Rev. Richard Baxter.* Vol. XXI. *The Reasons of the Christian Religion.* London: James Duncan, 1830.

BERNS, MICHAEL. *Altar der Atheisten, der Heyden, und der Christen . . . Wider die 3 Erz-Betrieger Herbert, Hobbes und Spinosa.* Hamburg: T. von Wiering, 1692.

[BLOUNT, CHARLES]. *Miracles, No Violations of the Laws of Nature.* London: Printed for Robert Sollers at the King's Arms and Bible in St Paul's Church-yard, 1683.

―― *The Oracles of Reason. In several letters to Mr Hobbs and other Persons of Eminent Quality, and Learning.* London: Printed 1693.

B[OYLE], R[OBERT]. *The Christian Virtuoso: Shewing That by Being addicted to Experimental Philosophy a Man is rather Assisted, than Indisposed, to be a good Christian.* London: In the Savoy: Printed by Edw. Jones for John Taylor at the Ship in St Paul's Church-yard, 1690.

BOYLE, ROBERT. *An Examen of Mr T. Hobbes his Dialogus Physicus De Natura Aeris.* London: Printed by J.G. for Thomas Robinson Bookseller in Oxon, 1662.

―― *New Experiments and Observations touching Cold, or an Experimental*

History of Cold Begun. To which are added An Examen of Antiperis-tasis and An Examen of Mr Hobs's Doctrine about Cold. London: Printed for John Crook, at the Sign of the Ship in St Paul's Church-yard, 1665.

BRAMHALL, JOHN. *Castigations of Mr Hobbes His Last Animadversions, in the Case concerning Liberty and Universal Necessity.* London: Printed by E.T. for J. Crook, 1658.

—— *The Catching of the Leviathan, or the Great Whale. Demonstrating out of Mr Hobbs his own Works, That no man who is thoroughly an Hobbist, can be a good Christian, or a Good Common-wealthsman, or reconcile himself to himself. . . .* London: Printed by E.T. for John Crooke, at the Sign of the Ship in St Paul's Church-yard, 1658.

—— *The Works of John Bramhall. Collected into One Volume.* Dublin: Printed by Benjamin Tooke Printer to the King's Most Excellent Majesty, 1677.

[BROWNE, REV. THOMAS]. *Miracles Work's Above and Contrary to Nature; or, An Answer to a late Translation out of Spinoza's Tract-atus Theologico-Politicus, Mr Hobb's Leviathan, &c. Published to undermine the Truth and Authority of Miracles, Scripture, and Religion.* London: Printed for Samuel Smith at the Princes Arms in St Paul's Church-yard, 1683.

BROWNE, SIR THOMAS. *Works.* Edited by Simon Wilkin. 3 vols. London: George Bell & Sons, 1901–1910.

BURNET, GILBERT. *History of His Own Time, from the Restoration of K. Charles II to the Conclusion of the Treaty of Peace at Utrecht.* 3rd ed. London: Printed for T. Davies, 1766.

BURTHOGGE, RICHARD. *ΤΑΓΑΘΟΝ, or, Divine Goodness Explicated and Vindicated From the Exceptions of the Atheist: Wherein also the Consent of the Gravest Philosophers, with the Holy, and Inspired Penmen, in many of the most important points of Christian Doctrine is fully evinced.* London: Printed by S. and B. Griffin, for James Collins, and are to be sold at the Kings-Armes in Ludgate-street, 1671.

CAMPAGNAC, ERNEST TRAFFORD (ed.) *The Cambridge Platonists; being Selections from the Writings of Benjamin Whichcote, John Smith and Nathaniel Culverwel.* Oxford: The Clarendon Press, 1901.

The Character of a Coffee House, with the Symptomes of a Town Wit. London: Printed for Jonathan Edwin, 1673.

The Character of a Town Gallant. London: Printed for W.L., 1675.

CLARENDON, EDWARD, Earl of. *A Brief View and Survey of the Dan-gerous and pernicious Errors to Church and State, In Mr Hobbes's Book Entitled Leviathan.* 2nd ed. Oxford: Printed at the Theater, 1676.

CLARK, GILBERT. *Tractatus de restitutione Corporum in quo experimenta Torricelliania & Boyliana explicantur & rarefactio Cartesiana defenditur. Una cum responsione ad clarissimi T. Hobbii dialogum.* Londini: excudebat J.H. pro S. Thomson, ad insigne Episcopi in coemeterio Paulino, 1662.

COKE, ROGER. *A Survey of the Politicks of Mr Thomas White, Mr Thomas Hobbs, and Mr Hugo Grotius.* London: Printed for G. Bedell and T. Collins, and are to be sold at Middle-Temple Gate in Fleetstreet, 1662.

COLLIER, JEREMY. *Essays Upon Several Moral Subjects. In Two Parts.* Essay IV, Pt. I, 'Upon General Kindness'. London: Printed for Richard Sare at Grays-Inn-Gate in Holborn, and H. Hindmarsh against the Royal Exchange in Cornhill, 1700.

[CONWAY, ANNE]. *The Principles of the most Ancient and Modern Philosophy, Concerning God, Christ, and the Creatures, viz. of Spirit and Matter in general; whereby may be resolved all those Problems or Difficulties, which neither by the School nor Common Modern Philosophy, nor by the Cartesian, Hobbesian, or Spinosian could be discussed. Being A littleTreatise published since the Author's Death, translated out of the English into Latin with Annotations taken from the Ancient Philosophy of the Hebrews; and now again made English by J.C.* [London]: Printed in Latin at Amsterdam by M. Brown, 1690, and Reprinted at London, 1692.

CONRINGIUS, HERMANN. *Conringiana Epistolica sive Animadversiones Variae Eruditionis.* Editio Nova. Helmstadii: Typis Salmonis Schnorrii, 1719.

COOPER, THOMAS. *The Mystery of Witch-craft; discovering the truth thereof.* London: Printed for N. Okes, 1617.

COSIN, JOHN. *Works.* 5 vols. Oxford: John Henry Parker, 1843.

COWLEY, ABRAHAM. *The Works of Mr Abraham Cowley.* London: Printed by J.M. for Henry Herringman, at the Sign of the Blew Anchor in the Lower Walk of the New Exchange, 1668.

CROWNE, JOHN. *Caligula.* London: Printed by J. Orme for R. Wellington and sold by Percival Gilborne and Bernard Lintott, 1698.

—— *City Politiques.* London: Printed for R. Bentley and Joseph Hindmarsh, 1683.

—— *The Dramatic Works.* 4 vols. Edited by J. Maidment and W. H. Logan. Edinburgh: W. Paterson *et al.* 1873–74.

CUDWORTH, RALPH. *A Sermon Preached before the Honourable House of Commons . . March 31, 1647.* New York: The Facsimile Text Society, 1930.

—— *The True Intellectual System of the Universe: Wherein All the Reason and Philosophy of Atheism is Confuted, and its Impossibility Demonstrated; With a Treatise Concerning Eternal and Immutable Morality.* Edited by J. L. Mosheim, with Mosheim's notes translated by John Harrison. 3 vols. London: Printed for Thomas Tegg, 1845.

CULVERWELL, NATHANAEL. *An Elegant and Learned Discourse of the Light of Nature.* Edited by John Brown. Edinburgh: Thomas Constable and Co., 1857.

CUMBERLAND, RICHARD. *De Legibus Naturae.* Londini: Typis E. Flesher, prostat vero apud Nathanaelem Hooke, 1672.

—— *A Treatise of the Laws of Nature.* Translated by John Maxwell. London: Printed by R. Phillips, 1727.

CUPERUS, FRANCISCUS. *Arcana Atheisme Revelata, Philosophice & Paradoxe refutata, examine tractatus theologico-politici.* Roderodami: Apud Isaacum Naeranum, 1676.

DESCARTES, RENÉ. *Oeuvres.* Tome 10, 'Lettres'. Edited by Victor Cousin. Paris: P. G. Levrault, 1825.

—— *Oeuvres.* Vol III. *Correspondance: Janvier 1640–Juin 1643.* Paris: Leopold Cerf, 1899.

—— *The Philosophical Works of Descartes.* Translated by Elizabeth Haldane and G. R. T. Ross. 2 vols. Cambridge: Cambridge University Press, 1934.

—— *Six Metaphysical Meditations; Wherein it is Proved That there is a God. Hereunto are added the Objections made against these Meditations by Thomas Hobbes.* Translated by William Molyneux. London: Printed by B.G. for Benj. Tooke at the Ship in St Paul's Church-yard, 1680.

D'EWES, SIR SIMONDS. *Autobiography and Correspondence during the Reigns of James I and Charles I.* Edited by J. O. Halliwell. 2 vols. London: Richard Bentley, 1845.

DOWEL, JOHN. *The Leviathan Heretical; or The Charge Exhibited in Parliament against M. Hobbs justified by the Refutation of a Book of his Entitled The Historical Narration of Heresie and the Punishments thereof.* Oxford: Printed by L. Lichfield, and are to be sold by A. Stephens Bookseller, 1683.

DRYDEN, JOHN. *Fables Ancient and Modern.* London: Printed for Jacob Tonson at Shakespear's Head over-against Katherine-street in the Strand, 1713.

—— *Works.* Vol. XVIII. 'Life of Lucian'. Edited by Walter Scott, revised by George Saintsbury. London: William Paterson, 1893.

EACHARD, JOHN. *The Grounds & Occasions of the Contempt of the Clergy and Religion Enquired into.* London: Printed by W. Godbid for N. Brooke at the Angel in Cornhill, 1670.

—— *Mr Hobbs's State of Nature Considered: in a Dialogue Between Philautus and Timothy.* 4th ed. London: Printed for E. Belgrave, and Sold by the Booksellers of London and Westminster, 1696.

—— *Some Observations Upon the Answer to an Enquiry into the Grounds and Occasions of the Contempt of the Clergy.* 6th ed. London: Printed for E. Belgrave, and Sold by the Booksellers of London and Westminster, 1696.

—— *Some Opinions of Mr Hobbs Considered.* London: Printed by Macock for Walter Kettilby, 1673.

EDWARDS, JOHN. *Socinianism Unmask'd.* London: Printed for J. Robinson at the Golden Lyon and J. Wyat at the Rose in St. Paul's Church-yard, 1696.

An Elegie upon Mr Thomas Hobbes. [n.p.]: Printed in the Year 1679. [Broadside.]

An Elegy upon Mr Hobbes. [n.p.]: Printed in the Year 1680. [Broadside.]

FALKNER, WILLIAM. *Christian Loyalty.* London: Printed by J.M. for Walter Kettilby, 1679.

[FAWN, LUKE]. *A Beacon Set On Fire: or the Humble Information of certain Stationers, Citizens of London, to the Parliament and Commonwealth of ENGLAND. Concerning the Vigilancy of Jesuits, Papists, and Apostates . . . by Writing and Publishing many Popish Books . . . and Blasphemous Books of another Nature.* London: Printed for the Subscribers hereof, 1652.

[——] *A Second Beacon Fired, Humbly Presented to the Lord Protector and the Parliament By the Publishers of the First. With their humble Petition, that they would do what may be expected from Christian Magistrates, in suppressing Blasphemous Books.* London: Printed for the Subscribers hereof, 1654.

F[ERGUSON], R[OBERT]. *A Sober Enquiry into the Nature, measure, and Principle of Moral Virtue, Its distinction from Gospel-Holiness.* London: Printed for D. Newman at the King-Arms in the Poultry, 1673.

[FILMER, ROBERT]. *Observations Concerning the Originall of Government, Upon Mr Hobs Leviathan. Mr Milton against Salmasius. H. Grotius De Jure Belli. Mr Huntons Treatise of Monarchy.* London: Printed for R. Royston, at the Angel in Ivie Lane, 1652.

Fürstellung vier neuer Welt-Weisen, nahmentlich, I. Renati Des Cartes, II. Thomae Hobbes, III. Benedicti Spinosa, IV. Balthasar Beckers, nach ihrem Leben und fürnehmsten Irrthümern. [Frankfurt A.M.?]: Gedruckt im Jahr, 1702.

BIBLIOGRAPHY

[GLANVILL, JOSEPH]. *A Blow at Modern Sadducism in some Philosophical Considerations About Witchcraft.* London: Printed by E. Cotes for James Collins at the Kings Head in Westminster-Hall, 1668.

—— *Essays on Several Important Subjects in Philosophy and Religion.* London; Printed by J.D. for John Baker, at the Three Pidgeons, and Henry Mortlock, at the Phoenix in St Paul's Church-yard, 1676.

[——] *Lux Orientalis, Or an Enquiry into the Opinion of the Eastern Sages Concerning the Prae-existence of Souls.* London: Printed for J. Collins, and S. Lowndes over against Exeter-exchange in the Strand, 1682.

—— *Sadducismus Triumphatus: Or, a full and plain Evidence, concerning Witches and Apparitions. In Two Parts. The First Treating of their Possibility. The Second of Their Real Existence.* 4th ed. London: Printed for A. Bettesworth, and J. Batley, in Pater-noster Row; W. Mears and J. Hooke, near Temple-bar, in Fleet-street, 1726.

—— *Seasonable Reflections and Discourses In Order to the Conviction, and Cure of the Scoffing, and Infidelity of a Degenerate Age.* London: Printed by R. W. for H. Mortlock at the Phoenix in St Paul's Church-yard, and the White-Hart in Westminster-Hall, 1676.

[——] *A Whip for the Droll Fidler to the Atheist: Being Reflections on Drollery & Atheism. Sent upon the occasion of the Drummer of Tedworth, in a Letter to the most Learned Dr Hen. More, D.D.* London: Printed by E. Cotes for James Collins at the Kings-Head in Westminster Hall, 1668.

Great Britain. Public Record Office. *Calendar of State Papers, Domestic Series, of the Reign of Charles II.* Vol. x. Edited by Mary E. V. Green. London: Eyre and Spottiswode, 1895.

HARRINGTON, JAMES. *The Common-wealth of Oceana.* London: Printed by J. Streeter for Livewell Chapman, 1656.

HOBBES, THOMAS. *Behemoth or the Long Parliament.* Edited by Ferdinand Tönnies. London: Simpkin, Marshall, and Co., 1889.

—— *Considerations upon the Reputation, Loyalty, Manners & Religion of Thomas Hobbes of Malmsbury. Written by himself By way of a Letter to a Learned Person.* London: Printed for William Crooke, at the Green Dragon without Temple-bar, 1680.

—— 'Considerations touching the facility or Difficulty of the Motions of a Horse on straight lines & Circular', in *A Catalogue of Letters and other Historical Documents Exhibited in the Library at Welbeck.* Compiled by S. Arthur Strong. London: John Murray, 1903.

—— *De Mirabilibus Pecci. Being the Wonders of the Peak in Darby-Shire, Commonly called The Devil's Arse of Peak. In English and*

Latine. The Latine Written by Thomas Hobs of Malmsbury. The English by a Person of Quality. London: Printed for William Crook at the Green Dragon without Temple-bar nigh Devereux Court, being the passage into the Middle-Temple, 1683.

—— *Dialogus Physicus, sive De Natura Aeris Conjectura sumpta ab Experimentis nuper Londini habitis in Collegio Greshamensi Item De Duplicatione Cubi.* Londini: Typis J.B. et prostant Venales apud A. Crook sub insigne Draconis in Caemeterio Paulino, 1661.

—— *The Elements of Law, Natural and Politic.* Edited by Ferdinand Tönnies. Cambridge: Cambridge University Press, 1928. [Reprint of original London, 1889 edition.]

—— *The English Works.* Edited by Sir William Molesworth. 11 vols. London: John Bohn, 1839–1845.

[——] *Memorable Sayings of Mr Hobbes in his Books and at the Table.* [n.p. 1680?] Broadside. No imprint.

[——] *The Last Sayings, or Dying Legacy of Mr Thomas Hobbs of Malmesbury, Who departed this life on Thursday, Decemb. 4, 1679.* London: Printed for the Author's Executors, 1680. [Broadside.]

—— *Leviathan or the Matter, Forme and Power of a Commonwealth Ecclesiasticall and Civil.* Edited by Michael Oakeshott. Oxford: Basil Blackwell, [1946].

[——] *The Life of Mr Thomas Hobbes of Malmesbury. Written by himself in a Latine Poem. And now Translated into English.* London: Printed for A.C. and are to be sold in Fleetstreet, and without Temple-bar, 1680.

—— *Tracts of Thomas Hobb's, Containing His Life in Latine, part written by himself, since his death finished by Dr R.B.* London: Printed for William Crooke at the Green Dragon without Temple-bar, 1681.

HOOKER, THOMAS. *Works.* Edited by W. S. Dobson. 2 vols. London: G. Gowie et al., 1825.

H[OWELL], W[ILLIAM]. *The Spirit of Prophecie. A Treatise To prove (By the Ways formerly in use among the Jews, in the Tryal of Pretenders to a Prophetic Spirit) That Christ and his Apostles were Prophets Together With the Divine Authority of Christian Religion & the Holy Scriptures . . . and the Reasonableness of the Christian Faith, Hope, and Practice, Deduced therefrom and asserted against Mr Hobbes, and the Treatise of Humane Reason.* London: Printed for W. Crooke at the Signe of the Green Dragon without Temple-bar, 1679.

Insolence and Impudence triumphant; Envy and Fury enthron'd: The Mirrour of Malice and Madness. In a late Treatise, Entituled a Discourse of Ecclesiastical Politie, Ec., Or, The Lively Portraiture of Mr S. P. Limn'd and drawn by his own hand; And A brief View of his

Tame and Softly, Alias, Wild and Savage Humour; As also, Some account of his cold and frigid, i.e. fiery Complexion. [n.p.]; Printed in the year 1669.

The Judgment and Decree of the University of Oxford Past in their Convocation July 21, 1683, Against certain Damnable Books and Damnable Doctrines Destructive to the Sacred Persons of Princes, their State and Government, and of all Humane Society. [Oxford]: Printed at the Theater, 1683.

KORTHOLT, CHRISTIAN. *De tribus Impostoribus Magnis—Herbert, Hobbes, Spinoza.* Kiloni: J. Reumannus, 1680.

LANEY, BENJAMIN. *A Letter About Liberty and Necessity: Written to the Duke of Newcastle, by Thomas Hobbes of Malmesbury: With Observations upon it, By a learned Prelate of the Church of England lately deceased.* London: Printed by J. Grover, for W. Crooke, at the Green Dragon without Temple-Bar, 1676.

LETSOME, SAMPSON, and NICHOLL, J. (editors). *A defence of Natural and Revealed Religion: Being a Collection of the Sermons Preached at the Lecture founded by the Honourable Robert Boyle, Esq. (from the year 1691 to the year 1732).* 3 vols. London: Printed for D. Midwinter, 1739.

LEVENS, CHRISTIANUS *Thomae Hobbesii Angelographian.* Hamburgi: Typis Conradi Neumanni, Senatus, gymnasdi atque Schol. Typogr., 1694.

The Life Records of John Milton. Edited by J. Milton French. 4 vols. New Brunswick: Rutgers University Press, 1949–1956.

LONG, THOMAS. *Mr Hale's Treatise of Schism Examined and Censured.* London: Printed for Walter Kettilby, at the Bishop's Head in St Paul's Church-yard, 1678.

LOWDE, JAMES. *A Discourse Concerning the Nature of Man, Both in His Natural and Political Capacity: Both as he is a Rational Creature and Member of a Civil Society. With an Examination of some of Mr Hobbs's Opinions relating hereunto.* London: Printed by T. Warren for Walter Kettilby at the Bishop's-head in St Paul's Church-yard, 1694.

LUCY, WILLIAM. *An Answer to Mr Hobbs His Leviathan: With Observations, Censures, and Confutations of Divers Errours, Beginning at the seventeenth chapter of that Book.* London: Printed by S.G. and B.G. for Edward Man at the White Swan in St Paul's Church-yard, 1673.

—— *Observations, Censures and Confutations of Notorious Errors in Mr Hobbes His Leviathan and other his Bookes.* London; Printed by J.G. for Nath. Brooke at the Angel in Cornhill, 1663.

MILTON, JOHN. *The Works of John Milton.* Edited by F. A. Patterson *et al.* 18 vols. New York: Columbia University Press, 1931–1938.

MORE, HENRY. *A Collection of Several Philosophical Writings of Dr Henry More.* 4th ed. London: Printed by Joseph Downing in Bartholomew-Close near West-Smithfield, 1712.

—— *Enchiridion Ethicum.* The English translation of 1690, reproduced from the first edition. New York: The Facsimile Text Society, 1930.

—— *Enchiridion Metaphysicum. pars prima.* Londini: typis E. Flesher, Prostat apud Guilielmum Morden, Cantabrigiensem, 1671.

—— *An Explanation of the Grand Mystery of Godliness; or, a True and Faithful Representation of the Everlasting Gospel of our Lord and Saviour Jesus Christ.* London: Printed by J. Flesher, for W. Morden Bookseller in Cambridge, 1660.

—— *Philosophical Poems.* Cambridge: Printed by Roger Daniel, Printer to the University, 1647.

NEDHAM, MARCHAMONT. *The Case of the Common-wealth of England Stated: or, The Equity, Utility, and Necessity, of a Submission to the present Government; against all the Scruples and Pretences of the opposite Parties; viz. Royalists, Scots, Presbyterians, Levellers.* 2nd ed. London: Printed for E. Blackmore, and R. Lowndes, 1650.

NEWCASTLE, MARGARET CAVENDISH, Duchess of. *Philosophical and Physical Opinions.* London: Printed by William Wilson, Anno Dom., 1663.

—— *Philosophical Letters: or, Modest Reflections Upon some Opinions in Natural Philosophy, Maintained by several Famous and Learned Authors of this Age Expressed by way of Letters.* London: Printed in the Year, 1664.

NEWTON, ISAAC. *Opticks.* 3rd ed. London: Printed for W. and J. Innys, 1721.

The Nicholas Papers. Edited by George Warner. London: Printed for the Camden Society, 1866.

NORRIS, JOHN. *A Collection of Miscellanies.* 4th ed. London: Printed for S. Manship, and are to be sold by Percivall Gilbourne, 1706.

—— *The Theory and Regulation of Love. A Moral Essay. In Two Parts. To which are added Letters Philosophical and Moral between the Author and Dr Henry More.* Oxford: Printed at the Theatre for Hen. Clements, 1688.

OWEN, JOHN. *Truth and Innocence Vindicated.* [London?, 1669.] [No t.p. in McAlpin copy.]

[PARKER, SAMUEL]. *A Defence and Continuation of the Ecclesiastical*

Politie. London: Printed by A. Clark for J. Martyn, at the Bell in St Paul's Church-yard and without Temple-Bar, 1671.

—— *A Demonstration of the Divine Authority of the Law of Nature, and of the Christian Religion*. London: Printed by M. Flesher, for R. Royston, Bookseller to His most Sacred Majesty, and R. Chiswell, at the Rose and Crown in St Paul's Church-yard, 1681.

[——] *A Discourse of Ecclesiastical Politie: Wherein The Authority of the Civil Magistrate Over the Consciences of Subjects in Matters of Religion is Asserted; The Michiefs and Inconveniences of Toleration are Represented, and all Pretences Pleaded in Behalf of Liberty of Conscience are Fully Answered*. London: Printed for John Martyn at the Bell without Temple-Bar, 1670.

PARSONS, ROBERT. *A Sermon Preached At the Funeral of the Rt Honorable John Earl of Rochester*. Oxford: Printed at the Theater for Richard Davis and Tho: Bowman, In the Year, 1680.

PAYNE, S. *A Brief Account of the Life, Character, and Writings of the Right Reverend Father in God, Richard Cumberland, D.D.* London: Printed by W.B. for R. Wilkin at the King's Head in St Paul's Church-yard, 1720.

Petty-Southwell Correspondence. Edited from the Bowood Papers by the Marquis of Lansdowne. London: Constable and Co., 1928.

PIERCE, THOMAS. *A Decad of Caveats to the People of England, of General Use in All Times, but most seasonable in These. To which is added an Appendix, In order to the Conviction of those Three Enemies to the Deity: The Atheist, the Infidel and the Setter up of Science to the Prejudice of Religion*. London: Printed for Richard Davis Bookseller in Oxford, 1679.

—— *ΕΑΥΤΟΝΤΙΜΩΡΟΥΜΕΝΟΣ, or, The Self-Revenger Exemplified in Mr William Barlee*. London: Printed by R. Daniel, for Richard Royston, at the Angel in Ivie-lane, 1658.

—— *ΑΥΤΟΚΑΤΑΚΡΙΣΙΣ, or, Self-Condemnation, Exemplified in Mr Whitfield, Mr Barlee, and Mr Hickman. With occasional Reflexions on Mr Calvin, Mr Beza, Mr Zuinglius, Mr Piscator, Mr Rivet and Mr Rollock: But More Especially on Doctor Twisse, and Master Hobbs*. London: Printed by J.G. for R. Royston at the Angel in Ivy-lane, 1658.

POPE, WALTER. *The Life of Right Reverend Father in God Seth, Lord Bishop of Salisbury, with a Brief Account of Bishop Wilkins, Mr Lawrence Rooke, Dr Isaac Barrow, Dr Turbervile and Others*. London: Printed for William Keblewhite, at the Swan in St Paul's Church-yard, 1697.

PRIDEAUX, HUMPHREY. *Letters to John Ellis: 1674–1722*. Edited by

E. M. Thompson. London: Printed for the Camden Society, 1875.

PRYNNE, WILLIAM. *Canterburies doome*. London: Printed by John Macock for Michael Spark senior, 1646.

ROCHESTER, JOHN WILMOT, Earl of. *Collected Works*. Edited by John Hayward. London: The Nonesuch Press, 1926.

ROSS, ALEXANDER. *Arcana Microcosmi: or the hid Secrets of Man's Body discovered; in an Anatomical Duel between Aristotle and Galen concerning the Parts thereof: With a Refutation of Doctor Brown's Vulgar Errors, The Lord Bacon's Natural History and Doctor Harvy's Book De Generatione, Comenius, and Others. . . .* London: Printed by Tho. Newcomb, and are to bee sold by John Clark, entring into Mercers-Chappel, at the lower end of Cheapside, 1658.

—— *Leviathan drawn out with a Hook, or Animadversions Upon Mr Hobbs His Leviathan*. London: Printed by Tho. Newcomb for Richard Royston at the Angel in Ivy-lane, 1653.

—— *The New Planet no Planet*. London: Printed by J. Young, and are to be sold by Mercy Meighen, and Gabriel Bedell, 1646.

RUST, George. *A Letter of Resolution Concerning Origen and the Chief of His Opinions*. Reproduced from the edition of 1661. New York: Facsimile Text Society, 1933.

SCARGILL, DANIEL. *The Recantation of Daniel Scargill publickly made before the University of Cambridge, in Great St Maries, July 25, 1669*. [Cambridge]: Printed by the printers to the University of Cambridge, 1669.

SCARISBRIKE, EDWARD. *Catholic Loyalty upon the Subject of Government and Obedience*. London: Printed for R. Booker, 1688.

SCOT, PHILIP. *A Treatise of the Schism of England. Wherein particularly Mr Hales and Mr Hobbs are modestly accosted*. Amsterdam: Printed Anno Dom., 1650.

SCOT, REGINALD. *The Discoverie of Witchcraft*. Edited by Brinsley Nicholson. London: E. Stock, 1886.

SEDLEY, SIR CHARLES. *The Poetical and Dramatic Works*. Edited by V. De Sola Pinto. 2 vols. London: Constable and Co., 1928.

SELDEN, JOHN. *Table-Talk: Being the Discourses of John Selden, Esq.; Or His Sence of Various Matters of Weight and High Consequence Relating especially to Religion and State*. London: Printed for E. Smith in the year 1689.

SETTLE, ELKANAH. *The Empress of Morocco. A Tragedy. With Sculptures. As it is Acted at the Duke's Theatre*. London: Printed for William Cademan, 1673.

SEWARD, WILLIAM. *Biographiana*. London: Printed for J. Johnson, 1799.

BIBLIOGRAPHY

[SHAFTO, JOHN]. *The Great Law of Nature, or Self-Preservation Examined, Asserted, and Vindicated from Mr Hobbes his Abuses. In a small Discourse; Part Moral, part Political; and part Religious.* London: Printed for the Author, and are to be sold by Will. Crook at the Green-Dragon without Temple-Bar, 1673.

S[HARROCK], R[OBERT]. *De Finibus Virtutis Christianae. The Ends of Christian Religion.* Oxford: Printed by Hen. Hall Printer to the University, for Ric. Davis. Anno Domini, 1673.

SHERLOCK, WILLIAM. *Their Present Majesties Government Prov'd to be Thoroughly Settled, and that we may Submit to it, Without Asserting the Principles of Mr Hobbes.* London: Printed for Robert Clavel, 1691.

SIDNEY, ALGERNON. *Discourses Concerning Government.* 2nd ed. London: Printed by J. Darby in Bartholomew-Close, 1704.

SMITH, JOHN. *Select Discourses.* Cambridge: Printed by John Hayes, for W. Morden Bookseller, 1673.

SORBIÈRE, SAMUEL. *A Voyage to England, Containing many Things relating to the State of Learning, Religion, and other Curiosities of that Kingdom.* London: Printed, and Sold by J. Woodward, in St Christopher's-Alley in Threadneedle-Street, 1709.

SOUTH, ROBERT. *Sermons Preached Upon Several Occasions.* 6 vols. London: Printed for H. Lintot, in Fleet-street, 1737.

SPRAT, THOMAS. *Observations on Mons. de Sorbiere's Voyage into England.* London: Printed in the Year 1708.

[STAALKOPFF, JACOBUS]. *Ab Impius Detersionibus Thomae Hobbesii & Benedicti de Spinoza.* Gryphiswaldiae: Typis G. H. Adolphi, Acad. Reg. Typogr. [1707].

STILLINGFLEET, EDWARD. *Irenicum: A Weapon-Salve for the Churches Wounds.* London: Printed by R.W. for Henry Mortlock, at the Phoenix in St Paul's Church-yard near the little North-door, 1661.

—— *Origines Sacrae, or a Rational Account of the Grounds of Christian Faith, as to the Truth and Divine Authority of the Scriptures, and the matters therein contained.* London: Printed by R.W. for Henry Mortlock at the sign of the Phoenix in St Paul's Church-yard near the little North-door, 1662.

STRIMESIUS, SAMUEL. *Praxiologia Apodictica, Seu Philosophia Moralis Demonstrativa, Pythanologiae Hobbesianae Opposita.* Francofurti ad Oderam: Sumptibus Heredum Jobi Wilhelmi Fincelli excudebant Haered. s. B. Johannis Ernesti. Acad. Typog. 1677.

STUBBE, HENRY. *Clamor, Rixa, Joci, Mendacia, Furta, Cachini, or, A Severe Enquiry into the late Oneirocritica.* London: 1657. [No other imprint.]

TAYLOR, JEREMY. *A Sermon Preached in Christ Church, Dublin: at the Funeral of the most Reverend Father in God, John, Late Lord Archbishop of Armagh and Primate of all Ireland; With a succinct Narrative of his whole Life.* London: Printed for John Crooke, at the Sign of the Ship in St Paul's Church-yard, 1663.

TEMPLER, JOHN. *Idea Theologiae Leviathanis.* Londini: Typis E. Flesher, Impensis G. Morden Bibliopolae Cantabr., 1673.

TENISON, THOMAS. *The Creed of Mr Hobbes Examined; in a feigned Conference Between Him And a Student in Divinty.* London: Printed for Francis Tyton, at the three Daggers in Fleet-street, 1670.

THORNDIKE, HERBERT. *The Theological Works.* 6 vols. Oxford: John Henry Parker, 1845.

TILLOTSON, JOHN *The Works of the Most Reverend Dr John Tillotson, Late Lord Archbishop of Canterbury: Containing Fifty-Four Sermons and Discourses, on Several Occasions. Together with the Rule of Faith.* 8th ed. London: Printed for T. Goodwin, B. Tooke and J. Pemberton in Fleetstreet; J. Round in Exchange Alley, and J. Tonson in the Strand, 1720.

TRAHERNE, THOMAS. *Christian Ethicks: or, Divine Morality. Opening the Way to Blessedness, By the Rules of Vertue and Reason.* London: Printed for Johnathan Edwin, at the Three Roses in Ludgate-street, 1675.

A Tryal of Witches, at the assizes held at Bury St Edmunds for the County of Suffolk; on the tenth day of March, 1664. London: Printed for William Shrewsbery, 1682.

The True Effigies of the Monster of Malmesbury; or, Thomas Hobbes in His True Colours. London: Printed in the Year, 1680.

VELTHUYSEN, LAMBERT VAN. *Epistolica dissertatis de principiis insti, et decori, continens apologiam pro tractatu clarissimi Hobbaei, De cive.* Amstelodami: L. Elzevirius, 1651.

VILVAIN, ROBERT. *Theoremata Theologica: Theological Theses.* London: Printed by R. Hodgkinsonne (for the Author) and are to be sold at his Hous in Thames-street neer Baynards-Castle, 1654.

The Visions of John Bunyan. London: Printed for J. Midwinter, 1711.

Visits From the Shades: or, Dialogues Serious, Comical, and Political. Calculated for these Times. London: Printed in the Year 1704.

WALLIS, JOHN. *The Doctrine of the Blessed Trinity Briefly Explained.* London: Printed for Tho. Parkhurst, at the Bible and Three Crowns, in Cheapside, 1690.

—— *Hobbius Heauton-timorumenos, or A Consideration of Mr Hobbes his Dialogues in an Epistolary Discourse, Addressed to the Honourable Robert Boyle. Esq.* Oxford: Printed by A. and L. Lichfield, for

Samuel Thomson, at the Bishops-Head in St Paul's Church-yard, London 1662.

—— *A Seventh Letter, Concerning the Sacred Trinity.* London: Printed for Tho. Parkhurst, at the Bible and Three Crowns, in Cheapside, 1691.

—— *Theological Discourses; Containing VIII Letters and III Sermons Concerning the Blessed Trinity.* London: Printed for Tho. Parkhurst at Bible and Three Crowns at the Lower End of Cheapside near Mercers-Chapel, 1692.

WARD, RICHARD. *The Life of the Learned and Pious Dr Henry More, Late Fellow of Christ's College in Cambridge.* London: Printed and Sold by Joseph Downing in Bartholomew-Close near West-Smithfield, 1710.

WARD, SETH. *Against Resistance of Lawful Powers: A Sermon Preached at White-Hall, Nov. Vth 1661.* London: Printed by Tho. Roycroft for John Martin, James Allestry, and Tho. Dicas, at the Bell in St Paul's Church-yard, 1661.

—— *In Thomae Hobbii Philosophiam Exercitatio Epistolica, cui subjicitur Appendicula ad calumnias ab eodem Hobbio (in sex Documentis nuperrime editis) in authorem congestas, responsoria.* Oxon., 1656.

—— *A Philosophicall Essay Towards an Eviction of the Being and Attributes of God, The Immortality of the Souls of Men, the Truth and Authority of Scripture.* 2nd ed. Oxford: Printed by Leonard Lichfield, and are to be sold by Edward Forrest, 1655.

—— *Vindiciae Academiarum containing Some briefe Animadversions upon Mr Websters Book, stiled, the Examination of Academies Together with an Appendix concerning what M. Hobbs, and M. Dell have published on this Argument.* Oxford: Printed by Leonard Lichfield, Printer to the University, for Thomas Robinson, 1654.

WHICHCOTE, BENJAMIN. *Moral and Religious Aphorisms. To which are added Eight Letters: which passed between Dr Whichcote and Dr Tuckney.* Edited by Samuel Salter. London: Printed for J. Payne at Pope's-Head, in Pater-Noster-Row, 1753.

WHITEHALL, John. *The Leviathan Found out: or The Answer to Mr Hobbes's Leviathan, in that which my Lord of Clarendon hath past over.* London: Printed by A. Godbid, and J. Playford, dwelling in Little-Britain, 1679.

WILKINS, JOHN. *Sermons Preached upon Several Occasions.* London: Printed for Tho. Basset, Ric. Chiswell and Will. Rogers, 1682.

WOLSELEY, SIR CHARLES. *The Reasonableness of Scripture-Belief. A Discourse Giving some account of those Rational Grounds upon which the Bible is received as the Word of God.* London: Printed by T.R. and

N.T. for Nathaniel Ponder at the Peacock in Chancery-lane near Fleet-street, 1672.

—— *The Unreasonablenesse of Atheism made manifest.* 2nd ed. London: Printed for Nathaniel Ponder, and are to be sold at his Shop, at the Sign of the Peacock in Chancery-lane, 1669.

WOOD, ANTHONY. *Athenae Oxonienses.* Edited by Philip Bliss. 4 vols. London: Printed for Rivington; Lackington, Allen; Payne *et al.*, 1813–1820.

WORTHINGTON, JOHN. *Diary and Correspondence.* Edited by James Crossley and R. C. Christie for the Chetham Society in *Remains Historical & Literary Connected with the Palatine Counties of Lancaster and Chester.* Vols. XIII, XXXVI, CXIV. Manchester: Printed for the Chetham Society, 1847, 1855, 1886.

WREN, MATTHEW. *Monarchy Asserted, or the State of Monarchicall and Popular Government; in Vindication of the Considerations upon Mr Harrington's Oceana.* 2nd ed. London: Printed by T.R. for Francis Bowman of Oxford, and are to be sold by Io. Martin, Ia. Allestry, and T. Dicas at the Bell in St Paul's Church-yard, 1660.

WYCHERLEY, WILLIAM. *The Complete Works.* Edited by Montague Summers. 4 vols. London: Nonesuch Press, 1924.

II. MODERN SCHOLARSHIP

AARON, R. I. 'A possible early draft of Hobbes' *De Corpore*', *Mind*, LIV (1945), 342–56.

ADDISON, WILLIAM. *Worthy Dr Fuller.* New York: Macmillan, 1951.

ANDERSON, PAUL RUSSELL. *Science in Defense of Liberal Religion: A Study of Henry More's Attempt to Link Seventeenth Century Religion with Science.* New York: Putnam, 1933.

ARMITAGE, ANGUS. 'René Descartes (1596–1650) and the Early Royal Society', *Notes and Records of the Royal Society*, VIII (1950), 1–19.

BAKER, JOHN TULL. *An Historical and Critical Examination of English Space and Time Theories from Henry More to Bishop Berkeley.* Bronxville, N.Y.: Sarah Lawrence College, 1930.

BEACH, JOSEPH WARREN. *The Concept of Nature in Nineteenth-Century English Poetry.* New York: Macmillan, 1936.

BICKLEY, FRANCIS. *The Cavendish Family.* Boston: Houghton Mifflin, 1914.

BOWLE, JOHN. *Hobbes and His Critics: A Study in Seventeenth Century Constitutionalism.* London: Jonathan Cape, 1951.

BOYCE, BENJAMIN. 'News from Hell', *P.M.L.A.*, LVIII (1943), 402–37.

BRANDT, FRITHIOF. *Thomas Hobbes' Mechanical Conception of Nature.* Copenhagen: Levin and Munksgaard, 1928.

BREDVOLD, LOUIS I. 'Dryden, Hobbes, and the Royal Society', *Modern Philology*, XXV (1928), 417–38.

—— *The Intellectual Milieu of John Dryden: Studies in Some Aspects of Seventeenth-Century Thought.* Ann Arbor: University of Michigan Press, 1934.

BROCKDORFF, CAY, BARON VON. 'Des Sir Charles Cavendish Bericht für Joachim Jungius über die Grundzuge der Hobbes'schen Naturphilosophie', *Societas Hobbesiana. Veröffentlichungen*, Nr. 3. Kiel, 1934.

—— 'Friedrich Maximilian Klinger und Hobbes', *Societas Hobbesiana. Veröffentlichungen*, Nr. 4. Kiel, 1935.

—— 'Eine Thomas Hobbes zugeschriebene Handschrift und ihr Verfasser. Ein Verehrer Thomas Hobbes' als Interpret des Aristotles'. *Societas Hobbesiana. Veröffentlichungen*, Nr. 1. Kiel, 1932.

BURTT, EDWIN ARTHUR. *The Metaphysical Foundations of Modern Physical Science: a Historical and Critical Essay.* Revised edition. New York: Doubleday Anchor Series, 1954.

—— *Religion in an Age of Science.* New York: Frederick Stokes, 1929.

BUSH, DOUGLAS. *English Literature in the Earlier Seventeenth Century.* Oxford: The Clarendon Press, 1945.

CAJORI, FLORIAN. *A History of Mathematics.* New York: Macmillan, 1894.

CARPENTER, EDWARD. *Thomas Tenison: Archbishop of Canterbury, His Life and Times.* London: S.P.C.K., 1948.

CARRÉ, MEYRICK. 'The New Philosophy and the Divines', *Church Quarterly Review*, CLVI (1955), 33–44.

—— *Phases of Thought in England.* Oxford: The Clarendon Press, 1949.

—— 'Ralph Cudworth', *The Philosophical Quarterly*, III (1953), 342–51.

CASSIRER, ERNST. *Die Platonische Renaissance in England und die Schule von Cambridge.* Leipzig: B.G. Teubner, 1932.

CATLIN, George E. G. *Thomas Hobbes as Philosopher, Publicist and Man of Letters.* Oxford: Basil Blackwell, 1922.

CLYDE, WILLIAM M. *The Struggle for the Freedom of the Press from Caxton to Cromwell.* St Andrews: Humphrey Milford, 1934.

COHEN, I BERNARD. 'A Lost Letter from Hobbes to Mersenne Found', *Harvard Library Bulletin*, I (1947), 112–13.

177

COLIE, ROSALIE L. *Light and Enlightenment: A Study of the Cambridge Platonists and the Dutch Arminians.* Cambridge: Cambridge University Press, 1957.

COPE, JACKSON I. *Joseph Glanvill: Anglican Apologist.* St Louis: Washington University Studies, 1956.

COURTHOPE, W. J. *A History of English Poetry.* Vol. III. London: Macmillan, 1903.

CRAGG, G. R. *From Puritanism to the Age of Reason: A Study of Changes in Religious Thought Within the Church of England,* 1660–1700. Cambridge: Cambridge University Press, 1950.

CRANE, R. S. 'Suggestions toward a Geneology of the "Man of Feeling"', *E.L.H.* I (1934), 205–30.

DE BEER, G. R. 'Some Letters of Thomas Hobbes', *Notes and Records of the Royal Society,* VII (1950), 195–206.

DE MORGAN, AUGUSTUS. *A Budget of Paradoxes.* 2 vols. 2nd ed. Edited by David Eugene Smith. Chicago: The Open Court Publishing Co., 1915.

DE PAULEY, W. C. *The Candle of the Lord: Studies in the Cambridge Platonists.* London: S.P.C.K., 1937.

DE WAARD, C. 'Un entretien avec Descartes en 1634 ou 1635', *Archives Internationales d'Histoire des Sciences,* XXII (1953), 14–16.

DEWEY, JOHN. 'The Motivation of Hobbes' Political Philosophy', vol I of *Studies in the History of Ideas.* New York: Columbia University Press, 1918, pp. 88–115.

DOWLIN, CORNELL MARCH. *Sir William Davenant's Gondibert, its preface, and Hobbes's answer.* Philadelphia: University of Pennsylvania Press, 1934.

EDELEN, GEORGE. 'Joseph Glanvill, Henry More, and the Phantom Drummer of Tedworth', *Harvard Library Bulletin,* X (1956), 186–92.

ELIOT, T. S. *Selected Essays.* 3rd ed. London: Faber and Faber, 1951.

FINCH, JEREMIAH S. *Sir Thomas Browne: A Doctor's Life of Science and Faith.* New York: Henry Schuman, 1950.

FIRTH, C. H. 'A Letter from Lord Saye and Sele to Lord Wharton, 29 Dec. 1657', *English Historical Review,* X (1895), 106–7.

FLETCHER, J. M. J. 'Seth Ward, Bishop of Salisbury, 1667–89', *Wiltshire Archeological and Natural History Magazine,* XLIX (1940), 1–16.

FUJIMURA, THOMAS H. *The Restoration Comedy of Wit.* Princeton: Princeton University Press, 1952.

GILLET, CHARLES R. *Burned Books.* 2 vols. New York: Columbia University Press, 1932.

GREENSLET, FERRIS. *Joseph Glanvill: A Study in English Thought and*

Letters of the Seventeenth Century. New York: Columbia University Press, 1900.

GÜTTLER, C. *Eduard Lord Herbert*. München: C. H. Beck, 1897.

HAM, ROSWELL GRAY. *Otway and Lee: Biography from a Baroque Age*. New Haven: Yale University Press, 1931.

HARRISON, A. W. *Arminianism*. London: Duckworth, 1937.

HARRISON, CHARLES T. 'Bacon, Hobbes, Boyle, and the Ancient Atomists', *Harvard Studies and Notes in Philology and Literature*, XV (1933), 191–218.

HARRISON, FRANK MOTT. *A Bibliography of the Works of John Bunyan*. Oxford: Printed at the University Press for the Bibliographical Society, 1932.

HAZARD, PAUL. *The European Mind: 1680–1715*. Translated by J. Lewis May. London: Hollis and Carter, 1953.

HUNT, JOHN. *Religious Thought in England From the Reformation to the End of The Last Century*. 3 vols. London: Strahan and Co., 1870.

HUXLEY, ALDOUS. *The Devils of Loudon*. New York: Harper and Brothers, 1953.

JACQUOT, JEAN. 'A Newly Discovered Manuscript of Hobbes', *Notes and Records of the Royal Society*, IX (1952), 188–95.

—— 'Sir Charles Cavendish and his Learned Friends', *Annals of Science*, VIII (1952), 13–27, 175–91.

JAMMER, MAX. *Concepts of Space: The History of Theories of Space in Physics*. Cambridge, Mass: Harvard University Press, 1954.

KOCHER, PAUL H. *Science and Religion in Elizabethan England*. San Marino: The Huntington Library, 1953.

KYLE, W. M. 'British Ethical Theories: The Intuitionist Reaction Against Hobbes', *The Australasian Journal of Psychology and Philosophy*, V (1927), 113–23.

KROOK, DOROTHEA. 'The Recantation of Daniel Scargill', *Notes and Queries*, CXCVIII (1953), 159–60.

—— 'Thomas Hobbes's Doctrine of Meaning and Truth', *Philosophy*, XXI (1956), 3–22.

LAIRD, JOHN. *Hobbes*. London: Ernest Benn Limited, 1934.

—— 'Hobbes et la Grande Bretagne Contemporaine', *Archives de Philosophie*, XII (1936), 61–72.

LAMPRECHT, STERLING. 'Hobbes and Hobbism', *American Political Science Review*, XXXIV (1940), 31–53.

—— 'Descartes in England', vol. III of *Studies in the History of Ideas*. New York: Columbia University Press, 1935, pp. 184–240.

LANDRY, B. *Hobbes*. Paris: Librairie Felix Alcan, 1930.

LINNELL, C. L. S. 'Daniel Scargill. A Penitent "Hobbist"', *Church Quarterly Review*, CLVI (1955), 256–65.

—— 'The Scargill Memorial, Mulbarton Church, Norfolk', *Transactions of the Monumental Brass Society*, LXV (1945), 91–3.

LIPS, JULIUS. *Die Stellung des Thomas Hobbes zu den Politischen Parteien der grossen Englischen Revolution.* Leipzig: Ernst Weigandt Verlagsbuchhandlung, 1927.

LOEWE, JOHANN HEINRICH. 'John Bramhall, Bischof von Derry, Und Sein Verhältnis zu Thomas Hobbes', *Čéské společnosti nauk. Rozpravy třídy pro filosofü, dějepis a filologü.* Prague, VII (1886), 3–16.

LOVEDAY, T. 'An Early Criticism of Hobbes', *Mind*, XVII (1908), 493–501.

LUBIENSKI, ZBIGNIEW. 'Hobbes' Philosophy and its Historical Background', *Journal of Philosophical Studies*, V (1930), 175–90.

—— *Die Grundlagen des ethisch-politischen Systems von Hobbes.* München: Ernest Reinhardt, 1932.

MACAULAY, THOMAS BABINGTON. *The History of England from the Accession of James II.* 2 vols. London: Longmans, Green, Reader, and Dyer, 1877.

MACDONALD, HUGH, and HARGREAVES, MARY. *Thomas Hobbes: A Bibliography.* London: The Bibliographical Society, 1952.

MALLOCH, ARCHIBALD. *Finch and Baines: A Seventeenth-Century Friendship.* Cambridge: Cambridge University Press, 1917.

MEYER, MARILYN. 'The Philosophy of Ralph Cudworth', unpublished doctoral dissertation, Columbia University, 1952.

MINTZ, SAMUEL I. 'A Broadside Attack on Hobbes', *History of Ideas News Letter*, I (1955), 19–20.

—— 'Hobbes, Galileo and the Circle of Perfection', *Isis*, XLIII (1952), 98–100.

MUIRHEAD, JOHN HENRY. *The Platonic Tradition in Anglo-Saxon Philosophy: Studies in the History of Idealism in England and America.* London: G. Allen and Unwin, 1931.

NICOLSON, MARJORIE HOPE. *The Breaking of the Circle: Studies in the Effect of the 'New Science' upon Seventeenth Century Poetry.* Evanston: Northwestern University Press, 1950.

—— *Conway Letters.* New Haven: Yale University Press, 1930.

—— 'Christ's College and the Latitude-Men', *Modern Philology*, XXVII (1929), 35–53.

—— 'The Early Stage of Cartesianism in England', *Studies in Philology*, XXVI (1929), 356–74.

—— 'George Keith and the Cambridge Platonists', *Philosophical Review*, XXXIX (1930), 36–55.

—— 'Milton and Hobbes', *Studies in Philology*, XXIII (1926), 405–33.

NOTESTEIN, WALLACE. *A History of Witchcraft in England*. Washington: American Historical Association, 1911.

NOTT, KATHLEEN. *The Emperor's Clothes*. Bloomington: Indiana University Press, 1954.

PAPINI, GIOVANNI. *The Devil*. Translated by Adrienne Foulke. New York: E. P. Dutton, 1954.

PARKER, WILLIAM RILEY. *Milton's Contemporary Reputation*. Columbus: Ohio State University Press, 1940.

PASSMORE, J. A. *Ralph Cudworth: An Interpretation*. Cambridge: Cambridge University Press, 1950.

PETERS, RICHARD. *Hobbes*. London: Penguin Books, 1956.

POLLOCK, SIR FREDERICK and HOLDSWORTH, W. S. 'Sir Matthew Hale on Hobbes: An Unpublished MS', *Law Quarterly Review*, XXXVII (1921), 274–303.

POWELL, ANTHONY. *John Aubrey and His Friends*. London: Eyre and Spottiswoode, 1948.

POWICKE, FREDERICK J. *The Reverend Richard Baxter Under the Cross (1662–91)*. London: Jonathan Cape, 1926.

PRINZ, JOHANNES. *John Wilmot Earl of Rochester*. Leipzig: Mayer and Müller, 1927.

PRIOR, MOODY E. 'Joseph Glanvill, Witchcraft, and Seventeenth-Century Science', *Modern Philology*, XXX (1932), 167–93.

RAVEN, CHARLES E. *Natural Religion and Christian Theology*. Vol. I. Gifford Lectures 1951. Cambridge: Cambridge University Press, 1953.

REESINK, H. J. *L'Angleterre et la Littérature Anglaise Dans Les Trois Plus Anciens Périodiques Francais de Hollande de 1684 à 1709*. Zutphen: W. J. Thieme et Cie, 1931.

REIMANN, HUGO. *Henry Mores Bedeutung für die Gegenwart*. Basel: Rudolf Geering, 1941.

ROBERTSON, GEORGE CROOM. *Hobbes*. Edinburgh: William Blackwood and Sons, 1886.

—— *Philosophical Remains*. Edited by Alexander Bain and T. Whittaker. 'Some Newly Discovered Letters of Hobbes', pp. 303–16. London: Williams and Norgate, 1894.

SCHRÖDINGER, ERWIN. *Science and Humanism*. Cambridge: Cambridge University Press, 1952.

SCOTT, J. F. *The Mathematical Work of John Wallis*. London: Taylor and Francis Ltd., 1938.

SHILLINGLAW, ARTHUR T. 'Hobbes and Ben Jonson', *London Times Literary Supplement*, 18 April, 1936.

STEPHEN, LESLIE. *Hobbes*. New York: Macmillan, 1904. (English Men of Letters Series.)

STOCKS, BETTY T. 'Two Broadsides on Hobbes', in *Elizabethan Studies and other Essays in Honor of George F. Reynolds*. University of Colorado Studies in the Humanities, vol. II, no. 4 (1945), 211–14.

STOYE, JOHN WALTER. *English Travellers Abroad, 1604–67: Their Influence in English Society and Politics*. London: Jonathan Cape, 1952.

STRAUSS, LEO. *Natural Right and History*. Chicago: University of Chicago Press, 1953.

—— *The Political Philosophy of Hobbes*. Translated by Elsa M. Sinclair. Oxford: The Clarendon Press, 1936.

STROUP, THOMAS B. 'Shadwell's Use of Hobbes', *Studies in Philology*, XXXV (1938), 405–32.

SYFRET, R. H. 'Some Early Critics of the Royal Society', *Notes and Records of the Royal Society*, VIII (1950), 20–64.

—— 'Some Early Reactions to the Royal Society', *Notes and Records of the Royal Society*, VII (1950), 207–58.

TAINE, HIPPOLYTE. *Histoire de la Littérature Anglaise*. Vol. III. 10th ed. Paris: L. Hatchette et cie, 1899.

TAYLOR, A. E. 'The Ethical Doctrine of Hobbes', *Philosophy*, XIII (1938), 406–24.

TEETER, LOUIS. 'The Dramatic Use of Hobbes's Political Ideas', *E.L.H.* III (1936), 140–69.

THORPE, CLARENCE D. *Aesthetic Theory of Thomas Hobbes*. Ann Arbor: University of Michigan Press, 1940.

THURSTON, HERBERT, S. J. *Ghosts and Poltergeists*. Chicago: Henry Regnery Company, 1954.

TÖNNIES, FERDINAND. 'Hobbes-Analekten', parts I and II, *Archiv für Geschichte der Philosophie*, XVII (1903), 291–317; XIX (1906), 153–75.

—— *Thomas Hobbes, der Mann und der Denker*. Osterwieck/Harz und Leipzig: U. W. Zickfeldt, 1912.

TULLOCH, JOHN. *Rational Theology and Christian Philosophy in England in the Seventeenth Century*. 2 vols. 2nd ed. Edinburgh and London: William Blackwood and Sons, 1874.

TURBERVILLE, A. S. *A History of Welbeck Abbey and its Owners*. 2 vols. London: Faber and Faber, 1938.

WARRENDER, HOWARD. *The Political Philosophy of Hobbes: His Theory of Obligation*. Oxford: The Clarendon Press, 1957.

WEISS, SAMUEL A. 'Hobbism and Restoration Comedy', unpublished doctoral dissertation, Columbia University, 1953.

WHITEMAN, E. A. O. 'Two Letter Books of Archbishops Sheldon and Sancroft', *Bodleian Library Record*, IV (1953), 209–15.

BIBLIOGRAPHY

WILLEY, BASIL. *The Seventeenth Century Background: Studies in the Thought of the Age in Relation to Poetry and Religion.* 5th impression. London: Chatto and Windus, 1950.

WILSON, JOHN HAROLD. *The Court Wits of the Restoration.* Princeton: Princeton University Press, 1952.

WOLFE, DON M. 'Milton and Hobbes: A Contrast in Social Temper', *Studies in Philology,* XLI (1944), 410–26.

YULE, G. UDNEY. 'John Wallis, D.D., F.R.S.: 1616–1703', *Notes and Records of the Royal Society,* II (1939), 74–82.

ZIMMERMAN, ROBERT. 'Henry More und die vierte Dimension des Raumes', *Kaiserliche Akademie der Wissenschaften. Sitzungsberichte der Philosophisch-Historischen Classe,* XCVIII (Wien, 1881), 403–48.

INDEX